Projecting Illusion offers a systematic analysis of the impression of reality in the cinema and the pleasure it provides the film spectator.

Film affords an especially compelling aesthetic experience that can be considered as a form of illusion akin to the experience of daydream and dream. Examining the concept of illusion and its relationship to fantasy in the experience of visual representation, Richard Allen situates his explanation within the context of an analytical criticism of contemporary film theory. Contrary to many critics, he argues that many contemporary film theorists correctly identify the significance of the impression of reality, although their explanation of it is incorrect because of an invalid philosophical understanding of the relationship between the mind, representation, and reality. Offering a clear presentation and critique of central arguments of contemporary film and critical theory, *Projecting Illusion* also touches on fundamental issues in the current discourses of philosophy, art history, and feminist theory.

PROJECTING ILLUSION

CAMBRIDGE
STUDIES
IN FILM

GENERAL EDITORS

Henry Breitrose, *Stanford University*
William Rothman, *University of Miami*

ADVISORY BOARD

Dudley Andrew, *University of Iowa*
Anthony Smith, *Magdalen College, Oxford*
Colin Young, *National Film School*

OTHER BOOKS IN THE SERIES

PROJECTING
ILLUSION

Film Spectatorship and the Impression of Reality

RICHARD ALLEN
New York University

CAMBRIDGE
UNIVERSITY PRESS

PUBLISHED BY THE PRESS SYNDICATE OF THE UNIVERSITY OF CAMBRIDGE
The Pitt Building, Trumpington Street, Cambridge CB2 1RP, United Kingdom

CAMBRIDGE UNIVERSITY PRESS
The Edinburgh Building, Cambridge, CB2 1RU, United Kingdom
40 West 20th Street, New York, NY 10011-4211, USA
10 Stamford Road, Oakleigh, Melbourne 3166, Australia

First published 1995
First paperback edition 1997

Printed in the United States of America

Typeset in Times

Library of Congress Cataloging-in-Publication Data
Allen, Richard, 1959–
    Projecting illusion: film spectatorship and the impression of reality / Richard Allen.
        p. cm. – (Cambridge studies in film)
    Includes index.
    ISBN 0-521-47015-3
    1. Motion pictures – Philosophy. 2. Motion picture audiences.
    I. Title. II. Series
    PN1995.A376 1995
    791.43'01 – dc20   94–22942
                                                                    CIP

A catalog record for this book is available from the British Library

ISBN 0-521-47015-3 hardback
ISBN 0-521-58715-8 paperback

Chapter 3 is a revised version of "Representation, Illusion, and the Cinema," *Cinema Journal* 32:2 (Winter 1993): 21–48.
Chapter 4 is a revised version of "Cinema, Psychoanalysis, and the Film Spectator," *Persistence of Vision* 10 (1993): 5–33.

For my mother,
Vera Allen

and in memory of my father,
Edward Allen

Contents

vii

Acknowledgments

It is a pleasure for me to acknowledge those individuals who have contributed to the evolution of this work. Its origins lie in my dissertation on film theory at UCLA. I wish to thank the members of my committee: my chair, Nick Browne, and Janet Bergstrom, Vincent Pecora, Teshome Gabriel, Bob Rosen, and Eric Rentschler. Thanks also to Miriam Hansen for her valuable encouragement at an early stage, as well as to my teachers at the University of East Anglia, Thomas Elsaesser and Don Ranvaud, who first encouraged me to pursue problems in film theory.

In drafting this manuscript I am much indebted to Ben Singer for his incisive and constructive criticisms, and I am grateful to Paul Willemen, who always seems to be around at the right time to provide a cogent commentary on my work. Also, for their advice, encouragement, and general willingness to give my ideas a hearing, I would like to thank John Belton, Nicola Galombik, Lee Gibson, Tom Gunning, Getrud Koch, Antonia Lant, Charles Musser, Bill Paul, Hector Rodriguez, Chris Straayer, and Michael Zryd.

My writing has been nourished by the intellectual stimulation of my graduate seminars in film theory in the Department of Cinema Studies at New York University, and I thank all those students who have participated. This book would not have been completed without the support of my departmental chairperson, Bill Simon, who, together with my colleagues at NYU, granted me a course reduction and relief from administrative burdens at a crucial period.

I thank Beatrice Rehl, Michael Gnat, and William Rothman at Cambridge University Press. Thanks also to Karen Katz for designing the cover. I am extremely grateful to Renata Jackson for her diligent proofreading of the manuscript, her compilation of the index, and, not least, for her unwavering enthusiasm for this project.

I owe a lot to Martha Liebman and the Thursday night group for taking some of the pain out of writing, and for much else besides. Finally, my thanks to Bridget Sisk for the material, emotional, and spiritual support she has given me over the years we have been together. Her restless, indomitable spirit showed me then, and shows me now, how to enjoy being alive.

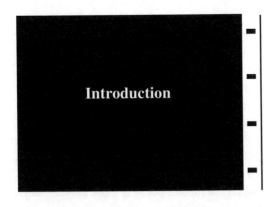

Introduction

In this monograph I seek to explain the impression of reality in the cinema. I begin by joining a number of recent writers in criticizing the way that contemporary film theory characterizes the impression of reality in the cinema with ideas drawn from Althusserian Marxism, Lacanian psychoanalysis, and Marxist literary modernism. I then offer my own explanation of the phenomenon through an analysis of the concept of illusion and its relationship to fantasy in the experience of visual representation.

I follow the usage of Noël Carroll and employ the term "contemporary film theory" to refer to Althusserian–Lacanian film theory, but the reader should bear in mind that this is a term of art.[1] The phrase "contemporary film theory," in my usage, does not describe all post-1960s film theory, some of which, like that of Stanley Cavell and Victor Perkins, is cast in the classical mold, and some of which, like the work of Edward Branigan or Carroll himself, has a distinctly analytical orientation. Nor does the term refer to the various theories of spectatorship and culture falling under the general rubric of "cultural studies" that currently occupy the field in the wake of the perceived failings of Althusserian–Lacanian film theory adequately to account for the social context in which films are produced and understood. What the term does describe is a film theory that has the following characteristics:

It is relatively recent in origin – the founding texts date from the late sixties.

It is united by certain common theoretical assumptions, central of which, I shall argue, is a certain understanding of the impression of reality in the cinema.

It is united in method by a self-conscious opposition to traditional or classical film aesthetics.

It has occupied a preeminent place in the theoretical literature on film in the past twenty years.

1

In order to characterize the power of movies upon the spectator's imagination, contemporary film theorists draw on Althusser's theory of ideology, which borrows certain ideas from Lacanian psychoanalysis. Contemporary film theorists conceive of ideology as a form of knowledge in which human beings are blind to the fact that what they believe to be true is a product not of the way the world is, but of the language they use. Language appears to provide humans with the capability of knowing reality, but only because its role in structuring the way that knowledge is produced is invisible or transparent. The effect of language upon the human being is more radical than a simple misunderstanding of the nature of reality; for the apprehension of reality that discourse appears to afford also produces a person who defines herself through the apparent ability to use language to refer to reality. Thus, human self-definition is deemed to be based upon a fundamental misunderstanding. The human subject, capable of knowledge, is formed through a necessary misrecognition of her radical dependency upon language.

The transparency of the cinematic image and its effect upon the spectator seems to contemporary film theorists to exemplify this conception of ideology. Contemporary film theorists argue that, for a number of reasons, the cinematic image appears to spectators as if it were reality, but this appearance is an illusion. In fact, the cinematic image provides an *impression* of reality; it is actually an image and not the reality it appears to be. In this way the spectator's response to the cinematic image exemplifies the way in which ideology in general functions. Cinema is a form of signification that creates the appearance of a knowable reality and hence confirms the self-definition of the human subject as someone capable of knowing that reality; but in fact both reality and the human subject who appears capable of knowing that reality are "effects" of a process of signification. The film theorists' exposure of the way in which the spectator experiences cinematic representation as an illusion thus seems to reveal the more fundamental illusion upon which subjectivity itself is based.

I argue that contemporary film theorists' characterization of the impression of reality in the cinema is logically incoherent. Contemporary film theorists claim that the spectator's response to cinematic discourse illuminates the manner in which the human being in general is constructed in discourse. However, it is only possible to understand the fact that knowledge is a function of discourse if a human being exists who is capable of knowing reality in a different way than in the manner described by the theory. There must be a film spectator who *can* see a film and his own relationship to it for what it actually is. If such a human or film spectator exists, then the theory is false. If such a human or film spectator does not exist, then the way in which the human being is constructed in discourse cannot be known and the theory is vacuous. Contemporary film theorists construe the film spectator as a passive observer of the image who is duped into believing that it is real. In fact, as I shall argue, the film spectator knows it is only a film and actively participates in the experience of illusion that the cinema affords. However, my arguments may not be convincing to those persuaded by the basic idea that the failure of language to offer a transparent grasp of reality serves to expose the way the human being is constructed out of language. Since it could be argued that the problems arising in film theory stem not from this basic idea but rather from its application, it is the idea itself that must be challenged.

I undertake this task by tracing the contemporary philosophical sources of this idea in the transcendental phenomenology of Edmund Husserl and Jacques Derrida's philosophy of deconstruction. I do not claim that these writers are the only philosophical sources for film theory – Georg Hegel and Jean-Paul Sartre are also significant – but I do contend that it is transcendental phenomenology and its deconstruction that provide the philosophical picture of representation and its critique that animates contemporary film theory. I argue that in contemporary film theory, the film spectator and, by extension, the human being in general, exemplifies Husserl's transcendental subject to whom representation appears transparent. The exposure of cinematic representation as a form of illusion illustrates Derrida's contention that representation is fundamentally opaque and not transparent in the manner that Husserl claims. Since Derrida, like Husserl, assumes that knowledge is possible only if representation is transparent, the opacity of representation entails that all knowledge is founded upon illusion. The idea of the "humanist" subject that rests on the possibility of shared knowledge of human experience is thus a fiction.

By invoking arguments made in the later philosophy of Wittgenstein, I argue that the theoretical discourse that informs arguments about cinematic illusion made within contemporary film theory embodies a mistaken picture of the relationship between human beings, representation, and the world. The error lies in the assumption shared by Husserl and Derrida alike that genuine knowledge is possible only if representation *is* transparent. I argue that contemporary film theorists' analyses of the impression of reality in the cinema illustrate not that knowledge is a function of representation, but embody, instead, a false conception of representation and its relationship to knowledge. Contemporary film theorists suggest that film spectators misunderstand their relationship to representation, but in fact it is the critical theorist who misconstrues the nature of representation and its role in affording us knowledge of the world. For Wittgenstein, the capacity to know the world is not an illusion fostered by forms of representation; instead, forms of representation are tools that allow us to interact with a world that we come to know through this interaction. Indeed, it is mistaken to speak of language as a form of representation at all in the sense that the use of language to represent the world is only one of its uses, and one that is no more privileged than others in affording us knowledge.

My arguments place some of the criticisms leveled by Noël Carroll at contemporary film theory and at the theory of subject construction that underlies it in a wider philosophical context. I also concur with Carroll's conclusion that contemporary film theorists' characterization of the impression of reality in the cinema is mistaken. Where my criticism of contemporary film theory differs sharply from Carroll's is in the implication that I draw from the failure of such theory. Carroll rejects entirely the applicability of the concept of illusion to the cinema, and together with his rejection of illusionism, he rejects the appropriateness of any kind of psychoanalytic theory for understanding the spectator's experience of the cinema. In place of psychoanalytic theory Carroll endorses the cognitively oriented theories of narrative comprehension offered by David Bordwell and others who conceptualize the spectator as an active participant in understanding the text. While I believe that cognitive theory illuminates the way in which we understand films, I also believe that by rejecting the idea of an impression of reality in the cinema and psychoanalytic theories of spectatorship that might explain it, Carroll is unable to account for central aspects of our pleasure in the cinema that contemporary film theorists correctly identify but incorrectly describe.

I seek to give the impression of reality in the cinema renewed significance through a detailed investigation of the different ways in which illusion may be experienced and the kind of belief that illusion entails. I argue that the form of illusion central to our experience of the cinema is one in which, while we know that what we are seeing is only a film, we nevertheless experience that film as a fully realized world. I call this form "projective illusion." The experience of projective illusion is not one that is imposed upon a passive spectator but an experience into which an active spectator voluntarily enters. The experience is characteristic of all media, not a property that is essential to cinema and cinema alone. However, I argue that projective illusion is most consistently afforded by the cinema because of the specific properties of the medium. In sum, I provide an analytical account of the "suspension of disbelief" as it functions in media that are based upon vision and/or sound, such as representational painting, photography, and theater, and I argue for the special significance of the cinema for understanding this phenomenon.

Contemporary film theory has tended to assimilate in its use of psychoanalysis the idea of the construction of the subject in discourse. Once stripped of this idea, psychoanalysis can illuminate the epistemology of film spectatorship.[2] I argue that the experience of the impression of reality in the cinema takes the form of a benign disavowal where spectators entertain in thought that what they see is real in a manner akin to the experience of a conscious fantasy. The difference lies in the fact that in cinema this conscious fantasy is fully realized for the spectator in the form of a projective illusion. Thus I argue that while I know that what I see is only a film, I can experience this film with the kind of realization that occurs in dreams. In this way a psychoanalytic theory of film can assign a proper place to consciousness in the experience of film.

The revision of psychoanalytic film theory I propose here has particular significance for feminist film theory. An influential paradigm of feminist theorizing about the cinema identifies the transcendental subject constructed by film with the male subject and assumes a connection between disavowal in the cinema and fetishistic disavowal that is predicated, according to Freud, upon the male perception of female lack. Feminist film theory thus offers a conception of the essentially masculine character of the cinematic apparatus that rests upon the theory of subject construction. In this way feminist theories of the gender-bound character of the cinematic apparatus are also implicated in the epistemological contradictions that underlie the theory of subject construction. Without a doubt, women go to the cinema, but this form of feminist film theory can account for their pleasure only in terms of a familiar double bind: The female spectator must either identify with an active masculine gaze or identify with woman as lack, the object of that gaze. However, I argue that the form of aesthetic disavowal I associate with the experience of the impression of reality in the cinema is not to be identified with fetishistic disavowal that focuses on the sight of sexual difference. It is a gender-indifferent experience that pertains to the child's original separation from her or his mother. I argue that once the gender indifference or neutrality of disavowal and the gaze in the cinema is recognized, proper account can then be taken of the way in which the activity of disavowal engages with specific kinds of image to produce an experience that, although it may be qualified by gender, allows room for different kinds of appropriation of the image by female and other spectators.

The shape of the argument of the book is not strictly linear. In Chapter 1 I outline and criticize the major arguments of contemporary film theory regarding the impression of reality in the cinema, and delineate the way in which contemporary film theory incorporates arguments from Althusserian

Marxism, Lacanian psychoanalysis, and Marxist literary modernism. Chapter 2 takes up the wider philosophical picture that informs the arguments introduced in Chapter 1. I trace the philosophical assumptions that underpin contemporary film theory to Husserl's transcendental phenomenology and Derrida's "deconstructive" philosophy. I explicate and criticize the work of both these philosophers in the light of the later philosophy of Wittgenstein, which I suggest is important for understanding the philosophical failings of contemporary film theory that result, in central respects, from their work.

In Chapter 3, I abandon the general philosophical issues of Chapter 2 and return to addressing the specific question of the impression of reality in the cinema. I develop an alternative explanation for the phenomenon of the impression of reality in the cinema in terms of projective illusion, which I situate in relationship both to other forms of visual experience that we might more readily call illusions and to the experience of projective illusion in other cultural practices. The argument of Chapter 4 proceeds from and complements that of Chapter 3. I suggest that the way we experience the impression of reality in the cinema can be understood through a psychoanalytic conception of the mind and, in particular, a conception of the role that fantasy plays in mental life. In the course of defending a psychoanalytic understanding of film spectatorship, I begin to explicate the relationship between character identification and the experience of cinema in the form of projective illusion. Finally, I reevaluate some of the central arguments of feminist film theory and join the attempt to cast feminist psychoanalytic film theory in a different theoretical mold than the one that has dominated its development.

The shape of the work affects the way it might be profitably read. The argument of Chapter 2 relates film theory to a wider philosophical framework, one that informs critical theory in the humanities in general; it thus will prove most interesting to those who seek to understand the connection between film theory and this broader theoretical discourse. Those whose interest is primarily in film can skip this chapter without losing the thread of my argument about the impression of reality in the cinema, how it has been conceived, and how it should be reconceived.

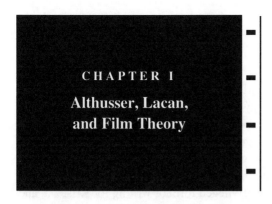

Anglo–French film theory of the 1970s and early 1980s sought to synthe-size Marxism and psychoanalysis in an explanation of the ideological, psy-chological, and cognitive effects of the cinema's apparent evocation of reali-ty. The impetus to theorize the psychological and social impact of cinema was nourished by events of May 1968 and their failure to provoke radical social change.[1] The outcome of these events rekindled the ongoing debate in Western Marxism about the failure of working-class revolution, which many Marxists imputed to the role of ideology in reproducing the class structure that governs the process of production. The immediate inspiration for radical film theorists in this period was the psychoanalytically inflected theory of ideology proposed by the French Marxist Louis Althusser. Althusser him-self did not write on the mass media; but the theory of ideology he proposed seemed to offer film theorists the basis for a detailed explanation of the in-fluence of movies upon the imagination. In particular, film theorists argued that the kind of deception that cinematic illusion wrought upon the film spectator was a precise instantiation of the kind of deception wrought by ideology upon the individual. Since Althusser's theory of ideology was pre-sented in a provisional and tentative form, and since cinematic illusion seemed to demonstrate his theory so well, the analysis of cinematic illusion promised to play a central role in bringing to fruition the Marxist project of explaining and criticizing the function of ideology in society.

Since the propagation of ideology in the cinema was said to have such a pivotal role in maintaining the status quo, the critique of cinematic illusion-ism also offered the hope of undermining that status quo and promoting so-cial change. In this respect, ideology critique meshes with a second tradition within Western Marxism, represented by figures such as Bertolt Brecht, György Lukács, and Theodor Adorno, that has promoted social change through the practice of art. Althusser's own essays on art contribute to this tradition, but their relationship to his theory of ideology is only very tenta-tively sketched. However, his psychoanalytically inflected theory of ideology was influential upon a group of writers associated with the French journal *Tel Quel* who, in the wake of the events of May 1968, promoted a political literary avant-garde within the Marxist tradition. The key to understanding the relationship between ideology and revolutionary art was, for these literary Marxists, language or, more specifically, signification or linguistic meaning. For theorists like Julia Kristeva, Althusser's theory of ideology could be used to illuminate the way in which signification itself was at once ideological and yet also, in the context of artistic practice, a source of liberation from the hold of ideology. The privileged form of writing for Kristeva, and other contributors to *Tel Quel*, was literary modernism, which echoed Adorno's own espousal of high modernism in the postwar decades.[2]

When film theorists applied Althusser's theory of ideology to understanding the cinema, some of them did so within this broader intellectual framework that equated signification itself with ideology. The effect of the impression of reality in the cinema upon the spectator was likened to the effect of language upon the individual in its ideological impact. In the case of the analysis of signification, it was necessary to turn to a distinctive use of language – literary language – in order to find a way to expose the ideological effects of language. The question for film theory was to identify and promote, in an analogous way, a form of filmmaking that would counter cinematic illusion. Certain filmmakers of the North American avant-garde who explored the material properties of film provided a model of filmmaking practice that was radically anti-illusionist in its form. However, an avant-garde practice rooted in the materiality or "ontology" of the medium was deemed insufficient, by itself, to transform the ideological effects of the apparatus, for it ignored the role of narrative in sustaining illusion and the ideological effect produced by it. It was the interaction between the impression of reality in the cinema and cinematic narration that engendered the ideological effects of the cinematic apparatus. Thus, within the framework of Althusserian film theory, contemporary film theorists turned to the work of Bertolt Brecht as a model for a modernist, reflexive filmmaking practice that challenged principles of narrative linearity, closure, and verisimilitude. This Brechtian modernism was considered to be exemplified in the work of Jean-Luc Godard and the collaborative films of Jean-Marie Straub and Danielle Huillet.[3]

Brecht, Lukács, and Adorno had all in their different ways sought to question the distinction between high art and mass culture. However, French political modernists of the 1960s betrayed scant interest in the mass media and tacitly upheld the dichotomy between the refined ennobling experience of high art and the debased manipulative character of the mass media that characterized literary modernism in general. The difference for the Marxist literary modernists lay in the fact that the ennoblement of the human spirit that characterized high art was defined as the capacity of certain forms of artistic practice to liberate the individual from the hold of ideology. When film theorists embraced political modernism, they carried this dichotomy over into their understanding of cinema. Mass culture – classical Hollywood cinema – was deemed illusionistic and manipulative, and an alternative film-making practice was celebrated in which cinematic illusionism and the pleasures of narrative involvement it afforded were eschewed in favor of the cerebral pleasures of films that sought to foreground the manner of their construction and undermine the effect of cinematic illusion.[4]

In this chapter I criticize contemporary film theorists' account of the impression of reality in the cinema and its foundations in the writings of Althusser, Lacan, and Marxist literary modernism. This task is a complicated one for two reasons. First, when the ideas of Althusser or Lacan are applied to film they are often oversimplified and misconstrued, particularly since they often enter into film theory through literary theory. Second, Althusser's own reference to Lacan's idea of "mirror misrecognition," from which contemporary film theorist's took inspiration, misconstrues Lacan's argument. However, even when freed from the distortions of film and literary theorists, the arguments of Althusser and Lacan on the topics that have been germane to contemporary film theorists' understanding of the impression of reality in the cinema and its effect on the spectator are not convincing.

Althusser's Theory of Ideology

Althusser developed his theory of ideology in the context of a wider criticism of the kind of Marxism that dominated European Marxism in the postwar period and had been inspired by the rediscovery of Marx's early writings. These early writings had grown out of Hegel's progressive, enlightenment view of history as the grand journey of the spirit of humankind through successive self-alienation toward self-realization and freedom. While retaining the overall shape of Hegel's story of history, Marx transforms the relationship posed by Hegel between consciousness and society. For Hegel, different forms of social organization are actual manifestations of the human spirit; for Marx, successive forms of social organization manifest the best available form, at any given level of technological development, for human beings to extract and transform the natural resources necessary to sustain their material existence. According to Marx, the beliefs about society that are held within any given form of social organization tend to promote and sustain that form of social organization. These beliefs are ideological because, although held to be true, they turn out to be false in the light of a wider view of history (historical materialism).[5] Thus, to use the classic example, the bourgeois state accords civil liberties to all its citizens, and these political rights bestow legitimacy upon the state. However, these political rights serve to mask the real state of affairs in civil society where one class (the bourgeoisie) exploits another class (the workers). The bourgeoisie is, characteristically, unaware that there is a contradiction between the conditions of life in political and civil society, for it is not in its own interests to perceive this contradiction (false consciousness). Since such a perception is not in its interests, the bourgeoisie will not necessarily be converted to the cause of social change by education alone. In order to recognize the conflict between apparent rights and actual exploitation, the intellectual must take the point of view of the worker, who actually experiences alienation.

Althusser's critique of Hegelian Marxism lies in its assumption of a domain of shared human experience unclouded by ideology to which one can appeal in support of the call for social change. Althusser argues that as Western Marxism embraced this humanist assumption in the postwar period it pursued the option of reform rather than revolution and abandoned its claim to be Marxist. He contends that in order to understand, once again, the necessity of revolutionary practice in Marxism, a reassessment of the revolutionary character of Marxist epistemology is required. Althusser claims that the later writings of Marx articulate an "epistemological break" with Hegelian philosophy and transform the relationship between theory and practice that it implies. It is because the later writings of Marx provide a new theory of knowledge that they offer a conception of political practice incompatible with reform. For Althusser, the early writings of Marx share with the tradition of philosophical epistemology from which they are derived a certain picture of how truth is established. Althusser discerns that this picture of truth underlies philosophy, science, and common sense. He refers to it as the "empiricist conception of knowledge":

The empiricist conception of knowledge presents a process that takes place between a given object and a given subject.... What defines it as such is the nature of the process of knowledge, in other words a certain relationship that defines knowledge as such, as a function of the real object of which it is said to be the knowledge.[6]

In an analogy that proved extremely important for film theory, Althusser compares the empiricist conception of knowledge to the metaphor of knowledge as vision. This metaphor describes an ideal of unclouded, transparent perception of the real object by the percipient when she has discovered the truth. For Althusser, the empiricist conception of knowledge describes the form that knowledge takes when it is ideology, and this is the form of knowledge that characterizes the early writings of Marx.

According to Althusser, truth is really a function of the system of concepts that produce it. In his view, the empiricist conception of knowledge is defined by its erroneous claim that truth is a function of reference. Within the empiricist conception of knowledge, truth-claims are grounded upon a failure to recognize their own conditions of existence, and this failure constitutes their ideological character. Althusser illustrates his equation of ideology with a certain conception of epistemology by analyzing the theory of ideology articulated in Marx's early writings as an exemplification of ideology. It turns out that the theory of ideology as false consciousness is itself ideological on the grounds that this theory embodies the same conception of epistemology as the ideas that it labels as "false consciousness"; that is, it fails to acknowledge its own historical conditions of existence as a theory.

Althusser argues that the later writings of Marx afford the possibility of genuine knowledge because they are premised upon a transformed conception of what constitutes knowledge. Genuine science self-consciously recognizes the fact that the object of its inquiry is a function of the system of concepts that produce it. The truths of genuine science are not judged by whether or not they correspond to the object, but according to the coherence of the system of concepts that produce knowledge of the object. Althusser writes that scientific discourse

contains in itself definite protocols with which to validate the quality of its product, i.e., the criteria of the scientificity of the products of scientific practice. . . . It has been possible to apply Marx's theory with success because it is "true": it is not true because it has been applied with success.[7]

The "epistemological break" between the early and later writings of Marx enacts the demarcation between science and ideology that remained largely untheorized until Althusser's reading of Marx's texts. Althusser argues that Marx articulates a method of analysis (dialectical materialism) that can comprehend the ideological character of knowledge and hence can comprehend its own historical conditions of existence as a discourse. By exposing the historical conditions of existence of ideology, the science of Marxism at once exposes the inherently conservative character of ideology and establishes its own importance for revolutionary practice. Ideology is the invisible cement that holds the structure of society together. By understanding how this structure is held together, Marxist theory exposes the cracks in the cement that revolutionary practice can then pry open.

Althusser suggests that the illusion underlying traditional epistemology and the ideological conception of knowledge it embodies can be diagnosed through reference to the concept of misrecognition articulated by Jacques Lacan. In his essay on Freud and Lacan, Althusser writes that psychoanalysis has discovered "that the human subject is de-centered, constituted by a structure which has no 'center' either, except in the imaginary misrecognition of the 'ego,' i.e. in the ideological formations in which it 'recognizes' itself."[8] Lacan's theory of misrecognition allows Althusser to conceptualize the way in which the empiricist conception of knowledge structures experience for the human subject. For Lacan, a child's sense of self-identity emerges in her early life only through her representation in a mirror or, less metaphorically, through seeing herself in the gaze of the other. The self is constituted in a state of disavowal or misrecognition because the subject really is thoroughly fragmented and is not the unified body image she appears to be in the mirror or in the gaze of the other.[9] For Althusser (though *not* for Lacan), the subject before the mirror is an individual who believes she is a subject, that is, an autonomous, free agent capable of discriminating truth from falsehood. However, this belief is produced within a loose system of ideas and values (i.e., a culture) whose function is precisely to produce in the subject a belief in her own agency, and thus necessarily renders opaque its own effects upon the subject. Ideology creates subjects who believe that they have the capacity to make judgments without presuppositions, but the capacity to make judgments takes place against a background of presuppositions concealed by the very exercise of that capacity. The human agent is someone whose capacity for judgment is founded upon a blindness to the arbitrary character of the ideas and values that define the field of possibilities within which opinions are expressed and decisions are made.

Althusser proposes that it is the role of several key institutions in society – the family, the church, the school, and the media – to reproduce the process of mirror misrecognition that transforms the individual into a subject in ideology. The discourses of these institutions assign the individual a specific role to play in society, and the individual comes to recognize herself as a subject in and through that role, as if the role itself were an authentic expression of subjectivity and agency. Althusser suggests this process is like the situation where someone is hailed in the street by a stranger – "Hey you there!" – and turns around and recognizes herself as the person called. Through this process, which he calls "interpellation," an individual's status as a social subject is achieved by subjection to authority that is misrecognized as the attainment of the capacity to act as a free agent. Because ideology is propagated through specific institutions, these become a central site of the class struggle. Depending on what discourse is promulgated and the means by which this is done, these "ideological state apparatuses," or ISAs, may create either individuals who are compliant to the ruling ideology or ideologically critical subjects. Althusser writes:

the ISAs represent the *form* in which the ideology of the ruling class must *necessarily* be realized, and the form in which the ideology of the ruled class must *necessarily* be measured and confronted[;] ideologies are not "born" in the ISAs but from the social classes at grips in the class struggle: from their conditions of existence, their practices, their experience of the struggle, etc.[10]

Now, Althusser's theory of ideology can be objected to on both political and epistemic grounds (i.e., on the grounds of its conception of knowledge). A central political objection to Althusser's theory stems from the fact that he seems to identify bourgeois ideology with ideology in general. For example, comparing the philosophical foundations of the early and later writings of Marx in his essay "Marxism and Humanism," Althusser writes:

Marx rejected the problematic of the earlier philosophy and adopted a new problematic in one and the same act. The earlier idealist ("bourgeois") philosophy depended in all its domains and arguments (its "theory of knowledge," its conception of history, its political economy, its ethics, its aesthetics, etc.) on a problematic of *human nature* (or the essence of man). For centuries, this problematic has been transparency itself, and no one had thought of questioning it even in its internal modifications.[11]

Here and elsewhere the identification of bourgeois humanism with the "transparency" implied by the empiricist conception of knowledge is so close that they become indistinguishable. If this equation is made, then in spite of Althusser's claim that the ISAs are a site of the class struggle, bourgeois ideology would seem to be inescapable, for it is this ideology that makes individuals into subjects. The class struggle against bourgeois ideology could never take hold because there would be no possibility of the subject recognizing and resisting the hold of ideology over him. At most, the subject might come to a scientific recognition of the necessary hold that bourgeois ideology has, but such a theory of ideology is certainly not useful to a Marxist who is committed to a political program of revolutionary social change.[12]

It is therefore ironic that Althusser's theory is explicitly designed to dramatize the importance of ideology as a site of the class struggle.[13] Althusser wishes to maintain a distinction between the form that all ideology takes (the empiricist conception of knowledge) and the content of a specific ideology – bourgeois ideology – that is challenged by the class struggle. In a classless society, ideology will remain indispensable as the glue that holds the social fabric together, but it will no longer have as its content a system of ideas and values that serve the interests of one class. In a class society, then, ideology is defined by two separate criteria: Ideas are ideological (1) when they take the form of the empiricist conception of knowledge, and hence are "false" in the sense that they fail to acknowledge their own historical conditions of existence; and (2) when they express the interests of a particular class.

The reason that Althusser tends to identify bourgeois ideology with ideology in general is that, for Althusser, the later writings of Marx expose for the first time the structure that ideology in general takes by revealing the character of bourgeois ideology. Althusser defines the structure of the empiricist conception of knowledge by defining the character of bourgeois ideology; thus the two conceptions of ideology tend to be discussed as if they were one and the same. Given this strategy – and in view of the absence of any guidelines as to what a definition of bourgeois ideology would comprise independent of the empiricist conception of knowledge and the idea of the human subject it entails – it is not surprising that film theorists and others assimilated the two as well.

I now turn to the epistemic objections to Althusser's characterization of ideology in terms of the empiricist conception of knowledge. Althusser's discussion of this conception could be defended as a description of the way in which both philosophers and scientists have understood the practice of making truth-claims about the world. For example, it could be argued that although many scientists proceed as if they are discovering something about the world, their discoveries actually reflect the background of presuppositions that govern their inquiries: the concepts they use to define their hypotheses, the kinds of hypotheses they formulate, and the methods of verification they use to confirm or deny them.[14] Furthermore, it is also true that Althusser's characterization of the empiricist conception of knowledge serves to define the way in which the practice of making truth-claims has often been conceived within the tradition of Western philosophy, as we shall see in Chapter 2. However, for Althusser, the empiricist conception does not simply describe a widespread misconception about the practice of making knowledge-claims, but also provides a way of demarcating categorically different forms of knowledge. Knowledge that takes an "empiricist" form is ideology; knowledge that understands its own conditions of existence is science. The epistemic objections to Althusser's theory stem from the fact that he takes the empiricist conception of knowledge to describe a categorical difference between scientific knowledge and ideology.

In the context of demarcating ideology from science, the empiricist conception of knowledge does not describe an erroneous understanding of the practice of making knowledge-claims; rather, it suggests that the day-to-day assertions we make about the world are founded upon error. That is, Althusser suggests that our customary practice of making knowledge-claims is undermined by a blindness to the background of presuppositions that enable us to make them. This argument is insupportable, however: The fact that we cannot include within any given knowledge-claim an acknowledgment of *all* the conditions that make that knowledge-claim possible does not mean that such a claim is thus irredeemably relative to the conditions under which it is made in such a way that undermines its veracity. It simply describes the way in which truth is attained; for without a background of presuppositions against which claims to knowledge are formulated, it would be impossible to make knowledge-claims at all. Scientific knowledge-claims are made in the context of a more rigorous account of the presuppositions that enable them, but they are no more immune from error than nonscientific ones.

Althusser's theory of knowledge as ideology involves an understanding of the way in which human beings, in order to become human beings, must necessarily misconstrue the nature of their own relationship to the world. Governed by the empiricist conception of knowledge, humans act as if they had the ability to make judgments that are free of presuppositions; but just as Althusser's theory of knowledge as ideology is based on a misguided conception of what it is to make a knowledge-claim, it is also based on a misguided conception of what it is to be free or to be a human agent. Human agency does indeed take place against a background of norms and values that shape human action, but this discovery is not something that robs human beings of their freedom; nor does it imply that their lives are determined, or, in the language of contemporary theory, that subjectivity is constructed by discourse. As Nöel Carroll has suggested in the context of his critique of Althusserian film theory, it is "absurd to suggest that humans are not shaped by social rules, roles, ideals, imperatives, guidelines, precedents, and so on. However, it seems equally problematic to think that society totally molds the agent, since social roles, rules, ideals, and so on are transformed by the interpretative activity of agents."[15] To be sure, the existence of some background set of norms, conventions, and values that comprise a culture is what makes human agency possible. However, human agency defines itself through the shaping of that culture, through the application and interpretation of norms and values.

I have challenged Althusser's distinction between science and ideology on the grounds that it cannot be drawn in relationship to the empiricist conception of knowledge, for this conception is a mistaken description of what it is to make a knowledge-claim. However, rejection of this criterion does not entail abandoning altogether a distinction between science and ideology. Certain critical theorists have also challenged Althusser's distinction between science and ideology, but on the grounds that the empiricist conception of knowledge describes the nature of all knowledge-claims, and hence that Althusser's critique of this conception applies to all knowledge-claims. Thus they abandon the distinction between science and ideology altogether: All knowledge-claims are compromised by the background conditions and circumstances in which they are produced. This radical skepticism underlies the social theory of Althusser's pupil Michel Foucault. Foucault embraces Friedrich Nietzsche's dictum that truth is a function of self-interest, but he redefines Nietzsche's individualistic account of the relationship between knowledge and power in terms of an Althusserian conception of the role of discourse in shaping social subjects and hence the distribution of power in society.[16] However, once it is accepted that knowledge-claims are merely a function of one's social or class position within a given discursive formation, there is in principle no way to adjudicate rival knowledge-claims, and so the pejorative sense attached to the concept of ideology must be abandoned. Reason becomes indistinguishable from sophistry: It is simply a strategic weapon for undermining the argument of one's opponent and maneuvering for a position of supremacy for one's class or social group. The distinction between being right and seeming to be right becomes a function of occupying a position where one can be heard.

The political consequences of a theory that precludes the possibility of distinguishing between the correctness of a knowledge-claim and access to power are invidious, for such a theory neutralizes the weapon foremost in the arsenal of the critic of ideology: namely, the fact that ideological beliefs are false. If the knowledge-claims of dominant ideology are relative to the position of the social agent who makes them, then the truth of ideological critique is also contaminated by the same relativity; and yet ideological assertions used to sustain forms of social domination are challenged most effectively on the grounds that they are false. Of course, demonstrating the falsity of ideological beliefs that are used to sustain forms of social domination does not guarantee access to state power. However, the failure of liberal democracies to measure up to the claims of reason provides the grounds for criticizing them, just as it provides grounds for criticizing those political cultures that have been defined by coercion and indoctrination – where the value of reason is undermined and truth is a function of social power.

In Chapter 2, I argue in detail that such a radically skeptical view of knowledge should be abandoned. The skeptic agrees with the Althusserian scientist that nonscientific knowledge-claims are based upon the assumption of an unclouded, presupposition-free presentation of the object of knowledge to the mind's eye, and that knowledge-claims are thus founded upon an illusion. Equally, the skeptic construes the fact that human action is shaped by norms and rules and values as a discovery that must radically change the way in which we conceive of human action, and disagrees with the Althusserian scientist only by denying that there is an Archimedian point from which the illusory character of these knowledge-claims can be judged. This view of knowledge and human agency is only supportable, however, if the empiricist conception of knowledge is accepted as an accurate description of the way in which knowledge-claims are made. Since that conception provides an erroneous characterization of the way we make knowledge-claims, the assertion that knowledge-claims are dependent upon or relative to a background of shared assumptions is not a discovery that licenses skepticism, nor should it undermine our conception of human agency; for it is the existence of assumptions and norms taken for granted that makes both knowledge and human agency possible.

I have argued that Althusser's redefinition of ideology in terms of epistemology should be rejected on political and epistemic grounds. To abandon Althusser, however, is not to abandon a theory of ideology. We need to begin with a narrower theory of ideology that is epistemically coherent and that retains the pejorative force of the term, thus rendering it politically useful. Such a theory of ideology has been put forward in the context of cultural studies by Terry Lovell in a significant though rather neglected monograph. "Ideology," Lovell writes, "may be defined as the production and dissemination of erroneous beliefs whose inadequacies are socially motivated."[17] Ideological beliefs are characterized not simply by the fact that they are beliefs motivated by social domination, but also by the fact that they are false. Of course, not all beliefs that are used for social domination are false. The fact that women, on average, have less muscular strength than men has been used to justify differences in the treatment of men and women that have worked to women's disadvantage. Prejudicial treatment of women is not justified by this belief, but the injustice of prejudicial attitudes toward women is not due to the fact that this belief is false. However, many beliefs that are used to justify forms of social domination *are* false, such as the belief that all black men are sexual predators, that the unemployed are essentially lazy, or that people are homosexual solely because they choose to be.

These beliefs can be countered not simply on the grounds that they are used to justify inequity and oppression but that they are false. At the same time, the falseness of certain beliefs is not sufficient to make them ideological, for many scientific propositions have turned out to be false.

The merit of Lovell's rational-agent theory of ideology is that it makes ideological beliefs "defeasible" (i.e., capable of being falsified). It assumes that individuals are not simply the dupe of ideology but have the capacity to recognize and resist its hold upon their lives. Of course, as Marx was well aware, reason alone is not sufficient to counter ideological beliefs where they support social privilege: Political action is also required. Furthermore, even where the iniquities of a social system are transparent, the system will not necessarily be challenged. However, this does not mean that compliance to the system is necessarily an irrational behavior explained by the fact that individuals are duped by ideology that has made them unable to recognize their own subjection to a situation inimical to their overall well-being. For example, drawing on empirical research into working-class beliefs, Carroll points out that, in general, workers are well aware of the false claims of capitalist ideology, and what binds them to the system is the imperative of earning a living: "Given the necessity of securing one's daily bread, and given the socially available means at one's disposal, it is a matter of rational choice, a simple practical syllogism, that the worker complies with capitalism."[18]

This kind of rational-agent theory of ideology cannot adequately explain the fact that ideological beliefs are often held to be true by those whom they serve to oppress, however. It must be complemented by a psychological explanation of the power of ideology. Such an explanation might take the form of specifying how a certain set of socially motivated false beliefs are sustained through their engagement with a citizen's imaginary conception of who she is or would like to be. It would seek to describe the way in which a political system may mobilize fantasies of its citizenry and the apparent wish fulfillment those fantasies afford in order to secure its own legitimation. Thus in so-called cultural imperialism the United States and its products are legitimized by projecting upon third-world peoples an illusory conception of what the United States is. However, what needs to be emphasized in the context of my criticism of Althusser's theory of ideology is that such a psychological explanation of the power of ideology takes place in the context of a conception of ideology as false belief. What sustains cultural imperialism is precisely a lack of education in or information about alternatives to the ideological belief that is purveyed through mass media. What ideology conceals is truth.

The Theory of the Cinematic Apparatus

Although Althusser is interested in demonstrating the pervasive role of ideology in reproducing the social relations of production, he does not equate art with ideology. On the one hand, art confronts us with everyday life in a manner that is akin to the way we experience everyday life, that is, in a manner unmediated by theoretical reflection. In this sense art is akin to ideology and opposed to science. On the other hand, art – at least what Althusser calls "authentic art" – presents us with everyday life in a manner that is mediated and circumscribed by an artistic form and medium. In this sense, art, like science, is at one remove from that everyday life, and provides us with a way of understanding ideology. However, the form of knowledge it produces is not the one that characterizes science. Althusser writes that "the real difference between art and science lies in the specific form in which they give us the same object in quite different ways: art in the form of 'seeing' and 'perceiving' or 'feeling,' science in the form of *knowledge* (in the strict sense, by concepts)."[19] Though he does not explain himself adequately, what Althusser seems to mean here is that art allows us to recognize that we live in ideology, but it does not, as science does, allow us to comprehend the historical conditions of existence of ideology; that is, it does not *explain* how ideology works.

In an influential essay entitled "Ideological Effects of the Basic Cinematographic Apparatus," published in the French film journal *Cinéthique* in the late sixties and subsequently translated into English in *Afterimage,* a journal of avant-garde film, Jean-Louis Baudry attempted to conceptualize the effect that the cinematic apparatus has upon the spectator in terms of Althusser's theory of ideology. He argues that the impression of reality created by the cinema literally reproduces the empiricist conception of knowledge in its ideal form: the absolutely transparent, presuppositionless vision of reality of a transcendental subject. Since the cinema reproduces the empiricist conception of knowledge, it offers a way for the critical spectator to understand how ideology creates an illusory relationship between subject and world. Baudry's argument comprises three interlocking components, which I shall discuss in turn.

The first part of Baudry's argument is that the conventions of monocular linear perspective enshrined in the camera provide a literal realization of the metaphor of knowledge as vision that underlies the empiricist conception of knowledge. The film spectator is positioned "ideologically" at the center of the visual field of the photographic image by the monocular perspective embodied in the camera lens. I shall call this argument "the thesis of perspec-

tival subject positioning." The second part of his argument is that the spectator in the cinema "identifies with the camera" and perceives the events that
are depicted in the image in the manner of a transcendental subject. That is,
the spectator is not simply positioned by the image but assimilates her own
vision to that of a camera-eye with limitless powers of vision and sees the
world viewed through this eye in a way that appears unmediated. I shall call
this argument, after Christian Metz, who echoes Baudry's contention, "the
thesis of primary cinematic identification." The third part of his argument is
that the spectator in the cinema is like the child before the mirror in Althusser's interpretation of Lacan's scenario. Since the spectator believes in the
reality of what he perceives, he is confirmed in the illusory sense of mastery
and self-coherence that defines the misrecognition of the subject and the
structure of the empiricist conception of knowledge. I shall call this
argument "the thesis of mirror misrecognition."

If Baudry were to conduct his argument in terms of Althusser's conception of authentic art, his claim might be cast in the following way: The cinema is ideological in its form because it is not authentic art; that is, it does not
present the world to us in a manner that appears mediated by artistic form.
In fact, the thesis of perspectival subject positioning contradicts Althusser's
attempt to differentiate ideology from authentic art. For, following a suggestion made by Marcelin Pleynet, Baudry claims that the conventions of
Renaissance perspective themselves provide a literal realization of the metaphor of knowledge as vision that underlies the empiricist conception of
knowledge:

Western easel painting, presenting as it does a motionless and continuous
whole, elaborates a total vision which corresponds to the idealist conception of
the fullness and homogeneity of "being," and is, so to speak, representative
of this conception. In this sense it contributes in a singularly emphatic way to
the ideological function of art, which is to provide the tangible representation
of metaphysics.[20]

Since the conventions of monocular perspective in Western art are reproduced by the camera lens, the empiricist conception of knowledge as ideology is also reproduced in the cinema. The film spectator is positioned "ideologically" at the center of the visual field of the photographic image by the
monocular perspective embodied in the camera lens.[21]

Let us assume, for the sake of argument, that Althusser's characterization
of ideology in terms of the empiricist conception of knowledge is cogent. If
the perspectival painting and the photograph serve to represent for the spectator the empiricist conception of knowledge (ideology) through embodying
the conventions of Renaissance perspective, they would also allow the spec-

tator to recognize ideology in a manner not unlike the idea of recognition proposed in Althusser's theory of "authentic" art. The premise of Althusser's theory of ideology is that the empiricist conception of knowledge conceals from the individual the nature of her own positioning in discourse as a subject. However, representational painting and photography per se do not entail that the spectator assent to or deny any truth-claims about the world, except in the sense that what the standard photograph depicts actually existed in front of the camera. If painting and photography are said to realize literally the metaphor of knowledge as vision, they also serve to unpack that metaphor, for they demonstrate to the spectator that her perception of "reality" is dependent upon a particular representation of that reality by the painter or photographer. Paintings or photographs *might* illustrate to the spectator an idea of how Althusserian ideology operates; but if they illustrate ideology to the spectator, they cannot operate ideologically upon her.

If ideology is to operate in cinematic representation in the manner required by the application of Althusser's theory, it must be shown that the spectator is deceived into believing that what is depicted is real. However, the argument about monocular perspective does not support the idea of cinematic illusion. As Carroll has argued, although monocular perspective is an accurate convention for mimetically depicting the distribution of objects in space, it does not necessarily compel us to experience the distribution of objects in space depicted by a painting or photograph as if they were real.[22] To claim that the painting or photograph of an object *resembles* the object itself does not entail our being deceived into thinking that the painting or photograph of the object *is* the object. I do not rule out the idea that representational paintings and photographs can be experienced as illusions. However, only under special circumstances do these objects *require* that we experience them as an illusion when we look at them. As Carroll correctly insists, there is no sense of illusion that can support the idea of monocular perspective as a form of representation that sustains the spectator's false beliefs about the world and her relationship to it.

The thesis of primary cinematic identification suggests a more explicit theory of illusion in the cinema that is independent of the thesis of perspectival subject positioning. According to Baudry a world of experience is created in the cinema, not quite analogous to the real world, but a "phantasmatization of objective reality," a world that is akin to the world of dream. Corresponding to this dreamlike world of experience, the cinema apparently augments the powers of the subject. The combination of recorded motion and mobile framing afforded by the cine-camera creates the condition of an eye that in Baudry's words "is no longer fettered by a body, by the laws of matter and time." He continues, "if there are no more assignable limits to its displacement – conditions fulfilled by the possibility of shooting and of film – the world will be constituted not only by this eye but for it. The mobility of the camera seems to fulfill the most favorable conditions for the manifestation of the transcendental subject."[23] The cinematic apparatus thus simultaneously creates a universe of perception and the position of the transcendental subject who perceives that universe. The spectator's identification with characters in a film and, more generally, his emotional response to what he sees, take place within and thus presuppose this transcendental perception. Baudry writes, "the second level [primary cinematic identification] permits the appearance of the first [secondary identification, or identification with an on-screen character] and places it 'in action' – this is the transcendental subject whose place is taken by the camera which constitutes and rules the objects in this 'world.'"[24]

In Chapter 4, I defend the idea that the spectator, in a certain sense, identifies with the position of the camera in the cinema. However, the thesis that the spectator in the cinema identifies with the camera does not necessarily imply the thesis of *primary* cinematic identification: Identification with the camera or the experience of the image as an illusion is not necessary in order for the spectator to have an emotional response to a film any more than it is necessary to experience a drama or representational painting as an illusion in order to have an emotional response to it. To be sure, my identification with characters in a film requires, first, that I recognize those characters and re-identify them over time. In *this* sense my identification with those whom I see presupposes that I see them; but this is not the sense in which the thesis of primary cinematic identification is proposed. The thesis of primary cinematic identification proposes that my emotional response to a character presupposes my gaze at that character in a manner predicated upon the particular quality of the gaze made possible by identification with the camera. It is this thesis that I contest.

The thesis of mirror misrecognition presupposes the full-blown thesis of primary cinematic identification and makes explicit the manner in which primary cinematic identification involves the ideological effects of the cinematic apparatus. The spectator in the cinema, perceiving the cinematic image in the form of an illusion of reality, is given what appears to be a transparent, unmediated perception of that world. However, the world that the spectator perceives, and hence the position from which she appears to perceive that world, are engendered by an apparatus. The cinematic apparatus produces a situation in which the subject's perception of reality is constituted together with the reality of the subject's experience. In this way the cinematic apparatus serves to perpetuate the spectator's disavowal of the fact that her perception of reality is determined only within and through representation:

> What emerges here (in outline) is the specific function fulfilled by the cinema as support and instrument of ideology. It constitutes the "subject" by the illusory delimitation of a central location – whether this be that of a god or of any other substitute. It is an apparatus destined to obtain a precise ideological effect, necessary to the dominant ideology: creating a phantasmatization of the subject, it collaborates with a marked efficacy in the maintenance of idealism.[25]

The thesis of mirror misrecognition exposes the position of the spectator who believes in the reality of what she sees, but for whom? Presumably the spectator in the cinema is not simply the dupe of cinematic illusionism but can recognize and resist the experience of illusion in the same manner as the theorist. The position of the spectator in the cinema is said to be "ideologically" constructed by the image; yet the spectator must simultaneously be capable of recognizing and resisting the ideological effect of the image. Although the theory of the cinematic apparatus is designed to demonstrate how the experiencing self is constructed in and through representation, it depends upon a subject who is not constructed in and through representation and who recognizes this process and can criticize it from the outside.[26] Thus the theory provides no basis to predict how any given spectator will experience the standard projected moving image as it occurs in narrative cinema. The spectator may equally experience the image illusionistically and hence "ideologically," or not illusionistically and hence as a critique of ideology. I shall argue in Chapter 3 that it is precisely this dual possibility that illuminates the character of cinematic illusionism, and thus also serves to undermine Baudry's attempt to apply Althusser's theory of ideology to the cinema.

I have centered my criticism of Baudry on the fact that it cannot be determined in advance that the spectator will experience any given image as an illusion, and still less as a transcendental subject. However, there is one kind of cinema in which the spectator's response to cinematic illusion *is* determined by the image, and that is where our capacity to see the projected moving image as an image of anything is precluded or attenuated, or when the material properties of the image are foregrounded. Baudry notes that the illusionistic effect of the cinematic apparatus is based upon the effacement of the materiality of the image, in particular the fact that the projected image is constituted out of a series of still photographic images on a two-dimensional strip of film. Baudry's essay thus appeared to lend an ideological significance to the work of certain practitioners within the American and British avant-gardes, such as Paul Sharits and Peter Gidal, whose concerns were to investigate and expose the material properties of the projected image – its basis in the still photograph, the film strip, and in projected light. These strategies of avant-garde practice differ from the moving image as it is presented in classical narrative film by forcing the spectator's awareness of the material basis of the image in such a way that may preclude entirely her illusionistic immersion within the image. These forms of filmmaking are misconstrued if they are considered to be in some way subversive of ideology, though they do conceivably undermine the hold of cinematic illusion upon the spectator, as I shall explore more fully in Chapter 3.

Baudry implies that there is a second sense in which the effect of cinematic illusion may be exposed that depends on the relationship established between the impression of reality in the cinema and continuity rules of cinematic narration. He suggests that while cutting, in the form of continuity editing, preserves the impression of reality in the cinema, it also threatens to draw the spectator's attention to the fact that the film is only a film and not the illusion of reality it appears to be, and thus threatens to expose the position of the transcendental ego to the spectator. Furthermore, Baudry argues that this potential level of discontinuity is directly related to the discontinuity produced by exposure of the material properties of film: "Continuity is an attribute of the subject. It supposes the subject and circumscribes its place. It appears in the cinema in the two complementary aspects of a 'formal' continuity established through a system of negated differences and narrative continuity in the filmic space."[27]

It is certainly true that, in order for continuity editing to preserve the impression of reality in the cinema, the illusion of continuous movement must first be established in the projected moving image. However, the impact of any given system of editing on the spectator's experience of illusion in the cinema is not predictable in the manner of an exposure of the material or technical basis of the medium, such as sprocket holes or scratches on the surface of the film. I would suggest that certain forms of storytelling facilitate the spectator's experience of illusion in the cinema and certain forms of storytelling in cinema attenuate it; but whether or not the spectator actually experiences a film or sequence of a film as an illusion cannot simply be read off the formal organization of a sequence of images.

Although Baudry's analysis of the cinematic image in terms of Althusser's theory of ideology collapses the distinction that Althusser wishes to draw between art and ideology, it does serve to clarify the problem that underlies Althusser's theory of ideology and the kind of thinking it represents. Baudry's theory of ideology conflates the form of the image with its content, the way we perceive an image with the way we understand it, and imputes this conflation to the spectator. As Noël Carroll has emphasized, ideology is not dependent on the fact that a picture is a picture; it is a function of particular kinds of representation and the form and context in which they are presented to us.[28] In a parallel way Althusser's theory of ideology understands ideology to be a function of the form that knowledge takes, of the way we make propositions about the world, rather than a function of the content of the propositions we make. However, ideology is not to be identified with the fact of making a knowledge-claim; rather, it describes particular kinds of knowledge-claims and the way we make them.

The Lacanian Subject

The theory of the cinematic apparatus suggests how the spectator is positioned ideologically by the cinematic apparatus; but as we have seen, it also raises the question of how the ideological effect of the apparatus is sustained or challenged by different practices of representation and narration. Film theorists turned to Lacanian psychoanalysis to extend apparatus theory, for it seemed to afford a theory of the way in which the subject is constructed in discourse over time. The idea of mirror misrecognition had already been borrowed from Lacan by Althusser to describe the interpellation of the subject in ideology, and was used in the context of this theory of ideology to describe the spectator's relationship to the cinematic apparatus. Thus it seemed to contemporary film theorists that Lacan's theory of the individual's relationship to language could be used to clarify and/or modify an Althusserian theory of the apparatus in order to understand the effect of the apparatus upon the subject, once images were edited together in a sequence for the purpose of storytelling. To understand the extension and modification of Althusserian film theory by Lacanian ideas, we must turn to Lacan's rereading of Freud.

Freud's central contribution to psychology was his discovery of the role that unconscious mental processes play in the mental life of human beings. Freudian psychoanalysis explains the place of the unconscious in mental life through a developmental account of the human being. Born into the world in a state of complete dependency on another, the human infant, provided he is nurtured, experiences a congruence between what he finds in the world and what he wants to find. The human infant is thus able to realize his desires in a manner that takes no heed of the external world. (Freud terms this activity "wish fulfillment.") Facing withdrawal of maternal support, the infant may sustain the fulfillment of his wishes through the exercise of his imagination. However, the mechanism of wish fulfillment threatens to debilitate the organism, since by affording it fulfillment of the wish, the imagination sustains and nurtures the wish itself, and so on ad infinitum. The development of language skills that emerge in conjunction with the infant's growing mastery over bodily processes allows the human being to subordinate his desires to beliefs about the world and thus to defer the apparent gratification of desires in imagination in favor of finding some measure of actual satisfaction in reality. This deferment of instinctual gratification involves repression and the formation of the unconscious, which consists of repressed – that is, unarticulated or idle – desires that constantly threaten to colonize rationally formulated beliefs about the world.

In his rereading of Freud, Lacan seeks to rescue him from his interpreters in a way that bears certain parallels to Althusser's attempt to rescue Marx. Lacan argues that latter-day interpretations of Freud have robbed Freudian psychoanalysis of the radical understanding of what it is to be a human being implied by the discovery of the unconscious. The school of ego psychology that developed in America in the postwar period sought to emphasize the extent to which the ego could be strengthened in analysis and the impact of the unconscious upon mental life minimized.[29] Ego psychology presumes that human communication (in particular, the psychoanalytic session) can take place in a manner that is unclouded by unconscious projections of what I would like the other to be (the transference). Lacan counters that such an interpretation of Freud gives the ego an apparent autonomy in mental life and in its transactions with the other that it actually lacks. According to Lacan, rather than being autonomous from the mechanism of the wish, the ego and the ego's perceptions of the other at once produce and are produced by that mechanism.

Lacan emphasizes the fact that the human infant's first moments of life are distinguished by a gap between her biological immaturity (characterized by her passive dependence on the environment and her intraorganic lack of coordination) and the highly developed state of her sensory faculties. Everything that the human being is, is due to the imposition of something that is alien or other. From the beginning of her life, the human attempts to overcome her biological deficiency by merging with an environment that she does not yet perceive as differentiated from her. She accomplishes this via the use of highly developed sensory organs – the mouth, anus, eyes, ears, and urinary duct – that enable the infant to forge a link between the as-yet undifferentiated inner and outer worlds by the movement of objects through them: the nipple, stool, the urinary stream, the gaze, and the voice (phoneme). Lacan calls these objects *objets petits a(utres),* objects that have only a "little otherness."[30] Lacan follows Melanie Klein in describing these objects as at once psychical and somatic, symbolic and substantive in character. For Klein, the movement of these objects are the operations of a mind governed by a corporeal conception of itself as a body or container. The mind conceives of thoughts as objects, and conceives of its own thought processes in terms of the incorporation and expulsion of objects.[31] For Lacan, however, the mind does not yet *conceive* of thoughts and thought processes, for it is constituted out of those processes. Thus the original condition of the subject is a state of no-thing-ness (the real) in which the subject is fragmented or dispersed across a field of symbol-substances.

Lacan's view of the development of the subject follows from this original condition of dispersal in a manner that is reminiscent of Hegel. For Hegel, the subject develops through successive stages of self-alienation in encounter with the other. The three stages of development that Lacan isolates are the real, the imaginary (the mirror stage), and the symbolic. However, since Lacan starts with a state of being in which symbol and substance, subject and object, are not yet differentiated, this has a radical effect upon how he conceptualizes "development," for the activity of describing already presupposes a distinction between symbol and substance, subject and object, that is not yet achieved. The original condition of the subject can be explained only by naming it as something: a broken egg or *homolette,* in Lacan's words. However, this original condition can only ever be described *after* the event. This point has been made by Jane Gallop in her discussion of the mirror stage: "The image of the body in bits and pieces is fabricated retrospectively from the mirror stage. It is only the anticipated 'orthopedic' form of its totality that can define – retrospectively – the body as insufficient."[32] In this way, Lacan gives an enlarged explanatory role to the Freudian concept of deferred action (*Nachträglichkeit*). In the history of the subject, what comes after determines the effect of what comes before.

Bearing in mind the inadequacy of a developmental account of the subject from the perspective of Lacanian psychoanalysis, we may describe the imaginary or the mirror stage as the moment when the distinction between the me and the not-me is constituted. According to Lacan, this occurs between the ages of 6 and 18 months, and coincides with what psychoanalysts would call the pre-Oedipal stage of development. For Lacan, the distinction between the me and not-me cannot be simply cast as an opposition between the ego and the other, since the ego itself is formed in a relationship of transference that occurs as a result of the encounter with the other. Lacan seizes on the common occurrence of the child's encounter with his image in the mirror as an allegory of the way in which the subject is divided in his encounter with the other. In the mirror (of the other) the self or ego anticipates a form for itself as an autonomous, unified entity that is distinct from the environment that surrounds it. The child pictures himself in the form that he thinks the other requires him to take. The encounter with the other in the mirror stage marks the coming into being for the subject of the distinction between subject and object out of the chaos of infantile body experience; but the ego's sense of itself as an autonomous, unified entity and the reality it appears to experience are both illusions. The real condition of the subject is no-thing-ness and not the unified, autonomous entity confronting a separate knowable reality that the ego conceives itself to be in the mirror. Because the subject is divided from himself in his encounter with the other, the experience of the imaginary is characterized by ambivalence. The child is captivated by the temporary image of himself that the other bestows, because of the concomitant sense of autonomy and agency; but he also experiences that self-image as an "armour of an alienating identity" that constrains and confines him.[33]

Lacan cannot be charged with the problem that besets Althusser's appropriation of his theory; namely, that recognition precedes misrecognition, or that there must be a subject before the mirror who misrecognizes herself in it. For Lacan, before the mirror, spatially and temporally, there is the subject as no-thing-ness. Only after the mirror does a subject exist as a thing with recognition capacities. The subject endowed with the capacity to recognize – the knowing subject – *is* a function of its representation in the gaze of the other; but what the subject recognizes is now always a misrecognition, for she is really no-thing-ness and not the ego that she thinks herself to be. However, although recognition does not precede misrecognition, the former is not, within the mirror stage or the imaginary, simply reducible to the latter. Since, in the mirror stage, the subject is endowed with recognition capacities, she is reminded of the no-thing-ness or lack that presupposes her existence. This possibility defines the drama of the imaginary and the inception of the Freudian wish, which Lacan calls "desire," in the life of the subject. The subject is driven by an awareness of her lack to become a whole under the gaze of the other, to make good her lack. Yet the experience of wholeness under the gaze of the other is predicated upon her lack. Desire is born of a search for integration that is impossible to satisfy, and this creates an ambivalence toward the subject's self-image that is permanent for her. In pre-Oedipal terms, this ambivalence is expressed in the impossible desire to merge with the mother. However, the reminder of no-thing-ness that defines the ambivalence of the imaginary is subsequently repressed. The cause of this secondary repression is the entry of the subject into the symbolic, which causes the mirror to become an opaque screen or wall.[34] The relationship between no-thing-ness before the mirror and the something that exists after the mirror is severed. Once again, it should be remembered that, for Lacan, just as the condition of no-thing-ness is retrospectively defined by the imaginary, so the condition of the subject in the imaginary is retrospectively defined by the symbolic order.

For Lacan, the symbolic order is closely associated with the acquisition of language and coincides with the Oedipus complex and the threat of castration: the child's encounter with sexual difference. Lacan uses another event common in the life of the child as a metaphor to describe how the encounter with the symbolic order affects the child's development. In *Beyond the Pleasure Principle,* Freud tells how his grandson plays with a wooden reel on a string that he throws away from himself and then pulls back, as he exclaims *fort* (gone) and *da* (here). For Freud, the *fort–da* or peekaboo game illustrates the way in which the little boy masters separation from his mother;[35] but for Lacan, as we have seen, separation is conceived as a process of intrapsychic division or self-alienation. Thus while the game remains one of mastery, the reel does not simply represent the mother but "a small part of the subject that detaches itself from him while still remaining his, still retained" or an *objet petit a(utre).*[36]

Any attempt to understand the significance of the *fort–da* game for Lacan is complicated by the fact that he gives it two interpretations with competing emphasis. In the first interpretation, given in his first seminar and in his essay "The Function and Field of Speech and Language," the significance of the *fort–da* game rests in the child's acquisition of language with which the symbolic order is identified.[37] The emphasis of this interpretation is on the relationship between the imaginary and symbolic. Although Lacan does not explicitly say this, the *fort–da* game, prior to the moment that language is uttered, may be considered analogous to the child's game involving its reflection in the mirror.[38] When the cotton reel is detached from the subject, it allows the subject to experience itself as a unified ego like the image in the mirror; when it is present to the subject and no longer provides the otherness in which the subject can be reflected, the subject experiences the sense of fragmentation that retrospectively defines its prespecular condition. For Lacan, the acquisition of language skills allows the subject to overcome this imaginary oscillation, but only at the cost of a radical self-alienation.

Lacan's second interpretation of the *fort–da* game is presented in his eleventh seminar, entitled *The Four Fundamental Concepts of Psychoanalysis.*[39] Here Lacan's concern is not with the acquisition of language per se; instead, the symbolic order is identified with the game of presence and absence itself that replaces the gap caused by the mother's departure.[40] In this interpretation of the *fort–da* game Lacan emphasizes the relationship between the real and the symbolic or between absence (no-thing-ness) and the binary signifying structure that supervenes. It is as if Lacan wants to stress the fact that there is no imaginary "stage" for the subject to pass through for the subject is "always-already" in the symbolic. The function of the cotton reel (the *objet petit a[utre]*) is only comprehensible in relationship to the symbolic structure that defines it. For this reason Lacan reads the symbolic into the game with the cotton reel itself or with the child's image in the mirror, rather than identifying the symbolic with something that comes after – namely, language acquisition. However, if we are to retain a concept of the imaginary at all, it has to be inserted somewhere between no-thing-ness or lack and the binary structure that supervenes. These two accounts may be reconciled with the suggestion that although the symbolic structure is anticipated by the game with the cotton reel, the functioning of that structure is still understood by Lacan in terms of language. Equally, although the game with the cotton reel can be identified with the symbolic structure, it can also represent the imaginary relation that pretends to exist outside this structure. The metaphor of the *fort–da* game is most illuminating when read from both sides, imaginary and symbolic. Thus I shall emphasize the distinction between the physical game with the reel and the utterance that accompanies it that is presupposed in Lacan's two different accounts of the game.

In the mirror of the imaginary, the imaginary ego's reflection in the gaze of the other stands in for or replaces no-thing-ness or lack. In this sense, the gaze of the other, whose function can be said to be taken up by the wooden reel, serves to represent the subject as lack. This representation is what Lacan calls the "unary signifier," a symbol that does not refer to anything outside itself. The child's utterance of *fort* (gone) is the hinge on which the transition from imaginary to symbolic takes place. Invoking a particular interpretation of Saussurian linguistics, Lacan argues that *fort* gains its meaning for the subject only through its differential relation to *da* (here). It is what Lacan calls a "binary signifier." The subject establishes his identity in relationship to otherness through the linguistic assertion of *fort;* but the capacity of this assertion to sustain the subject's identity is contingent on the utterance of *da,* the expression that serves to define the meaning of *fort.* Only when the subject utters *da* is his identity, expressed through *fort,* retrospectively ensured. However, the same logic applies to the subject's self-definition as he utters *da,* and so on ad infinitum. The integrity of the speaking subject is only as good as his last utterance, and that is never good enough to sustain him. Thus the subject is caught or sutured in the endless network of signifiers out of which the language system is comprised, as the ego seeks to maintain its sense of self-mastery and coherence.

This final condition of the subject as the speaking, socialized ego (the *je* or I) is characterized by the fact that it is doubly alienated from the original condition of the subject. The cotton reel qua unary signifier, along with the imaginary reflection of the subject it affords, disappears and is replaced by the symbolic structure. It is the child's utterance of *fort* (gone), a symbolic action, that now makes the reel disappear for him. When the reel is here, the utterance of *fort* anticipates its subsequent movement away. Likewise, the child's utterance *da* (here) anticipates the reel's return after it has been made absent by the first utterance.[41] A binary signifier now represents the subject, displacing the unary signifier. When the subject asserts himself through the utterance *fort,* the "I" necessarily disappears (together with the object referred to), and that disappearance is a condition of its reappearance (together with the object referred to) when he utters *da.* Symbolic mastery allows the subject to transcend the condition of imaginary identity and pre-Oedipal merger – the unstable oscillation between a sense of wholeness and dissolution – only by making the sense of lack internal to the subject's sense of wholeness and mastery. Lacan labels the process of double repression from the primordial self to the imaginary ego (the *moi*) to the social speaking subject (the *je*) the "aphanisis," or disappearance, of the subject:

[T]he subject appears first in the Other, insofar as the first signifier, the unary signifier, emerges in the field of the Other and represents the subject for another signifier, which other signifier has as its effect the *aphanisis* of the subject. Hence the division of the subject – when the subject appears somewhere as meaning he is manifested elsewhere as "fading," as disappearance. There is, then, one might say, a matter of life and death between the unary signifier and the subject, *qua* binary signifier, cause of his disappearance.[42]

Lacan's allegory of the subject's entry into and position within language is heavily dependent upon the theory of meaning that he extracts from Saussure's *Course in General Linguistics.*[43] In the *Course,* Saussure argues that, in order to be an autonomous field of inquiry, linguistics must conceive of language as a system of signs (*langue*) rather than as the totality of speech acts or token sentences made within a language (*langage*). As a result, a sharp distinction must also be drawn between the language system (*langue*) and the speech act (*parole*) that the existence of the system allows the individual to make. Saussure conceives of *langue* as a system of relations between signs that consists of correlations between sound-images (signifiers) and concepts (signifieds). The meaning of any sign is established diacritically or differentially in relationship to the other signs that together form the language system. There is thus, Saussure argues, no intrinsic bond between a given signifier and what it signifies. Differences at the semantic level are often, though not always, expressed through differences at the phonemic level. Thus the difference in meanings between the words "bat" and "cat" is signaled by the phonemic difference of the "b" and "c"; but the alignment of the word "bat" with the meaning of a small, black, nocturnal, winged creature, as opposed to a medium-sized, furry, domestic animal, is unmotivated or arbitrary.

Some interpreters of Saussure have taken this to imply that the meaning of a sign is a product solely of its differential relationship to other signs; in fact, this idea is central to Lacan's conception of the relationship of the subject to language. However, such an understanding of meaning severs meaning from reference, and thereby fails to explain how it is possible to learn a language and communicate in it. Saussure offers a diacritical conception of meaning because he writes from the point of view of a linguist who is concerned with mapping the system of phonemic differences that constitute a *langue*. However, it would scarcely be possible for the word "bat" to mean a small, black, nocturnal, winged creature if there did not already exist the practice of using the word "bat" to refer to a small, black, nocturnal, winged creature. The ability to define the word "bat" as such a creature, as opposed to a medium-sized, furry, domestic animal, is evidence that someone understands the meaning of the word "bat." What my ability to define the word "bat" amounts to is precisely my ability to use the word "bat" to refer to the creatures that hang out in the belfry, rather than in reference to the medium-sized, furry, domestic pet that curls up at the foot of my bed. If I consistently and seriously used the word "bat" to refer to my medium-sized, furry, domestic pet, it would be natural to conclude that I did not understand the meaning of the word, even if I were able to parrot a formal definition of the word as a "small, black, nocturnal, winged creature."

The view that the meaning of a word arises out of its use as a tool of communication is elaborated and defended in the later philosophy of Wittgenstein, which I discuss in the next chapter. However, one does not have to be a disciple of Wittgenstein to recognize the centrality of reference to meaning. Any view of word meaning that takes seriously the role of reference offers a challenge to Lacan's account of the relationship of the subject to language. The basic shift charted by Lacan's account of the child's relationship to language is a plausible one. That relationship begins in a context where words often carry a subjective emotional charge governed by the transferential relationship that the child has with the other; but when she begins to master language more fully as a tool of communication, the subjective meaning that a signifier might have had for the subject is lost beneath its objective meaning and becomes unconscious. We might conclude, with Lacan, that this subjective, transferential meaning is *potentially* at stake in any utterance, without undermining the possibility of communication. However, Lacan wishes to undermine the autonomy of rationality entirely: He contends that every communication is miscommunication because the speaking subject expresses herself only at the cost of the disappearance of the real. The mechanism that guarantees that the subject is never exactly whence she speaks is the diacritical theory of meaning; but the fact that this theory of meaning serves to support Lacan's theory of the subject is no reason to assent to it.

Lacan writes within the Freudian tradition of psychoanalysis in the sense that he emphasizes the permanent effectivity of the unconscious over mental life; but his characterization of the way in which the effect of the unconscious mental processes over mental life is to be conceived is idiosyncratic. For Lacan, the ego and rational mental life are strictly dependent upon and relative to the impersonal mechanism of the Freudian wish produced by the encounter with the other that forms the subject. From a more developmental view of the subject, the mechanism of the wish is a function of the limited cognitive powers of the infant at a certain stage of the growth of the human organism. If the mechanism of the wish continues to exert its force on the life of the mind, it is by virtue of the fact that the characteristics of mental life that serve to sustain it – in particular the capacity of iconic mental states to simulate the effect upon the mind of actual experiences – persist in adult mental life alongside rational mental processes. Lacan's view does not ignore development – after all, mirror misrecognition is a function of the individual's cognitive capacity to discriminate the contours of solid objects – but these developmental considerations are always subsumed into the dialectic of the other in a way that undermines the autonomy of rationality.

Although there exists a condition of mental life that is *genetically* prior to the development of rationality, it does not follow that this condition of mental life should have *explanatory* primacy over rational mental life. Yet by recasting developmental achievements into the dialectic of the subject, Lacan guarantees that what is genetically prior *is* given explanatory priority in the explanation of mental life. However, from a developmental perspective, the capacity of adult mental life to regress to more primitive forms of mental functioning does not entail that adult mental life is strictly governed by those forms. It is as unwarranted to conclude from the existence of unconscious mental processes that the development of cognitive faculties are determined by them as it would be to conclude that cognitive powers remain unaffected by them. In my view, Lacan is correct in wanting to emphasize the role that the overvaluation of mental life and mental capacities continues to play in the life history of the individual, in contradistinction to those post-Freudian analysts who focused their attention on the relationship between the ego and reality; but Lacan's interpretation of Freud radically undervalues the role that ego functions play in mental life. The appropriate response to an ego psychology that claims autonomy for the ego is not to deny autonomy altogether, but to understand the way in which the ego is more or less autonomous from or, conversely, more or less dependent upon unconscious mental processes.

The Theory of Cinematic Suture

Jacques-Alain Miller, one of Lacan's pupils, describes the relation of the subject to her discourse, illustrated by Lacan in the allegory of the *fort–da* game, as the suturing of the subject in language.[44] The word "suture" connotes the idea that the subject is stitched together by language, but it also suggests that, as in surgery, a wound or hole is covered over that always leaves a scar. The French theorist and critic Jean-Pierre Oudart uses the theory of the subject's sutured relationship to discourse to explain the relationship of the spectator to the image sequence of narrative cinema. Oudart focuses on one of narrative cinema's basic building blocks – the shot/reverse shot – where images whose visual fields are complementary with one another are alternated in sequence. In shot/reverse shot sequences, the first shot is typically connected to the second by an eyeline match on a character's look. For Oudart, the shot/reverse shot presupposes a role for the spectator in comprehending it that provides a model or analogue for the dialectic of the subject's relationship to language as it is described by Lacan.

Oudart posits a "mythical" moment in the spectator's encounter with the first image of the shot/reverse shot sequence when she does not see the image as an image but experiences it as a fluid, fantasmatic reality and recognizes the frame in a manner that is only fleeting and unstable. The spectator's vacillation between a fantasy of engulfment and awareness of the frame corresponds to the relationship of the child to the image in the mirror or to the cotton reel in the *fort–da* allegory prior to the utterance of *fort*. This oscillation ceases when the spectator realizes that the contents of the image are framed in a manner that is relative to the point of view of an ideal off-screen observer, "the subject of a vision which is not his own," which Oudart calls the Absent One.[45] This revelation is equivalent to the child's initial utterance of *fort,* for the spectator's mastery of the image is established at the cost of her own disappearance: The position of mastery is not the spectator's own but that of the Absent One. However, when the image is embedded in a shot/reverse shot sequence the imaginary position of the Absent One is converted into the real space of the reverse shot, which functions for the spectator like the utterance of *da*. The first image is retrospectively endowed with meaning as the visual field of a character who occupies the reverse shot: "[T]he appearance of a lack perceived as a Some One (the Absent One) is followed by its abolition by someone (or something) placed within the same field."[46] In this way the lack upon which the subject's relationship to cinematic discourse is founded – the position of the Absent One – is elided. The spectator's anticipation of the second image and recollection of the first binds the spectator into the discourse of the film in a manner that parallels the suturing of the subject into language.

Oudart provides a rudimentary outline of three kinds of shot/reverse shot sequences according to whether or not they successfully dramatize for the spectator the role that the Absent One plays in her comprehension of the image sequence. Oudart notes that the shot/reverse shot structure is a common editing strategy of "subjective cinema" (Oudart's term for classical Hollywood cinema), where it is employed without being brought to the consciousness of the spectator. In classical cinema the field of the Absent One (and hence the cut that divides the shots) is not drawn to our attention, for the Absent One is consistently identified with the glance of a character that covers over the cut. Oudart contrasts classical narration with the style of Robert Bresson in *The Trial of Joan of Arc* (1962). Bresson composes shots in shot/reverse shot sequences at oblique angles in relationship to the profilmic space that vary from shot to shot. In this way the space of the first shot does not correspond to the eyeline of a character in the second shot despite the presence of a character in the second shot. While the position of the Absent One is absorbed into the reverse field through the presence of the character, the space of the Absent One (and hence of the cut) is also highlighted by the obliqueness of the angle. A third kind of narration would consist in films that did not display shot/reverse shot articulations. The example Oudart gives is Bresson's *Au hazard, Balthazar* (1966), whose protagonist is a donkey. Once shot/reverse shot articulations are abandoned the position of the Absent One is indicated at the expense of the suturing of the subject into the film. Oudart makes clear in a later article that when the position of the Absent One is made overt, it may be identified by the spectator with the narrator of the film.[47]

The relationship between Oudart's theory of cinematic suture and the application of Althusser's theory of ideology to understanding spectatorship in the cinema is not made explicit in Oudart's essay. However, elsewhere in his writings, Oudart does discuss the ideological implications of what I have called the "thesis of perspectival subject positioning" in relationship to representational painting.[48] Oudart's discussion of ideology was brought together with his theory of cinematic suture by Daniel Dayan. The thesis of perspectival subject positioning suggests that the ideological effect of the perspectival image is to establish the field of the image as the apparent gaze of an all-seeing, transcendental subject. The spectator necessarily inhabits this visual field once she understands the relationship between the elements in the image relative to its frame. For Dayan, the ideological effect of classical cinema is to conceal from the spectator the fact that she inhabits the gaze of the Absent One or the other. Through the reverse shot the spectator does not view the image as an image produced from somewhere but as the visual field of a character within the fiction and thus produced from nowhere. The filmed fiction thus appears unauthored or even authored by the spectator. For Dayan, Oudart's analysis "deconstructs" the illusion of an unauthored fiction by exposing the mechanism upon which it is constructed. Dayan makes no distinction among the different ways in which the suturing process might work. He reduces Oudart's three options to two: Either the spectator is sutured into the narrative unaware of the cut, or the film that refuses reverse-field cutting undoes suturing – such as, for example, Jean-Luc Godard's *Wind from the East* (1970), in which "the shot tends to constitute a complete statement, and . . . the absent-one is continuously perceived by the spectator."[49]

It is evident that Dayan's interpretation of suture differs from Oudart's. For Oudart the central case of suture is precisely the case of Bresson's *Trial of Joan of Arc,* in which he argues that the position of the Absent One is made evident to the spectator even as suturing occurs. His account suggests that even in classical Hollywood cinema there is a latent awareness of the suturing operation. The assumption that the spectator is so readily made aware that her field of vision is the field of the Absent One seems contrary to the assumption that underpins the claim of apparatus theory and Dayan's account; namely, that the spectator in the cinema is not medium aware until her attention is drawn to the image as an image. Perhaps the two accounts can be provisionally reconciled in the following way: When the spectator occupies the position of the Absent One and takes its imaginary field as her own, she disavows the lack on which her perception of the image is based. When the shot is embedded in a shot/reverse shot sequence the cut threatens to lay bare the position of the Absent One, but such a revelation is thwarted as the place of the Absent One is taken by a character in the fiction. In this way the impression of reality created by the image is sustained across the cut through reverse-field cutting.

However, whether or not the theory of the spectator's ideological absorption in the cinematic image is compatible in this way with the theory of cinematic suture, the equivocation that besets the first theory also undermines the attempt to discriminate different narrational systems on the basis of whether or not the position of the Absent One is made evident or concealed to the spectator. Oudart and Dayan describe classical Hollywood cinema as a form of narration that elides the spectator's awareness of the Absent One and hence binds the spectator to the film in a manner of which she remains unaware. Why is it, however, that classical Hollywood cinema disguises the cut rather than dramatizing the nature of the spectator's relation to representation in the way that Oudart claims for Bresson? The editing pattern of the shot/reverse shot is certainly ubiquitous in classical Hollywood cinema, but it does not comprise the entirety of any one film and it does not typically take the form that Dayan ascribes to it.[50] Because the figure of reverse-field cutting is not a uniform one as Oudart's theory suggests, it will sometimes tend to draw attention to itself and at other times tend to be invisible, depending on how it is used. There is, in principle, no way to determine in a shot-by-shot, blow-by-blow fashion that any given system of narration reveals or conceals the position of the Absent One for the spectator, just as in the theory of the apparatus there is no way to establish that any given spectator will perceive an image as an illusion.

The process by which the subject is sutured in discourse – described by Miller, after Lacan – is essentially unconscious. Oudart and Dayan want to argue that this unconscious process is exemplified in the spectator's response to the reverse-field cut; but how can the spectator's response to such cutting exemplify this unconscious process? Lacanian theory would illuminate nothing about the spectator's response to the image in the cinema were that response considered merely a metaphorical illustration or model of that theory. If Lacanian theory were used in this way, spectatorship would act as an illumination of suture only for those theorists who have a grasp of the theory. The task of Oudart and Dayan must be to describe the way in which the *spectator* in the cinema can become conscious of this process; but this condition inevitably conflicts with the requirement that cinema spectatorship *illustrate* Lacan's theory. Beyond the question of whether or not Lacan's theory is true, this conflict leads suture theory to founder. Even where the intention is to describe a process that is conscious, the way in which psy-

choanalytic theory is deployed by suture theorists results in a theory that illuminates the character of spectatorship in the cinema only for those in the
grip of the theory. The kind of psychoanalytic theory required to explain the
spectator's psychological response to the image is one that builds into the
theory itself an acknowledgment of the role of the conscious spectator. I try
to offer such a theory in Chapter 4.

A final objection to suture theory is that it collapses two different dimensions of a spectator's response to film that must be distinguished. Oudart's
analysis of the shot/reverse shot sequence is offered as a rationalization of
the way in which we understand narrative. It is also a theory of the way in
which we respond emotionally to a film, in particular, how our emotional
response governs medium awareness. However, his theory of narrative
comprehension is explained through the theory of emotional response and
medium awareness; yet as David Bordwell has suggested, the cognitive processes that govern a spectator's comprehension of a sequence of images in
the cinema are not dependent, in this way, upon emotional response.[51] The
two aspects of spectator response to narrative cinema require separate explanation before their relationship in any given case can be understood. My
concern here is with how suture theory illuminates our understanding of
medium awareness in the cinema, whereas loss of medium awareness and
immersion in the image do not affect those aspects of spectator response ex-
plicated by a theory of narrative comprehension such as the one proposed
by Bordwell.

For my purposes, then, the value of Oudart's theory (as opposed to that
of Dayan) lies in its suggestion that a movement in and out of medium
awareness is possible in all cinema. He also suggests that a loss of medium
awareness may take two distinct forms: one a sense of identification with a
masterful gaze, the other a sense of loss or immersion in the image. Whether it does take place will depend partly on the character of the narrational
system. For example, we might contrast, in the manner of Oudart, the relatively impersonal systematic, formulaic character of Hollywood narration,
whose rationale is to maximize the spectator's experience of illusion, with
the highly anti-illusionist style of Soviet montage and certain films of the experimental avant-garde. However, whether or not a spectator actually views
a film as a medium-aware spectator is not strictly predictable. Hence the
metaphor of suture that implies the force of a binding or tying up is not
appropriate to describe the spectator's relationship to the experience of the
impression of reality in the cinema. Furthermore, what exactly medium
awareness is, or conversely, how it is that the cinema and other forms of

aesthetic representation allow us to experience them in the form of an illusion, remains to be conceptualized. I attempt to address these issues in Chapter 3.

Marxist Literary Modernism and Cinematic Enunciation

As we have seen, Dayan's theory of suture suggests a parallel between the ideological effect of the individual image and that of the text as a whole. Just as the spectator misrecognizes the image as an illusory world and hence a product of his own transcendental viewpoint, he also misrecognizes the classic Hollywood film as something that appears to lack a narrator and therefore appears to be a product of his own consciousness. Some of the limitations of the Oudart–Dayan analysis of suture were apparent to film theorists like Stephen Heath who sought to develop the theory. Heath rejects these theorists' dependence on the figure of the shot/reverse shot and the blow-by-blow account of suturing it implies in favor of a broader theory of narration that is strongly influenced by the Marxist literary modernism of Julia Kristeva.

For Kristeva, literature has the capacity to expose the subject's relationship to language in broadly the same way that the cinema functions for Oudart. However, her conception of this relationship differs from suture theory for she does not identify language simply with the symbolic. In a speculative interpretation of Lacan's theory of the subject, Kristeva argues that the subject has two kinds of relationship to signification, of which suture theory names only one: that of the subject to the symbolic. However, Kristeva contends that where the real meets the imaginary there exists "a modality of signification in which the linguistic sign is not yet articulated as the absence of an object and as the distinction between real and symbolic."[52] Kristeva calls this form of signification the "semiotic" and the realm of prespecular maternal body experience in which it functions the "chora." Within this realm of body experience, subjectivity is a process, a condition of constant fluidity, reversibility, and transformation. Kristeva contrasts this fluid, as-yet undifferentiated subject to that constructed in the symbolic, where "multiple constraints – which are ultimately socio-political – stop the signifying process . . . ; they knot it and lock it into a given surface or structure."[53] Within the realm of the symbolic, the subject is constructed "ideologically" as the transcendental subject in the manner described by Althusser. Between the semiotic and symbolic lies the process of misrecognition that marks the coming into being of the distinction between sign and substance, subject and object. Kristeva conceives of mirror misrecognition as the moment in which the subject uses language to make an assertion. She writes:

The sign can be conceived as the voice that is projected from the agitated body (from the semiotic *chora*) onto the facing *imago* or onto the object, which simultaneously detach from the surrounding continuity [the moment of misrecognition]. . . . On the bases of this positing, which constitutes a *break*, signification becomes established as a digital system with a double articulation combining discrete elements [entry into the symbolic].[54]

The relationship that the subject bears to language when it enters into rational thought is a precarious and provisional one, according to Kristeva. Language allows the subject to categorize and circumscribe the world and, in the same gesture, to become a speaking subject. Through the process of making sense, the subject creates the world of objects to experience, and creates herself, as a subject, to experience that world of objects in accordance with the empiricist conception of knowledge. However, this process of making sense is always a reification of the spatiotemporal flux of experience that characterizes the chora. The subject's assertion of itself in the symbolic always falls short of expressing the subject's desire and is undercut by the heterogeneity and disunity that defines the chora, until the speaking subject reasserts herself once again.

In Kristeva's conception of the subject's relationship to language, the concept of ideology is regrounded in the Hegelian dialectic; but whereas in Marx ideology is a manifestation of false consciousness, for Kristeva ideology is a manifestation of the falsity of consciousness itself. The historical understanding that provides the corrective to the falsity of consciousness is not the history of humankind's reproduction of its material conditions of existence, but rather the ceaseless movement of the subject between semiotic heterogeneity and symbolic closure that is at stake every time an individual makes an assertion.

For Kristeva, literature, the making of assertions in a nonserious or fictional way, has the capacity to expose to the subject the form by which it is held together by language in a manner that is unavailable to the individual when she is speaking seriously. Kristeva's analysis of literature draws on the same theory of narration invoked by Dayan, which has its origins in the writings of the phenomenological linguistics of Emile Benveniste. In the course of exploring the function of personal pronouns in language, Benveniste draws a distinction between two aspects of a spoken or written sentence: the "enunciation" (*l'énonciation*) and the "enounced" (*l'énoncé*). The enunciation consists of the context of an utterance, including place, time, and person. The enounced is the statement considered as a syntactically and grammatically coherent string of words. Benveniste makes a further discrimination between those spoken or written sentences that contain explicit markers of person and those that do not. "Discourse" (*discours*) designates those forms of speech or writing that contain a reference to "I" or "you," as in "I met Robin at the movies." It is a form of enunciation that does not hide the fact that it is an enunciation. "Story" (*histoire*) designates those forms of speech or writing that lack reference to "I" or "you," as in "Once upon a time, Robin met Paul at the movies." It is a form of enunciation that is detached from a communicative situation and does not refer to a subject of enunciation or a narrator. Benveniste writes that in the historic mode of narration "there is then no longer even a narrator. The events are set forth chronologically, as they occurred. No one speaks here; the events seem to narrate themselves."[55]

Kristeva and other literary Marxists characterize, in the terms of Benveniste's categories, the effect of literary realism as it was embodied in the nineteenth-century historical novel. Rather than conceiving *histoire* and *discours* as mutually exclusive forms of narration, as Benveniste had done, they see the novel as a form of *histoire* that conceals itself as *discours*. In the historical novel that Roland Barthes called *écriture classique* and, later, the "readerly" text, the author's voice is concealed: The events narrated by the novel appear to be transparently presented to the reader.[56] For Kristeva, the classical text's effacement of its own signs of enunciation is ideological in the sense that it mimes the empiricist conception of knowledge. However, Kristeva argues that the reader is not simply the dupe of this process, for he must assume the position of the implied narrator, and must therefore understand that *histoire* is really *discours,* in order to be a reader. Realist fiction thus draws attention to the position of the transcendental subject who makes sense, but it does not challenge the position of that subject who is the condition of the text's intelligibility.

Marxist literary modernists contrast the novel with the modernist (or what Barthes called the "writerly") text. The writerly text wears the signs that it is an enunciation on its sleeve and takes as its subject matter the process of its own writing in such a way that the reader is refused a stable position of knowledge from which to comprehend the story world. For Kristeva, modernist or "poetic" discourse, such as the writings of Joyce, Artaud, and Mallarmé, in contrast to the classical novel, stages the relationship between the transcendental subject and the object known in or as its content. Realist fiction imitates the empiricist conception of knowledge, where the knowing subject is constituted in a position that is separated and detached from the object known, even as it shows that position to be a function of discourse. In contrast, according to Kristeva, the modernist text demonstrates to the reader the impossibility or illusion of such a position of knowledge: "[I]t attacks not only denotation (the positing of the object) but meaning (the positing of the enunciating subject) as well, . . . [and] puts the subject in process/on trial through a network of marks and semiotic facilitations."[57]

In the early applications of this theory of narration to the cinema, such as the suture theory of Dayan, the distinction between the realist and modernist text is cast as a crude opposition between illusionism and reflexivity in a manner that reproduces the epistemological dilemmas of apparatus theory. Kristeva's theory of the realist text moves beyond this conception by recognizing that the way in which the realist text represents reality also demonstrates to the reader that the relationship between subject and reality is a function of signification. In this way, as I have suggested, Kristeva's theory of the reader parallels Oudart's analysis of the image sequence in the cinema that draws attention to the position of the viewer; but, by the same token, Kristeva's theory is open to the objections that I have already leveled at the Oudart–Dayan theory. In particular, Kristeva's reader, like Oudart or Dayan's viewer, must be made conscious of the process by which she is ideologically constructed in language if her encounter with the text is to free her from the hold of ideology. However, the only person who could be made conscious of this process through her encounter with the text is the analyst who believes in the theory.

Stephen Heath's film theory can be understood in general terms as an extension of the kind of analysis begun by Oudart and Dayan to an understanding of classical Hollywood cinema, in light of Kristeva's theory of narration. Unlike Oudart and Dayan, Heath resists characterizing the spectator's relationship to cinematic illusion in terms of a specific shot-by-shot process, and thus avoids the problems that stem from such an account; however, he does seek to discriminate different systems of narration according to the way they "manage" the process by which the spectator is absorbed in the story world depicted in a film. The general distinction that informs much of Heath's writing on the cinema is between the classical Hollywood text and the avant-garde film, which parallels Kristeva's distinction between the realist and modernist text. The classical Hollywood film draws the spectator's attention to the techniques by which it is constructed, but it does so in a way that is thoroughly conventionalized or naturalized. For Heath, classical film maintains the spectator in a certain ideal balance or "economy" between absorption and distanciation, in which the spectator's awareness of the techniques of cinematic enunciation is "contained" within and does not go beyond the limits circumscribed by the classical Hollywood style. In this way the spectator's pleasure in cinematic narration meshes seamlessly with his comprehension of it. By contrast, certain experimental films challenge this predictable positioning of the spectator in relationship to the text by refusing the standard protocols of continuity editing that define classical Hollywood cinema. One of Heath's examples is Chantal Akerman's *News from Home* (1977), which comprises a series of long takes of the streets and subways of New York City accompanied by the voice-over narration of the letters of a mother in France addressed to her daughter in New York. In contrast to the classical Hollywood film, *News from Home* consistently draws the spectator's attention to the two-dimensionality of the image space and the way that a story is told through that space.

It is more difficult to characterize Heath's film theory once one moves beyond this general framework to the details of his arguments, because Heath's explicit statements often seem to contradict his implicit positions and vice versa. In explicit reference to Metz's thesis of primary cinematic identification, Heath writes that "the spectator must *see* and this structuring vision is the condition of the possibility of the disposition of the images via the relay of the character look and viewpoint."[58] Yet he seems to endorse the idea of "identification with the camera" only in the trivial sense that identification with a character in any film is predicated on the fact that I must first of all see him or her. While he refers in other places to the spectator's absorption in the image or image sequence as a fantasmatic or dreamlike world, he does not explicitly state that identification with character is dependent upon the spectator's absorption in that world.[59] This reading of Heath appears to be supported by the fact that he does explicitly reject the thesis of mirror misrecognition. He writes: "[C]inema is not the mirror-phase, which any spectator-subject of a film has already accomplished (as against the little infant who can come to the film but not come as its spectator), being always-already a reading."[60]

However, while Heath does not appear to endorse the theses of primary cinematic identification and mirror misrecognition explicitly, he does emphatically endorse the first and central thesis of apparatus theory: that of perspectival subject positioning. He writes:

There is no brute vision to be isolated from the visual experience of the individual inevitably engaged in a specific socio-historical situation. In a real sense, the ideological force of the photograph has been to "ignore" this in its presentation as a coherent image of vision, an image that then carries over into a suggestion of the world as a kind of sum total of possible photographs, a spectacle to be recorded in its essence in an instantaneous objectification for the eye; . . . a world, that is, conceived outside of process and practice, empirical scene of the confirmed and central master-spectator, serenely "present" in tranquil rectilinearity.[61]

Heath suggests that this ideological "positioning" of the spectator in the photograph that is a function of monocular linear perspective is reproduced in the cinematic image. In addition, he suggests that this position of the transcendental subject is reproduced and restored by the completion of the performance of the film narrative. In spite of Heath's explicit disclaimer of the thesis of mirror misrecognition, the implication of his analysis is that the spectator in the cinema does ideologically misrecognize himself as the transcendental subject in the manner described by apparatus theory. Given the arguments I have already made concerning the logical structure of that theory, it seems to me that one would be hard pressed to defend the thesis of perspectival subject positioning as an exemplification of Althusser's theory of ideology without also accepting the theses of primary cinematic identification and mirror misrecognition. Furthermore, at the level of the completed film, the position of the transcendental subject is reproduced by the classical text in a manner that recalls Dayan's analysis. Heath's difference from Dayan, which marks the influence of Kristeva, lies in his explanation of the process by which the transcendental subject is restored in the viewing of a classical Hollywood film.

Heath follows Baudry's analysis of the fate of the transcendental subject in the cinema when he suggests that this subject's position of security and mastery is challenged by "the continual wealth of movements and details" that threatens to exceed the spectator's capacity to make sense of them. This "disruption" can be overcome through movement of the frame (camera movement, reframing) and movement between frames (editing). However, the problem remains of "achieving a coherence of place and positioning the spectator as the unified and unifying subject of its vision."[62] The particular economy of classical continuity editing is characterized by the manner in which it works to regulate and contain this threat of disruption by casting the image as the visual field of a character with whom the spectator identifies.

The drama of vision in the film returns the drama of vision of the film: the spectator will be bound to the film as spectacle as the world of the film is itself revealed as spectacle on the basis of a narrative organization of look and point of view that moves space into place through the image-flow; the character, figure of the look, is a kind of perspective within the perspective system, regulating the world, orienting space, providing directions – and for the spectator.[63]

Heath's analysis here recalls that of Dayan. The difference lies in the fact that he recognizes that this orchestration of looks is never seamless, nor does it use up all the space in a film. During the course of any film, the spectator-subject is put "in process/on trial" in the manner described by Kristeva. In the classical Hollywood text, the transcendental subject is restored through the predictability that governs the way that the film unfolds and the satisfaction of narrative closure. In a film like *News from Home,* however, the unpredictability of the text and its open-endedness strips the transcendental subject of her position of mastery and security.

The thesis of perspectival subject positioning and its metaphoric extension to refer to the positioning of the spectator by the completed performance of the classical narrative is not a contingent, dispensable part of Heath's theory.[64] Heath wishes to distinguish his own theory from Lacanian poetics. For Kristeva and Oudart (at least in his article on suture), textuality dramatizes the tragedy that underlies human existence in a manner that is theological rather than political in the sense that it provides an insight into the essential nature of what it is to be a human being. The overriding motivation of Heath's film theory is politics and an understanding of the ideological importance of discourse and, in particular, the cinema. Heath must follow apparatus theory in viewing the cinema as a medium that reproduces the empiricist conception of knowledge and the ideological construction of the transcendental subject it entails; for apparatus theory gives the cinematic image, in its production of the impression of reality, a direct political importance that the literary signifier lacks. By reproducing the ideological, transcendental subject, cinema can also transform that subject and thereby change the world. Heath turns to Lacan's theory of the construction of the subject to preserve apparatus theory and avoid the contradictions that arise from apparatus theory in explaining how the subject, if ideologically reproduced by the apparatus, can recognize and resist the hold of ideology.

Lacanian theory suggests that there is no subject outside discourse; thus there is no spectator in the cinema who is in a position to react to or resist the hold of cinematic illusion. The cinematic image is a simulacrum where the impression of reality is understood in two senses: The cinematic image engenders at one and the same moment an image of reality and an impression or mold of the spectator-subject who experiences that reality. Hollywood narrative cinema exemplifies how the construction of the subject in discourse serves to sustain the position of the transcendental subject. Other forms of cinema can break the ideological hold of discourse on the subject and expose her essential lack and the absence of the mastery that is illusorily furnished by the cinematic image. Although Heath's recourse to Lacan in this way resolves the problem of agency, it is ultimately self-defeating. Since, in this account of the subject, the experiencing subject is actually a fabrication of the process of representation, the possibility of that subject recognizing her conditions of existence and releasing the hold of ideology is ruled out entirely. The spectator's responses to cinematic discourse are determined in advance, and her conscious activities are wholly eclipsed. The contradictions of apparatus theory are resolved only by robbing the spectator of any agency at all.

Heath's film theory is most valuable once it is stripped of its Althussarian–Lacanian premises. Like Oudart, Heath builds a theory of narrative comprehension in a manner that is too closely dependent upon a theory of illusion or medium awareness in the cinema. Nonetheless, from the point of view of understanding the spectator's experience of medium awareness in the cinema, Heath's emphasis upon its relationship to narrative comprehension is helpful; for Heath does not insist upon a shot-by-shot account of the spectator's relationship to the Absent One, but instead makes medium awareness dependent upon the ease of narrative comprehension afforded by a given narrational system in relationship to a spectator's general familiarity with conventions of narration. Yet to remove from Heath's film theory its Althussarian–Lacanian premises is to make it unrecognizable; for at the core of this theory, and contemporary critical theory in general, lies the conviction that the human subject is constructed or imprisoned in discourse and can only illusorily refer to a referent or a self outside that discourse. If the challenge to contemporary film theory is to be persuasive, it is this underlying conviction that must be examined.

CHAPTER II

The Lure of
Metaphysics

In Chapter 1 I demonstrated the way in which the Althusserian–Lacanian paradigm in film theory is governed by a conception of the cinematic apparatus as a mechanism that reproduces what Althusser terms the empiricist conception of knowledge, and I sought to show how this conception of the apparatus cannot account for the spectator's experience of the impression of reality in the cinema. However, those who are persuaded by a view of the human subject as the prisoner of language for whom reference and self-knowledge are an illusion are unlikely to be convinced by my arguments against this view, tied as they have been thus far to an investigation of their application of it in the domain of film theory. Thus in this chapter I seek to unravel the epistemological assumptions that underlie the Althusserian–Lacanian paradigm. I try to demonstrate that a description of truth in terms of the empiricist conception of knowledge misconstrues the nature of truth itself. Since the empiricist conception of knowledge misconstrues what it is to make a knowledge-claim, one should reject the assertion of contemporary theorists that any knowledge-claim referring to the way things actually are undercuts its own validity. The cinematic apparatus does not provide a model of the way in which we erroneously make knowledge-claims about the world; rather, contemporary film theory construes the cinematic apparatus upon an erroneous conception of the way in which we make knowledge-claims about the world.

The philosopher whose writings provide the model for the way in which the empiricist conception of knowledge is characterized and criticized in contemporary critical theory, and exemplified and "deconstructed" by the cinematic apparatus, is the German phenomenologist Edmund Husserl. Althusser's own references to Husserl in *Reading Capital* are brief and occur in the context of references to other philosophers in the tradition of Western philosophy. However, for Althusser, Husserl does mark the culmination of the philosophical tradition that conceives epistemology in terms of the empiricist conception of knowledge. He writes:

The whole history of the "theory of knowledge" in Western philosophy from the famous "Cartesian Circle" to the circle of Hegelian or Husserlian teleology of Reason shows us that this "problem of knowledge" is a closed space, i.e., a vicious circle (the vicious circle of the mirror relation of ideological recognition). Its high point of consciousness and honesty was reached precisely with the philosophy (Husserl) which was prepared to take theoretical responsibility for the necessary existence of this *circle,* i.e., to think it as essential to its ideological undertaking; however, this did not *make it leave the circle,* did not deliver it from its ideological captivity.[1]

As we have seen, Althusser is a philosopher who seeks to deliver knowledge from its captivity in the circle. However, his argument is not a logical one that seeks to demonstrate that knowledge-claims are simply not made in the manner described by the empiricist conception of knowledge. Rather, he seeks to argue that knowledge does frequently, even typically, take the form that is described by the empiricist conception, and that this form of knowledge is ideology.

In his essay "Ideological Effects of the Basic Cinematographic Apparatus," Jean-Louis Baudry derives his conception of the transcendental ego that is said to be constituted by the cinematic apparatus from Husserlian phenomenology. Baudry describes the way in which the cinematic apparatus instantiates the empiricist conception of knowledge in its ideal form of a transparent or unclouded vision of the object by constituting the transcendental subject who seems to have an unmediated grasp of the referent. For Baudry, the cinema becomes a kind of metaphysical machine that produces the transcendental subject: "Limited by the framing, lined up, put at the proper distance, the world offers up an object endowed with meaning, an intentional object, implied by and implying the action of the subject which sights it." Quoting from Husserl's *Cartesian Meditations,* Baudry continues:

For Husserl, "the original operation [of intentional analysis] is to *unmask the potentialities implied* in the present state of consciousness. And it is by this that will be carried out, from the noematic point of view, the eventual *explication, definition,* and elucidation of what is meant by consciousness, that is, its objective *meaning.*" And again in the *Cartesian Meditations:* "A second type of polarization presents itself to us, another type of synthesis which embraces the particular multiplicities of *cogitationes,* which embraces them all and in a special manner, namely as *cogitationes* of an identical self which, *active* or *passive,* lives in all the lived states of consciousness and which, through them, relates to all objects."

Thus is articulated the relation between the continuity necessary to the constitution of meaning and the "subject" which constitutes this meaning: continuity is an attribute of the subject. It supposes the subject and it circumscribes its place. It appears in the cinema in the two complementary aspects of a "formal" continuity established through a system of negated differences and narrative continuity in the filmic space.[2]

The "system of negated differences" refers to the effacement of the differences between images on the film strip in projection. As I suggested in Chapter 1, Baudry claims that in a parallel way "narrative continuity in the filmic space" effaces the potential discontinuities in the perception of movement. By suggesting that the transcendental subject in the cinema is constituted only by the effacement of difference, Baudry invokes the writings of Jacques Derrida. Despite the fact that Derrida's influence on contemporary film theory is rarely explicit, his writings are central to Marxist literary modernism, and it was through the philosophy of Derrida that Husserl's influence upon contemporary critical theory was established. For Derrida, Husserl makes explicit the fact that the empiricist conception of knowledge is governed by a temporal structure, as well as by a spatial structure implied by the metaphor of knowledge as vision. Thus Derrida's term for the empiricist conception of knowledge is the "philosophy of presence" that emphasizes the idea of temporality. Since, for Derrida, all truth-claims depend upon temporal presence, they necessarily undermine themselves from within, for the object is never temporally present to the subject in the manner required by Husserl's theory of knowledge.

As we saw in Chapter 1, the dominant influence upon contemporary film theory is Lacanian psychoanalysis. It is invoked by Julia Kristeva, however, within the framework of a Husserlian conception of epistemology and Derrida's critique of that epistemology:

From our own perspective . . . recourse to phenomenology is useful . . . for demonstrating the insurmountable necessity of positing an ego as the single, unique constraint which is constitutive of all linguistic acts as well as all trans-linguistic practice. In this sense in the light of modern language theory [Derrida], we see that Husserlian phenomenology might serve as the bridge leading to an interrogation of the very positionality of the speaking subject: . . . in short, an interrogation to be used hereafter on another – dialectical and psychoanalytic – horizon.[3]

Kristeva casts the Lacanian ego in terms of the transcendental subject who through the act of assertion posits itself and the knowable object. This transcendental ego and the world it surveys are constituted through representation in the manner that is described by mirror misrecognition. At the same time, Derrida's critique of the transcendental subject influences Kristeva's reinterpretation of the relationship between the real and the imaginary in terms of the semiotic. She writes:

The functioning of writing (*écriture*), the trace, and the gramme, introduced by Derrida in his critique of phenomenology and its linguistic substitutes, points to an essential aspect of the semiotic: *Of Grammatology* specifies that which escapes *Bedeutung* [the transcendental subject's positing of the object]. We shall nevertheless keep the term semiotic to designate the operation that logically and chronologically precedes the establishment of the symbolic and its subject.[4]

Derrida's critique of Husserl is thus recast by Kristeva in terms of the relationship between a transcendental subject constructed in representation and a psychoanalytic conception of the subject that simultaneously resists this construction.

As we have seen, Stephen Heath's conceptualization of classical Hollywood narrative takes place within the framework of both apparatus theory and Kristeva's theory of narrative. Heath borrows from Baudry the idea that the transcendental ego is constituted by the cinematic apparatus, but his account of cinema is more complex than Baudry's because, borrowing from Kristeva's theory of narrative, he attempts to take account of how narrative affords the spectator an awareness of the manner in which he is constructed. However, this argument does not suggest a rejection of the idea of the transcendental ego; rather, it suggests that the transcendental ego is sustained over time by the classical Hollywood text through making known to that ego the conditions under which it is constructed. Heath is not explicit in his references to Kristeva in his film theory, and he does not refer to Husserl; however, I contend that his theory of the subject in the cinema is based upon the idea of the transcendental ego and its deconstruction through Lacanian psychoanalysis.[5]

Husserl's Transcendental Phenomenology

Husserl's transcendental phenomenology takes as its point of departure the picture of the mind that Althusser describes as the empiricist conception of knowledge, in which the relationship of the thinking subject to the contents of its consciousness is modeled on the relationship of the empirical subject to the external world. Ideas are considered to be perceived in the "mind's eye" in a way that is analogous to the perception of objects in the external world. The "inner world" is modeled upon the "outer world." The mind is a mirror of nature. The philosopher is someone who investigates the contents of consciousness to arrive at the foundations of knowledge by isolating the clear and distinct ideas from those that are vague, and by clarifying the pathways of association that distinguish true from false inferences. This picture of the mind and philosophical activity underlies both Descartes's conception of self-consciousness and the empiricist philosophy of mind as a storehouse of sense impressions or ideas. However, neither Cartesianism nor empiricism satisfactorily exorcise skepticism and relativism. Borrowing both from Cartesianism and empiricism, Husserl seeks to transcend their limitations in order to establish the foundations of knowledge.

Like Descartes, Husserl believes that the foundations of knowledge are to be located in an examination of that which is immediately given to consciousness, if only the "clear and distinct" ideas can be filtered out from those that are uncertain. Descartes proceeded by doubting the existence of the external world and concluded that what I can know for certain is only the fact that I am a thinking being or substance (*res cogitans*). Having situated the grounds of certainty in consciousness of a self, Descartes hoped to repair the damage that had been done by his method of doubting the existence of the external world; yet the effect of Descartes's argument ran contrary to his intent. If I have unique and privileged access only to the contents of my consciousness, then I only have indirect access to the minds of others through their behavior, and a gap is opened up between mind and body. Furthermore, if I only come to have knowledge of the external world through its impact upon the contents of immediate consciousness that I perceive directly, then I cannot be sure that the external world exists, I can only infer its existence, and a gap is opened up between self and world. Instead of rebuilding the bridge between inner and outer, idea and object, self and world, Descartes's philosophy established philosophical dualism and gave license to skepticism.

Husserl believes that the Cartesian quest for certainty can be fulfilled and the disease of skepticism eradicated from philosophy through what he calls the "phenomenological reduction" or "bracketing" (*epoché,* after the Greek). The phenomenological reduction is an attempt to generate a description of the contents of consciousness that excludes all reference to what Husserl calls the "natural standpoint" – that is, the attitude toward the status of the external world taken by both science and common sense. Husserl describes the attitude of the natural standpoint in terms of an empiricist philosophy of mind. When I look upon an object, what I actually perceive are discrete, partial, perspectival views of the object. I associate one sense-datum with the next and thereby infer, by induction, the existence of the object. Thus conceived, the natural standpoint opens up the specter of Cartesian doubt. Although Husserl identifies the natural standpoint with that of science and common sense, it already embodies a certain philosophical conception of the relationship between mind and reality. Husserl's natural standpoint describes Althusser's empiricist conception of knowledge from the perspective in which it appears to fail to guarantee certainty. In this sense, as Althusser suggests, Husserl recognizes the epistemological dilemma posed by the empiricist conception of knowledge. However, for Husserl, unlike Althusser, this dilemma is a function of the way in which the empiricist conception of knowledge has been described.

When Husserl relinquishes the natural standpoint through the phenomenological reduction, he is, like Descartes, suspending reference to the empirical world. However, since the natural standpoint, for Husserl, already embodies the idea of a relationship between mind and reality, when Husserl gives up the natural standpoint he gives up more than does Descartes. Both the *res cogitans* and the material object are assumed to be bracketed in the phenomenological reduction. Descartes failed to exorcise doubt because he tried to locate the grounds of certainty in the empirical ego, and thereby opened up the unbridgeable divide between the inner world of mental images and the outer world of objects. By bracketing both the *res cogitans* and the material object, as it is conceived from the natural standpoint, Husserl proposes to close off the possibility of doubt. What is left after the reduction is the "transcendental standpoint" – the relationship of the agency that thinks to the contents of its consciousness – that is free of any reference to the world from the natural standpoint, and hence free of the philosophical dilemmas to which the natural standpoint gives rise.

Husserl invokes the concept of intentionality to describe the transcendental standpoint. This is a source of some confusion, for the idea of intentionality is customarily used to account for the fact that the object I see may be different from the actual object. If "*P* sees *x*," where *x* is an illusion, *x* is the intentional object of *P*'s perception. *P*'s visual experience of *x* remains whether or not an empirical object corresponding to *x* exists. However, if the intentional object of transcendental consciousness is understood in this way, it clearly has all the psychological attributes of the natural standpoint that Husserl wishes to bracket. In *Ideas,* Husserl consistently emphasizes that the relationship between transcendental consciousness and empirical consciousness is not parallel to the relationship between an inner world of mental images or sense impressions and an outer world of objects. He writes:

[if we try] to separate the real object (in the case of outer perception, the perceived thing of nature) from the intentional object, placing the latter as "immanent" to perception within experience as a real factor, we are beset by the difficulty that now *two* realities must confront each other, whereas only *one* of these is present and possible.[6]

For Husserl, the intentional object, the object as it is perceived from the transcendental viewpoint, *is* the real object:

I perceive the thing, the object of nature, the tree there in the garden; that and nothing else is the real object of the perceiving "intention." A second immanent tree, or even an "inner image" of the real tree that stands out there before me, is nowise given, and to suppose such a thing by way of assumption only leads to absurdity.[7]

How can we square Husserl's insistence that the object perceived from the transcendental viewpoint is the real object with his claim that reference to empirical existence, as it is conceived from the natural standpoint, is relinquished in the transcendental viewpoint?

What is given up in the shift to the transcendental standpoint is not reference to the empirical world of objects, but the relation of the subject to that empirical world of objects as it is conceived by the natural standpoint. What is gained is an understanding of the fact that when I perceive an object from the natural standpoint, it is a real object that I perceive. When I shift to the transcendental standpoint and reflect upon my perception of the object, what I "see" is the appearing of the object to perception. What is gained by this shift in standpoint is a perception of the object not as a series of partial perspectives as it is described by an empiricist philosophy of mind from the natural standpoint, but a "perception" of the object as the intentional object of a single mental glance ("noesis," after the Greek, *nous,* meaning mind or spirit), as an object-appearing-to-consciousness or as a being-for-consciousness. This phenomenological or "noematic" object constituted in the "noetic" act is what Husserl calls "sense." The phenomenological object is the object as it appears "objectively" in pure consciousness – the idea or sense – that enables the subject to identify and reidentify the object in the external world. From the natural standpoint the object in the external world is apprehended only "subjectively" through a series of discrete and partial glances. The object as it appears to consciousness, revealed by the phenomenological reduction, is what enables those series of discrete and partial glances to be synthesized as views of the same object.

The phenomenological reduction does not involve actually giving up the empirical consciousness that is believed inadequate to ensure the existence of the external world in favor of a transcendental realm whose contents bear no relationship to the empirical world. On the contrary, when we return to consider the natural standpoint after an understanding of the transcendental standpoint has been achieved by the phenomenological reduction, something is added to our understanding of the relationship between consciousness and the world that cannot be taken into account from the natural standpoint, although that standpoint presupposes it. When Husserl shifts to the transcendental standpoint, his purpose is not to doubt the existence of the object known by empirical consciousness, but rather to understand the grounds of our knowledge of the object in a way that cannot be established by an empiricist philosophy of mind. We know that the object whose existence is inferred by empirical consciousness exists, but how do we know that it exists? This question cannot be answered from the natural, empirical standpoint, for if we attempt to answer it, doubt enters in. This is the lesson of Cartesianism. The transcendental standpoint is designed to show us what we knew all along but could not be grasped within a philosophy that remained wedded to the natural standpoint.

It is thus Husserl's introduction of the concept of the noematic object or "noema" through the phenomenological reduction that allows him to mediate between subjective sense-data that cannot guarantee our access to the object and the object itself. Transcendental phenomenology seems to reconcile the idea of an empirical, psychological consciousness embedded in the world with the idea of consciousness as a domain of objective ideas (objects) that are independent of a given perception at a given moment in time. The gaze of the transcendental subject constitutes the object that we perceive in the natural standpoint from a series of partial perspectives as the ideal object of sense. Conversely, the existence of the ideal object of sense under the gaze of the transcendental subject guarantees the existence of the agency that perceives. The phenomenological reduction creates

an essentially *twofold point of view.* In the *one,* the apprehending glance is turned towards the apperceived object through the very act of apprehending, as it were, through which the transcendent object is set up; in the *other,* the apprehending look passes back in reflection to the pure apprehending consciousness itself.[8]

However, can a coherent account of the noema be given? In many places Husserl equates the noema with the object itself. Such an identification of sense with the referent ensures that it is the same object referred to over time. However, it also entails an idealist conclusion that Husserl wishes to avoid: The existence of the object is dependent upon the activity of perception – to be is to be perceived. In other places Husserl makes the distinction between the noema and the referent that is required in order to avoid idealism; but such a distinction introduces precisely the inferential gap that transcendental phenomenology was designed to overcome between the mode of the appearance of the object or the way it is perceived and the object itself. It is no surprise that Husserl insists in some places that the noema is the object and in other places that it is not, for he requires both assertions to be true for the phenomenological reduction to overcome skepticism without falling into idealism. Husserl seeks a middle ground between an identification of noema and object and a separation between the two, but there is no middle ground to be had.[9]

Derrida's Deconstruction of Transcendental Phenomenology

Husserl purports to present a solution to the problems of philosophical epistemology through the idea of a transcendental subject who has an objective grasp of the referent as the object of sense. However, Husserlian phenomenology as such was not embraced by critical theorists in general and contemporary film theorists in particular as a solution to the problems of philosophical epistemology. Rather, it was embraced in the context of Jacques Derrida's critique of the enterprise of philosophical epistemology. For Derrida, Husserl's transcendental phenomenology marks the culmination of the philosophical tradition that seeks the foundations of knowledge in that which lies present to consciousness. In his book on Husserl's philosophy of language, *Speech and Phenomena,* Derrida introduces his approach to the criticism of that philosophical tradition through a criticism of the philosophy of language Husserl sets out in the first chapter of the *Logical Investigations.* It is well known that Derrida's central criticism of the tradition of Western philosophy is that it privileges a certain conception of spoken language at the expense of the spatiotemporal properties of the material sign; but insufficient attention has been paid to the fact that it is in and through a critique of Husserl's transcendental phenomenology that Derrida's deconstruction of Western philosophy is elaborated.[10] The way in which deconstruction entered into film theory through transcendental phenomenology serves to highlight the way in which the assumptions of transcendental phenomenology underlie the enterprise of deconstruction itself.

We have seen how the intended object of sense that is constituted within transcendental consciousness guarantees the existence of the sensuous object over time; but how is the identity of the object of sense itself guaranteed? Language is required to fulfill this role. We define a word, it seems, by correlating the word with an idea – for example, "red" with the idea of red – and then we use the word to pick out the idea in the future. However, from Husserl's point of view, ordinary language is inadequate to the task, for we can only infer, indirectly, the sense of another's utterance from the words she uses; hence we can only infer whether or not a word is being used with the same sense we would give it. In order to be present to transcendental consciousness, the object of sense must be unmediated, the linguistic sign must somehow be purified and stripped entirely of its sensuous aspect. The skepticism that Husserl endeavored to exorcise threatens to return at the level of language. Once again, it appears there are two distinct "objects" present, the material aspect of the sign and the object of sense, although only one "object" is possible. As Derrida points out, the whole dilemma of Husserlian philosophy to reconcile the transcendental and empirical is anticipated by Husserl's treatment of language.

Derrida's criticism of Husserl's philosophy of language takes two paths. First, he tries to refine and clarify Husserl's conception of a purified sign that functions to identify the object of sense in pure presence and that lacks in itself a sensuous aspect. Second, he endeavors to show that such a sign, and the conception of presence it supports, is only made possible by that which it must exclude: the sign as a spatial and temporal entity, and hence as something that cannot be present in the sense required by Husserl.

In order to purify language for phenomenology, Husserl proposes a distinction between the indicative and expressive functions of signs. A sign in its purely indicative function is a sensuous object lacking meaning. It may serve to point something out to a subject – as, for example, a highway sign indicates the presence of workers – but it is not a vehicle of sense. The sign in its expressive function is the sign as a vehicle of sense. In the communicative context of speech, the sign functions in expressive and indicative terms: For the speaker, the sign expresses its meaning; for the listener, the sign indicates the meaning that is being expressed. In the context of communication, the sign has sensuous reality and must play an indicative role in order for the communicative act to be completed. Husserl proposes to purify language for the purpose of the phenomenological reduction by eliminating the indicative aspect of the sign; but since this aspect is part and parcel of communication, it can be eliminated only in what he terms "solitary mental life." In solitary mental life the meaning of a sign is not indicated to the "speaker" indirectly, but is directly intuited: Sign and intended sense are somehow experienced as a unity. When this sense is communicated and the sign becomes indicative, the speaker's sense is not directly experienced but only inferred by the listener. However, the possibility of using language to communicate presupposes the possibility of using language in solitary mental life.

How exactly, then, are the sign and the intended sense experienced as a unity in solitary mental life? Husserl argues that in this circumstance I do not communicate with myself via language because I experience the sense directly; I only imagine or pretend that I communicate with myself via language.

One of course speaks, in a certain sense, even in soliloquy, and it is certainly possible to think of oneself as speaking, and even as speaking to oneself. . . . But in the genuine sense of communication there is no speech in such cases, nor does one tell oneself anything: one merely conceives of oneself as speaking and communicating.[11]

Derrida suggests that Husserl's ideal of pure presence is exemplified in the phenomenon of hearing oneself speak, and he equates this phenomenon with understanding one's own speech. In hearing someone else speak, I can only infer the other's sense, indirectly, from the words that he uses. When I hear myself speak, however, my intended sense is borne by my own voice as it utters each word. Here, according to Derrida, the sense of a word is experienced immediately from within and not inferred from the word as something external: "[T]he subject can hear or speak to himself and be affected by the signifier he produces, without passing through an external detour, the world, the sphere of what is not 'his own.'"[12] In hearing oneself speak, the relationship between inner and outer, transcendental and empirical, seems momentarily bridged.

Following Husserl's method in this way, Derrida suggests that we can achieve a reduction of the indicative aspects of the sign and describe the way in which the object of sense can appear to be directly present to transcendental consciousness through the medium of speech. However, this opposition between the indicative sign and the expressive sign – the one described from the inside and the other described from the outside – overlooks what makes the sign in general possible. Regardless of whether the sign is considered a real indicative sign that is used to communicate, or whether the material aspects of the sign are bracketed when one hears oneself speak in solitary mental life, if sense is actually to be conveyed in any given case, whatever conveys sense must also conserve it. That which makes possible the conservation of sense is repetition or iterability. Derrida writes: "[A] sign is never an event, if by event we mean an irreplaceable and irreversible empirical particular. . . . it can function as a sign, and in general as language, only if a formal identity enables it to be issued again and to be recognized."[13]

The purpose of Husserl's phenomenological reduction is to preserve the moment of pure presence where the object of sense or being-for-consciousness exists for the subject under the transcendental gaze. In order to do this, Husserl has set up a distinction between the purified and contaminated sign; but he preserves the moment of pure presence only by overlooking the fact that the presence of being-for-consciousness is itself made possible by the characteristics it shares with the contaminated sign. Repetition is the antithesis of pure presence: It implies multiplicity rather than singularity, difference rather than uniqueness, and an elsewhere both in time and space. It is as if Husserl strategically avoids the implications of repetition for the idea of presence by dividing the sign in two and casting out the repetitious aspects of the sign along with its material, sensuous characteristics. Even if pure presence can exclude the sensuous sign, however, it cannot exclude the repetition that makes the sensuous sign possible. The presence of the object of sense is thus made possible only through its antithesis, repetition, which undermines the possibility of presence from within. "This pure difference, which constitutes the self-presence of the living present," writes Derrida, "introduces into self-presence from the beginning all the impurity putatively excluded from it. The living present springs forth out of its non-identity with itself."[14]

The presence of the object of sense or being-for-consciousness is thus constituted by the iterable structure of the sign. Derrida calls this sign structure or general form of the sign "the trace," in order to distinguish it from the impoverished, contaminated idea of the material sign, which is counterposed to the idea of presence. For Husserl there is nothing present to consciousness other than the object of sense, nothing, that is, that mediates sense to the subject; thus the sign as it founds the possibility of the object of sense or being-for-consciousness is not something exterior to the object but the object itself. As Derrida writes, *"The thing itself is a sign."*[15] Being-for-consciousness as a sign is thus radically divided from itself: Its presence is founded on its absence, both in the sense of being not-here and not-now. Derrida coins the neologism *différance* as a way of capturing in a word the paradoxical structure of this sign that negates itself in the very act of being stated. *Différance* combines both meanings of the French verb *différer,* in that it refers simultaneously to the concepts of spatial difference and temporal deferral. Furthermore, it sounds the same as *différence* (difference) but is different when written, and thus represents in its form the sameness that is not identical and the identity that is not the same – the twofold function that is characteristic of the sign.

In an important sense, Derrida accepts that phenomenology defines the foundational or original structure of consciousness – the possibility of the experience of the world – and hence vindicates the picture of the mind that animates phenomenology. He accepts that Husserl's move to "bracket" the natural standpoint avoids altogether the traditional problems of philosophical epistemology concerning the existence or nonexistence of the objective world. It is from this perspective that Derrida confronts the problems that language raises for foundational philosophy. Husserl's failure is that he did not reduce the transcendental standpoint in the manner he reduced the natural standpoint. Husserl reduces experience in order to discover its conditions of existence in pure presence; however, he stops short of understanding the conditions of existence of pure presence in the sign. Husserl recognizes that the sign is needed in order to grasp the object of sense, but he fails to understand the fact that presence is presupposed by the sign. Reducing the idea of presence, understanding its constitution by the sign, requires a metadiscursive move that phenomenology was unable to make: namely, the reduction of phenomenology itself and of foundational philosophical discourse in general. This is the character of Derrida's "deconstructive" move, a "reduction of the reduction," which elaborates a description of the conditions of existence of presence in the sign.[16]

The presence of the transcendental object of sense, the possibility of synthesizing our sense impressions into a perception of the object itself, is dependent upon a structure of repetition unfolding through time. This structure of repetition "intervenes" as a kind of baffle between the transcendental subject and the object perceived under the transcendental gaze. The moment of pure presence in which the subject purports to perceive, identify, and name the object (and thereby "asserts" her own intentionality as a subject) is evanescent and illusory, the product of an imaginary freezing of the temporal structure of the sign that entails the object of sense being neither absolutely here nor absolutely now. Derrida "posits presence – and specifically consciousness, no longer as the absolutely central form of Being but as a 'determination' and as an 'effect.' A determination and an effect within a system which is no longer that of presence but of *différance*."[17] The method of deconstructive criticism serves to unfreeze this temporal structure of the sign, in order to demonstrate that the philosopher's claim of determinate meaning and hence determinable reference is founded only upon an exclusion that serves to undercut its own possibility.

Deconstruction emerges from the framework of phenomenology to become a general theory of "signification," partly through the fact that Derrida develops his theory in relationship to a discussion of certain aspects of Saussurian linguistics. For Saussure, a sign consists of the correlation of a sound-image (signifier) and concept (signified), between which there is no intrinsic bond; but if we attend to Saussure's definition of the sign, we can see that the correlation is not so straightforward. Saussure writes:

The linguistic sign unites, not a thing and a name, but a concept and a sound image. The latter is not the material sound, a purely physical thing, but the psychological imprint of the sound, the impression that it makes on our senses. The sound-image is sensory, and if I happen to call it "material," it is only in that sense, and by way of opposing it to the other term of the association, the concept, which is generally more abstract.[18]

Saussure defines the signifier not as the sound of a word, but as its psychic imprint or trace that intervenes between thought and its external manifestation in language. Derrida suggests that in this way Saussure's definition of the sign reproduces the Cartesian standpoint of an empirical, psychological ego. The psychic imprint stands in for the word as a sense-impression stands in for an object. An inferential gap exists between the objective material signifier and the psychological imprint that phenomenology sought to overcome. Thus in his interpretation of Saussure's theory of the sign, Derrida first performs a phenomenological reduction. The psychic imprint is conceived by Derrida in Husserlian terms as the noema or the expressive kernel of the signifier in the pure presence of transcendental consciousness. However, as we have seen, the presence of the noema to transcendental consciousness is made possible only by the characteristics of repetition as *différance* that it shares with the material sign. Thus the material signifier itself is made possible only by the structure of the trace or *différance,* and hence the structure of the trace or *différance* founds the Saussurian sign: "*The trace is in fact the absolute origin of sense in general. Which amounts to saying once again there is no absolute origin of sense in general.*"[19]

Derrida is not a skeptic in the traditional sense of the term, but his reading of phenomenology does bear a certain relationship to skepticism. Skepticism arises from the assumption that evidence of the existence of objects in the external world is provided by our visual experiences of those objects in the form of sense-data or sense-impressions. The skeptic points out that the sense-data upon which we base our inferences about the external world are unreliable, for we may be wrong in our perceptual judgments in any given case. Since we may be wrong in any given case, how can we be sure we are ever right? If, in order to check the veracity of a given sense-impression of an object, we try to compare it with a case where we did see the object, we run up against the problem that the putative veridical perception is itself a sense-impression that requires checking, and so on ad infinitum. The character of this ad infinitum marks the apparent impossibility of ever grasping the referent – an imprisonment in the "veil of ideas."

As we have seen, this skeptical dilemma characterizes the position of the subject from the natural standpoint. Furthermore, although Husserl believes that he has overcome this dilemma through the phenomenological reduction, it could be argued that it returns to haunt him in his treatment of the sign. It seems there is a fundamental contradiction between the fact that the object of sense can only be picked out at the transcendental level through the material indicative sign having the requisite characteristics of repeatability, and the fact that the material sign is precisely what must be bracketed in order to achieve pure presence. It seems that Husserl's whole enterprise must presuppose what it excludes in order to make sense. Faced with this contradiction, the phenomenological reduction collapses. The transcendental standpoint reproduces the skeptical dilemmas of the natural standpoint. The criticism of phenomenology returns us to the position of the skeptic that Husserl had worked so hard to exorcise.

However, this conclusion is not implied by Derrida's criticism of Husserl. Derrida takes as his starting point the coherence of the phenomenological reduction and of the idea of presence upon which the reduction is based. He thereby inoculates himself against skepticism as it is traditionally conceived. However, deconstruction can be seen as a kind of skepticism of a high power. It is as if Derrida tries to demonstrate once and for all the impossibility of knowledge of the world – to demonstrate, paradoxically, that skepticism is true. The skeptic is imprisoned in the veil of ideas or representations, unable to get out; nevertheless, he continues to believe in the possibility that there is a way out, that he can finally hook up his sense-impressions to the world. For Derrida, this belief animates the entire history of philosophy in its effort to secure the foundations of knowledge. Husserl's philosophy is the culmination of that history, in that he finally demonstrates the vantage point from which skepticism could be overcome. However, in Derrida's reading of Husserl, the overcoming of the philosophical problem of skepticism leads not to certainty, but to the undermining of certainty once and for all.

The infinite regress of the skeptic along the chain of sense-impressions was driven by the possibility of an identity between sense-impression and object. For Derrida, Husserl's philosophy demonstrates what this elusive identity between sense-impression and object would look like. Derrida, then, suggests that the possibility of such an identity is founded only upon the freezing of an infinite regress: the structure of the sign or *différance*. Thus it turns out that the philosopher's belief in the possibility of an identity between sense-impression and object is an illusion. The quest for this identity in the history of philosophy has finally been superseded by a discourse that demonstrates that this quest has been founded all along upon its own impossibility. Derrida's is thus a skepticism to end all skepticism. To the extent that skepticism has driven the quest for the foundation of knowledge and that this quest constitutes the history of Western philosophy, Derrida's is a skepticism that purports to bring an end to the history of philosophy itself.

As I have already suggested, it is in the context of Derrida's deconstruction of Husserlian phenomenology that the idea of the transcendental subject was embraced by Marxist literary modernism and the film theory that it influenced. Baudry's claim that the position of the transcendental subject is actually realized in the cinematic apparatus is founded upon the idea that the apparatus literalizes the Derridean trace in such a way that the position of the transcendental subject in the cinema is founded upon its own impossibility. Baudry assimilates the idea of the trace to the image on the filmstrip, which, like the material signifier, is defined by the boundaries dividing it from other images. The materiality of the image is repressed in the act of projection that creates a continuity out of discontinuity. The cinema is a kind of metaphysical machine, or consciousness machine, producing the transcendental subject and the object perceived by that subject in a temporal present through an erasure of the material basis of the medium. The exposure of the material basis of the medium could therefore be said to deconstruct the position of the transcendental subject. If considered just as a metaphor, rather than a metaphor that is literally realized, the analogy between the cinematic apparatus and metaphysics illuminates the relationship between the transcendental subject and its deconstruction.

It is one thing to understand how deconstruction emerges from transcendental phenomenology; it is quite another to assent to Derrida's argument. As we have seen, the essence of that argument is a critique of the idea of truth as an identity between representation and object. He does not deny this conception of truth in the name of an alternative theory of truth, as Althusser attempts to do; but he claims that this concept of truth is a paradox that undermines itself from within. One way in which the assumptions that underpin Derrida's critique of Husserl can be illuminated is by discriminating between two distinct forms of identity and difference: qualitative identity and difference, and numerical identity and difference. A statement of "qualitative identity" is made on the basis that two different particulars are alike with respect to specific properties. "Numerical identity" refers to individuation of particulars in space and over time. Thus the two marks x and x are qualitatively identical but numerically distinct. A statement that a given mental representation mirrors what it represents would appear to be a statement of qualitative rather than numerical identity. For Husserl such an identity claim licenses skepticism. It could be argued, at least on the basis of Derrida's analysis, that Husserl defends against skepticism by stipulating that any pure identity claim must also be a statement of numerical identity. In pure presence, sign and thing appear as a unity. Derrida accepts the premise of Husserl's argument, and then goes on to demonstrate that any pure identity claim is inherently paradoxical; for in order for *a* to be declared qualitatively identical to *b*, *a* and *b* must be numerically different. Yet the concept of pure presence implies that if *a* and *b* are numerically different, *a* and *b* are not qualitatively identical.

However, the only reason we should accept the essentially paradoxical character of truth is if we assent in the first place to the idea of pure presence that lies at the basis of transcendental phenomenology, and to the underlying picture of mind that it exemplifies; and the only reason we have to assent to the concept of pure presence is if Husserl's strategy is the only way to defeat the argument of the skeptic. It might be contended that Derrida's embrace of the concept of presence is a strategic move that enables him to undo a philosophical tradition that bases itself on the concept of presence. Giving provisional assent to the concept of presence allows Derrida to enter inside Husserl's discourse and undo it from within. However, if it made no sense to postulate the idea of pure presence in the first place, then Derrida's assent to the concept of presence, even if strategic, would be fatal for his critique. Instead of being trapped with Derrida within the metaphysics of presence, forever dismantling it from the inside, one could be positioned outside the enclosure of metaphysics upon different ground. I suggest that this is the challenge to deconstruction offered by Wittgenstein's later philosophy. If that philosophy is correct, Derrida and his fellow travelers are simply barking up the wrong philosophical tree, and the philosophical framework that underpins the discourse of contemporary theory should therefore be abandoned.[20] In order to trace the challenge of Wittgenstein's later philosophy to deconstruction we must return once again to Husserl.

Wittgenstein's Private Language Argument

In his later philosophy, Wittgenstein subjects to systematic criticism the picture, embodied in the empiricist conception of knowledge, of the mind as the mirror of nature, as well as the conception of the activity of philosophy that it serves to support. Husserl's philosophy is not an explicit target of Wittgenstein's criticism; however, as we shall see, it is an ideal target, for it corresponds in detail to the position of Wittgenstein's imaginary antagonist. At the core of Wittgenstein's criticism of the empiricist conception of knowledge lies the so-called private language argument that is developed in the

Philosophical Investigations. In this argument Wittgenstein entertains the idea that the picture of the mind that Husserl defends is true. Suppose that we *do* come to understand the world through introspection, through identifying and reidentifying ideas in our mind's eye; or, to use the language of Husserl, suppose we do come to synthesize our array of sense-impressions into a knowledge of the object through constituting and reconstituting the object as the object of sense in transcendental consciousness. For example, we develop the idea of red through synthesizing our red sense-impressions into the idea of red, and we then use this idea of red to identify and reidentify red objects in the world. In order for us to be able to identify and reidentify objects in the world with the idea, we must first be able to identify and reidentify the idea itself, and for this we use language; but, Wittgenstein argues, were language to play this role of consistently identifying the idea that is used to pick out the object in the world, only a certain kind of language would do. This kind of language is what Wittgenstein terms a "private language." Wittgenstein's argument demonstrates that such a private language is impossible to conceive, and hence the picture of the mind that seems to necessitate the existence of such a private language must be incoherent. The empiricist conception of knowledge is an erroneous description of the way in which we make knowledge-claims.

Wittgenstein defines a private language as one whose words "are to refer to what can only be known to the person speaking, to his immediate private sensations. So another person cannot understand the language."[21] At first sight this definition seems at variance with Husserl's account of language as it is used in solitary mental life. Husserl argues that in solitary mental life words have "the same meanings as in dialogue," and thus another person *can* understand the language that is used.[22] The difference between Husserl and Wittgenstein here stems from their respective approaches to the idea of a private language. Husserl's strategy with respect to language exemplifies his overall strategy to reconcile the transcendental and empirical viewpoint. Husserl wishes to draw a distinction between private and public language in order to purify language of its sensuous aspect, but at the same time he wishes to maintain the connection between the two in an effort to preserve the coherence of phenomenology. The implication of Husserl's model of communication is that we all have our own "private" language whose words we define by reference to the ideas we have in our mind's eye. Presumably, our common language results from the fact that all our different private languages happen to coincide, so that what I mean by red is qualitatively the same as what you mean by red, even though our respective ideas of red are located in different minds.

This conception of the relationship between private and public language is manifestly inadequate, as P. M. S. Hacker points out, for there is no way to determine if the ideas that each of the private linguists uses to define his or her use of words are the same ideas.[23] As soon as we enter the public domain of communication, skeptical doubt is once again introduced. Thus Husserl's effort to describe a purified conception of language that underlies the possibility of communication fails to provide the requisite grounds for certainty. Husserl's failure notwithstanding, it is the assumption of the empiricist conception of knowledge and the conception of language supporting it that seems persuasive. This conception of language is, once again, one in which words are defined according to private ideas or samples that exist in the mind's eye. The association of word and idea provides the basis for identifying and reidentifying the object of sense as the same object. What the private language allows me to explain is how I understand *my* ideas. If this conception of language fails to explain how we can communicate with each other, this failure can be imputed to inadequate philosophical argument or even insufficient empirical research. Either way, the resolution of this problem can be deferred to some future date.

What *is* essential to the idea of a private language is that it must, at a minimum, be understood by the person using it. If it cannot, then it certainly cannot be understood by others. Wittgenstein defines the private language as a language that is understood only by the person using it, in order to prevent assumptions that presuppose a language that *is* public and sharable creeping into the understanding of how the private linguist goes about defining the meaning of the words that she uses. This is merely a more rigorous application of the principles that Husserl himself fails to follow. Since a language that is public and sharable must have a sensuous character, the assumption of a public and sharable language must be suspended by the phenomenological reduction. Husserl's account of the use of language in solitary mental life must be shown to be coherent, irrespective of whether it is communicable.

It might still appear that by defining the private language as one that is necessarily private Wittgenstein builds into the premises of his argument that which it is designed to prove. The conclusion of the argument is that the idea of a language that can be understood only by the person using it makes no sense; but surely this conclusion is made inevitable by a definition of a private language as one that is necessarily incommunicable. After all, we all know that the word "language" already implies something that *is* communicable! However, it follows from what I have already said that the premise of the private language argument is distinct from its conclusion, for the question of the coherence of the private language is independent from that of its communicability. Wittgenstein argues that the idea of the private language fails not because the private language cannot be communicated, but because the private language cannot be understood by the person using it. The apparent plausibility of the idea of a private language and the picture of the mind it supports stems from the fact that, in the manner of Husserl, the idea of a private language constantly trades on the idea of a language that is public and sharable.

Wittgenstein mounts his argument against the idea of a private language by asking, How do the words of the private language stand for or refer to the ideas in my mind? The particular example from mental experience on which Wittgenstein focuses is the sensation of pain, which provides a particularly potent illustration of something to which we seem to have a unique and privileged access, although any private experience, such as a visual impression of red, would serve equally well as an example. The words that I use to describe my mental experiences cannot be correlated with the natural expressions (such as trembling with fear or smiling with joy) that accompany these experiences. If the words I use could be correlated with natural expressions, then the language that we were seeking to describe would no longer be a private one, for someone else could understand my use of the term and apply it as I do. However, suppose I try to construct a concept of the sensation S, independent of its public expression, by associating the word "S" with the occurrence of the sensation S. I cannot give an ordinary – that is, a public – definition of the word, but perhaps I can impress it upon myself that the correlation obtains. In fact, this is precisely the kind of performance that Husserl imagines to take place. He writes that when we understand the sense of a word "a peculiar act-experience relating to the expression is present that . . . shines through the expression, that . . . lends it meaning and thereby a relation to objects."[24] Wittgenstein points out, however, that the purpose of impressing the correlation upon myself is in order to be able to pick out the sensation S at future times; but how can this process of "impressing upon myself" establish a criterion of correctness or a rule for my future identification of S? How can it help me to identify a future occurrence of S as the same S? In order for the mental activity of "impressing it upon myself" that "S" corresponds with S to establish a rule for the use of "S," I must already have individuated S. The internal performance presupposes that I already possess the concept of an S, and this we can only obtain from ordinary, public language. By itself, it provides no way of telling whether we *seem* to be right or whether we *are* right. Hence we can no longer speak of "being right" at all. There is no concept of S, no rule for the use of an expression "S," and no language.[25]

Perhaps the failure to establish a definition of "S" results from the "content" of this performance being inadequately specified. Suppose, then, instead of trying to impress upon himself the connection between "S" and S, the private linguist uses a mental dictionary of sensation samples or definitions, which can be called upon to justify a given application of "S." This cannot be a public dictionary, since then the language would no longer be private, but could we not use an imaginary table in our minds? For example, I can check on the time of a train by imagining the page of a real timetable, and thereby remember correctly the time of the train. However, in the case with which we are concerned the dictionary is wholly imaginary. How could a purely imaginary timetable enable me to remember the time of the train correctly? In the case of the imaginary dictionary I can only check whether I remember what "S" means against a table that itself consists of my memory of what "S" means. Wittgenstein writes:

If the mental image of the time-table could not itself be *tested* for correctness, how could it confirm the correctness of the first memory? (As if someone were to buy several copies of the morning paper to assure himself that what it said was true.) Looking up a table in the imagination is no more looking up a table than the image of the result of an imagined experiment is the result of an experiment.[26]

As we have seen, Husserl tries to conceptualize the use of language in solitary mental life in a fashion very similar to that imagined by Wittgenstein. He suggests that in solitary mental life our ideas are correlated with pretend or imaginary signs. "In imagination," he writes, "a spoken or printed word floats before us, though in reality it has no existence. . . . The imagined verbal sound, or the imagined printed word, does not exist, only its imaginative presentation does so."[27] Here, Husserl equivocates between something real that is entertained in the imagination and what is purely imaginary. If these words in imagination are the words of a public language that are imagined, though not uttered, they serve the purpose of securing sense through being material signs. To imagine real words is not to bracket their reality in the manner required by phenomenology, but only to imagine that they are bracketed. This procedure fails to purify language in the manner required by Husserl. If these words do not actually exist in reality – that is, if they are wholly imaginary in the sense described by Wittgenstein – then they cannot perform the function required of them to individuate the object of sense. Language has been purified to the point of extinction. Either way, this invocation of imagination accomplishes nothing for Husserl.

Husserl believes that the possibility of communication is grounded in our capacity to define our words by reference to the ideas in our mind's eye; but the implication of the private language argument is that the character of the ideas in our mind's eye is irrelevant to ensuring that you and I mean the same thing by our use of an expression. Wittgenstein asks us to imagine a person who could not remember to *what* private object the word "pain" referred, yet who used the word in a way that fit in with usual pain behavior and pain expressions. Were she to refer to a different private object every time, would it make a difference? "A wheel that can be turned though nothing else moves with it, is not part of the mechanism."[28] Imagine that everyone had a box with something inside it they call "beetle." No one can see inside another's box, and everyone claims to know what a beetle is only by looking inside his own box. If the word "beetle" has a use in the language, then it does not matter whether there is an object in the box and what its character is: "The thing in the box has no place in the language-game at all; not even as a *something*: for the box might even be empty."[29] Conversely, if the object in the box were to play a role in establishing the meaning of the word, then communication would be impossible.

To use a language requires following rules for the use of words, and to follow a rule presupposes the possibility of justifying applications of the rule, and to justify its applications there must be a criterion of correctness for what constitutes following the rule (in this case, a criterion of correctness for identifying this particular sensation as a sensation of S). The immediate lesson of the private language argument is that there is no such thing as following a private rule or understanding a language whose rules could not receive public expression. The distinction between following a rule and failing to follow a rule makes sense only in the context of a *practice* of rule following. Rule following is the exercise of an ability whose mastery is manifest in the performance or action of applying the rule correctly. "'Obeying a rule,'" Wittgenstein writes, "is a practice. And to *think* one is obeying a rule is not to obey a rule. Hence it is not possible to obey a rule 'privately': otherwise thinking one was obeying a rule would be the same thing as obeying it."[30] By "practice," Wittgenstein does not mean *social* practice, as some commentators have maintained, but the regular performance of the ability to apply the rule correctly.[31] The distinction between whether someone understands or fails to understand the meaning of a word turns on whether he manifests the ability to use the word appropriately in the appropriate context. It does not turn on the presence of a concept in the mind's eye.

If the private language argument is correct, then Husserl's Cartesian quest to secure the foundations of knowledge in that which lies present to consciousness is a failed quest; but how is this failure to be characterized? A cursory reading of the private language argument might suggest that it offers an argument in support of skepticism. I have already noted that Husserl fails to sustain a coherent distinction between the expressive sign used in solitary mental life and the indicative sign used in public communication, and that without such a distinction language cannot be purified to meet the standards of the phenomenological reduction. It might seem that this is precisely the argument elaborated by Wittgenstein. The private language argument might seem to run as follows: In order to constitute a rule for the use of the word, or to establish its sense, we must be able to establish a correlation between the word and the concept or idea in our mind's eye. Since we are unable to do this with certainty, we can never be sure that our application of a rule is the correct one. Indeed, we can never be sure that the rule we are following in any given case is the right rule.

This is clearly not the private language argument. This is a skeptical argument that shares with a foundationalist like Husserl the assumption that the sense of a word is established through the correlation of word and concept in the mind's eye. However, the point of the private language argument is not to demonstrate that the "private rules" formed by the correlation of word and concept fall short of providing us with the certainty required by Husserl to secure the foundations of knowledge. Rather, the point of this argument is to demonstrate that the idea of following a "private" rule is senseless. The private language argument suggests not that a skeptical view of foundationalist arguments is right, but that the picture of the mind and its relationship to language that underpins the argument of both the foundationalist and the skeptic is incoherent.

Husserl's quest was, once again, to understand what were the grounds of our knowledge of the object that we perceive from a natural standpoint, when our knowledge of the object appears indirect and therefore open to doubt. By exposing that foundationalist arguments fail to make sense, the private language argument does not license a return to the skepticism that is entailed by the natural standpoint; rather, it exposes the false dilemma that founded Husserl's quest in the first place. This is the epistemological dilemma posed by a picture of the mind as mirroring in its representations a world that can only be inferred by them, a picture that would make sense only if the idea of a private language made sense. By exposing the incoherence of this picture of the mind's relationship to reality, Wittgenstein thus leads us outside the metaphysics of presence altogether to a position from which the whole edifice of Husserl's transcendental philosophy collapses. The private language argument does not expose the incoherence of the transcendental standpoint only to return us to the natural standpoint as defined by Husserl or the empiricist conception of knowledge as defined by Althusser; it exposes the incoherence of the philosophical picture of the mind's relationship to the world that called into being the distinction between the transcendental and the natural standpoint in the first place.

The implications of Wittgenstein's later philosophy for Derrida's critique of Husserl should now be apparent. Derrida's critique of Husserl presupposes the necessity of phenomenological reduction: "[A] thought of the trace," he writes, "can no more break with a transcendental phenomenology than be reduced to it."[32] Derrida thereby also presupposes the coherence of the picture of the mind's relationship to the world that Husserl calls the natural standpoint, that is, the picture of the mind as mirroring in its contents objects in the outside world that can only be inferred from those contents. While, for Derrida, this picture of the mind is no longer grounds for traditional skepticism, since he assumes that skepticism has been superseded by the phenomenological reduction, that reduction provides the basis for his own higher-order skepticism. Rather than undoing the philosophy of presence, Derrida's perpetual deconstruction of presence only serves to reassert its apparent inescapability. However, when Wittgenstein criticizes the impossibility of the private language, his point of attack does not take place from within the philosophy of presence. Hence it does not presuppose the intelligibility of the picture of the mind's relationship to reality that defines the natural standpoint and that underpins the philosophy of presence. On the contrary, the private language argument demonstrates that this picture of the mind's relationship to reality is unintelligible. Hence the logic of deconstruction that presupposes the coherence of this picture of the mind is a meaningless performance, a philosophically empty, rhetorical charade.

Just as Derrida's critique of Husserl spreads beyond the confines of Husserlian phenomenology to define a conception of the sign in general that has had a great influence on contemporary theory, so Wittgenstein's later philosophy has profound implications for the idea of theory in the humanities; for the philosophical linchpin of contemporary critical theory in general, and of film theory in particular, has been the philosophical critique of "humanism," which is identified with an epistemology in which the mind is conceived as a mirror of nature and truth is conceived in the form of what Althusser terms the empiricist conception of knowledge. The critique of humanism in the humanities purports to demonstrate that this conception of the humanist subject is an illusion, and that the possibility of reference and the guarantee that it appears to afford of self-identity is merely an effect of representation. Wittgenstein's later philosophy suggests that this conception of the humanist subject is merely a fabrication of theory. Althusser and contemporary film theorists after him make an error when they equate this fabrication with the operation of ideology. Ideological illusions are false; the empiricist conception of knowledge is meaningless.

The "Subject" of Theory

As we have seen, the phenomenological reduction establishes the object of sense – the noema – under the transcendental gaze of the subject, and thus purports to guarantee both that the object is known by the subject and that there is a subject who knows the object. We have also investigated the way in which the solution to the problem of knowledge proposed by transcendental phenomenology can be challenged by considering how it is that the objectivity of sense is guaranteed by language. Depending on how this question is answered, the response may lead either to skepticism, to deconstruction, or, as I have argued, following Wittgenstein, to a restoration of the idea of the objectivity of sense but on different grounds from those of transcendental phenomenology. So far, I have considered this argument from the standpoint of the object; that is, I have considered the different possibilities of challenging the objectivity of sense from the standpoint of whether or not the object can be successfully picked out or identified in the manner that purports to be guaranteed by transcendental phenomenology. However, it might be objected that this discussion is beside the point, in view of the fact that the question of my ability to reidentify the object is not what is at stake in the critique of humanism, but rather my self-identity as a subject.

This objection, however, fails to acknowledge the way in which my self-identity as a subject is dependent upon my ability successfully to identify and reidentify objects. If the latter is not secured, then the former is necessarily jeopardized. Nevertheless, the epistemological challenge to the "humanist" subject is often mounted in a direct fashion within contemporary film theory. Thus it is important to make explicit how the structure of my argument impinges directly on the question of how the self-identity of the subject should be conceived. The problem posed by the phenomenological reduction on the side of the subject is in fact identical in its structure to the problem posed on the side of the object. Instead of how to individuate the object of sense, on the side of the subject the question is this: How is the transcendental subject, whose integrity transcendental phenomenology purports to guarantee, actually going to be identified and individuated?

In ordinary language, the personal pronoun is used to individuate the subject. Consistent with his overall examination of language, Husserl wishes to abstract the indicative shell of "I" from its expressive kernel, where "in solitary speech the meaning of 'I' is essentially realized in the immediate idea of one's own personality." However, unlike expressions describing objects or properties of objects, like words for colors that allow us to pick out the same color in different contexts, the personal pronoun – like other so-called deictic expressions such as "this" and "here" – is dependent on context for its meaning. Husserl writes: "The word 'I' names a different person from case to case, and does so by way of an ever altering meaning." The indicative function is not an external, contingent aspect of the personal pronoun and deictic expressions that can simply be discarded: "[A]n essentially indicating character naturally spreads to all expressions which include these and similar presentations as parts." One cannot abstract the indicative shell from the expressive kernel of the word "I," for once one isolates "I" from the context of utterance, one is left without an objective idea of to what "I" refers. Husserl recognizes that the personal pronoun and deictic expressions challenge his attempt to determine the objectivity of sense by separating the indicative and expressive aspects of language, but he insists that in cases such as these, ordinary language is simply inadequate. "Ideally speaking," he writes, "each subjective expression is replaceable by an objective expression which will preserve the identity of each momentary meaning-intention."[33] Does this mean "I" must be replaced by a different mark every time it is used? While that would deal with the problem of the "ambiguity" of the word "I," it would also entail an infinite multiplicity of subjects and a radical skepticism concerning the unity of the ego.

Husserl's analysis of the personal pronoun enters into contemporary film theory through the writings of the French phenomenologist-linguist Emile Benveniste. Benveniste tries to argue that it is precisely because the personal pronoun uniquely fuses the indicative and expressive aspects of the sign that it becomes the key to the phenomenological enterprise of securing the foundations of knowledge. He writes:

What then is the reality to which "I" or "you" refers? It is solely a "reality of discourse" and this is a very strange thing. . . . The form of "I" has no linguistic existence except in the act of speaking in which it is uttered. There is thus a combined double instance in this process: the instance of "I" as referent and the instance of discourse containing "I" as the referee. . . . "I" is "the individual who utters the present instance of discourse containing the linguistic instance 'I'."[34]

Through this "combined double instance" of the personal pronoun, the speaker appropriates the system of language (*langue*) and in that act of appropriation is constituted as the transcendental subject, "as the psychic unity that transcends the totality of the actual experiences it assembles and that makes the permanence of consciousness."[35] For Benveniste, it is through the assertion of the self in language that the transcendental subject is hooked up to the field of possible reference mapped by the system of signs that constitute the language system. Through sentences containing "I," the subject at once uses language to refer and to identify herself as a subject. Thus, it is through the personal pronoun that the gap between the expressive and indicative aspects of language, subject and object, ideal and real, are bridged.

Benveniste's analysis of the personal pronoun simply replicates Husserl's analysis of the dependence of the expressive function of the personal pronoun on its indicative, linguistic function, but he seems less aware than Husserl of the philosophical consequences of his analysis. If the referent "I" exists only as a function of the "present discourse containing the linguistic instance 'I'," then how can I be sure that the individual who utters a discourse containing the linguistic instance "I" at time t is the same individual who utters the linguistic instance "I" at time t'? A skeptical conclusion about the possibility of individuating the transcendental ego is the inevitable corollary of Benveniste's analysis, though it is a conclusion repugnant to Husserl's entire theory, and it is not, I would surmise, the conclusion that Benveniste means to establish. On the basis of Benveniste's analysis of the personal pronoun, critical theorist Kaja Silverman writes that "the subject has an even more provisional status in Benveniste's writings than it does in Lacan's, since it has no existence outside of the specific discursive moments in which it emerges. The subject must be constantly reconstructed through discourse."[36] The subject, in this view, does indeed have a provisional status: One is a different subject every time one speaks. Certainly, even Lacan would not embrace *this* conclusion!

The skeptical response to the dilemma thrown up by the personal pronoun is not the response of Derrida. In a manner consistent with his reading of Husserl, Derrida suggests that Husserl's resorting to the indicative sign in order to explain how it is we can identify and individuate the self constitutes a failure to follow through on the premise of the phenomenological reduction. Once again, Derrida's strategy is to accept the terms of the phenomenological reduction. In this case, he accepts the idea that the use of the word "I" in solitary mental life must signify the same thing every time it is uttered. This should have been Husserl's conclusion if he had consistently followed on the premises of his own argument. However, Derrida argues, the very sameness that guarantees the self-presence of the subject is founded upon repetition and therefore *différance*. The conclusion to be drawn from this analysis of the personal pronoun is not that the subject is potentially a different subject in every utterance, but that the self-presence of the subject to itself is always excluded by the personal pronoun. The presence of the self to itself, like the presence of the object to the self, is only made possible by absence, the not-here and not-now that defines the structure of the sign. Derrida writes:

My nonperception, my nonintuition, my *hic et nunc* absence are expressed by that very thing that I say, by *that* which I say and *because* I say it. This structure will never form an "intimately blended unity" with intuition. The absence of intuition – and therefore of the subject of the intuition – is not only *tolerated* by speech; it is *required* by the general structure of signification.[37]

For Derrida, it is not that the subject exists from moment to moment in discourse, but that the subject exists in discourse only in a manner in which it is necessarily divided from itself.

I have already challenged Derrida's account of *différance* and the dependence of his theory upon transcendental phenomenology through the philosophy of Wittgenstein. Once again, in contrast to Derrida, in his analysis of the subject in *The Blue Book,* Wittgenstein steers a path between foundationalism and skepticism in a manner that parallels the structure of the private language argument. Let us assume that the phenomenologist's picture of how the objectivity of sense is guaranteed within the mind's eye is a correct one. Modeling the relationship between the transcendental ego and the noema in terms of a mental glance, the phenomenologist reasonably infers that the noema can be apprehended by the subject from a point of view that is not itself represented in the glance of the transcendental subject. However, the problem for the phenomenologist is how, within this picture of the mind, the transcendental ego is to be individuated. "Now let us ask ourselves," Wittgenstein writes, "what sort of identity of personality it is we are referring to when we say 'when anything is seen, it is always I who see.'" These cases of seeing do not have in common a reference to a body, nor even to a common memory; thus it seems that "what continued during all the experiences of seeing was not any particular entity 'I' but the experience of seeing itself."[38] The phenomenologist believes that the fact that the transcendental ego "perceives" the noema in transcendental consciousness will afford a criterion of identity for that ego, but it turns out that all that is available is a series of disconnected experiences of seeing that belong to no one.

Wittgenstein offers an ingenious diagnosis of this failure of reasoning by drawing a distinction between the geometrical and the physical eye. The transcendental phenomenologist assumes that the eye itself figures in the act of seeing as the anchoring point of the cone of the visual field; but Witt-genstein points out that there are two kinds of eye with different criteria of identity or individuation. The "physical eye" is the physical object that col-lects light rays; it may be identified by touch. The "geometrical eye" refers to the center of my visual field; for it to be identified, I have to open at least one eye and orient my finger along the axis of my visual field in order to find the point at which my vision is centered. Since these two criteria are distinct, it is conceivable that the geometrical eye could be located in another place than the physical eye: "I may see with what according to other criteria is the tip of my nose, or places on my forehead; or I might in this way point to a place outside my body."[39] It is thus only because we see – that is, we identify our visual field – with our physical eyes that the geometrical eye has a consistently identifiable location in space. The transcendental phenomenol-ogist, however, cannot make reference to the physical eye: She can refer on-ly to the geometrical eye. Thus the thing to which she refers does not have a consistently identifiable location and therefore is not something that can count as an ego. The argument of the transcendental phenomenologist thus seems plausible only because she smuggles in the concept of the physical eye or an ego defined by bodily criteria on the back of the concept of the geometrical eye or "geometrical ego" that lacks bodily criteria.[40]

Wittgenstein continues with an explanation of how the use of the person-al pronoun deceives us into thinking that "the self" is something located at the tip of the cone of our visual field, or something immaterial that is hidden inside our bodies like a transcendental ego. There are different uses of the word "I" that need to be distinguished. When I use the word "I" to express my thoughts (e.g., "I think it will rain") or to refer to physical states that have a psychological component (e.g., "I have a toothache"), it seems that I am making a direct observation or description of states that belong to my-self. Now, in the case of purely physical observations such as "I have grown six feet tall," I do make an observation or description of myself. Sentences within this category "involve the recognition of a particular per-son, and there is in these cases the possibility of an error, or as I should rather put it: The possibility of an error has been provided for." However, in the case of sentences that express thoughts and other psychological states I make no individuating reference to myself: "There is no question of recog-nizing a person when I say I have a toothache. To ask 'are you sure that it is you who have pains?' would be nonsensical."[41] The reason I cannot be mistaken that I have a toothache is not because I always *recognize* that it is I who am in pain, but because the first-person pronoun does not typically have a referential function. More generally, self-consciousness is not consciousness of one's self, a putative entity: It is consciousness that such-and-such holds of oneself (the indirect form of the reflexive pronoun "myself").[42] Expressed in the form that is least misleading, self-consciousness is simply the capacity to give expression in language to thoughts, beliefs, feelings, and wishes.[43]

Wittgenstein encourages us to view self-consciousness and the language skills that afford the articulation of self-consciousness as arising out of natural patterns of behavior. Our ability to express our own sense of self-identity through making reference to our own thoughts and feelings is simply an extension of our natural expressions when we tremble with fear, cry with rage, groan in pain, or smile with delight. Statements containing the first-person pronoun that report on thoughts and feelings function in a manner that is akin to natural expression. For example, the statement "I have a toothache" is akin to a moan of pain. Our capacity to discriminate our psychological states and articulate them through language presupposes the fact that we are persons with bodies that display a characteristic range of behavior patterns. This does not mean that pain is reducible to pain behavior or the expression of pain in the manner of behaviorism. It does means that our ability to discriminate our pain presupposes our capacity to express it. Equally it is because we share a common range of natural expressions of behavior with other people that we can refer to the mental states of others. Of course, the degree to which these natural expressions of behavior are mediated by cultural forms that are alien to us may impede our understanding. However, miscommunication or misunderstanding, in this sense, is a contingent part of human communication; but human communication is not predicated upon miscommunication or misunderstanding in the manner assumed by contemporary critical theorists.

We have examined the quest of Husserl to find a purified form of language that would allow reality to appear to consciousness in pristine form in the mind's eye. Philosophy could then establish once and for all the grounds of truth. Derrida – and following Derrida, much of contemporary theory – holds this philosophical quest to be an illusion. Language intervenes between mind and the world, structuring the relationship between them. The subject, in his efforts to comprehend himself and the world, is imprisoned by this system of language in such a way that knowledge of the world and hence a secure sense of self is an illusion. Contemporary theorists like Derrida are not traditional skeptics; they are, so to speak, modernist skeptics who manifest and valorize a particular kind of self-consciousness that knows only too well the chimerical claims of knowledge and hence the illusory claim of the individual to self-knowledge or self-coherence. As I have shown in Chapter 1, this kind of modernist skepticism is given political credibility within contemporary film theory through the identification of the empiricist conception of knowledge or presence with the ideological effect of the apparatus reinforced by classical narration, and of the avant-garde text with the radical subversion of the subject who is constructed by the apparatus and reinforced by the classical text.

Wittgenstein presents a conception of the relationship between the mind, language, and reality that is very different from the conception that underpins the discourse of much of contemporary literary and film theory. Wittgenstein's later philosophy implies that the problem at the heart of contemporary theory's conception of the mind's relationship to reality is precisely the nostalgia for an imagined unity between subject and object, self and world. This nostalgia no doubt has psychological, even psychoanalytic, explanation. It manifests itself in a philosophical craving to reinvent language in a form where it can have a transparent representational function. Realizing that this quest must fail, philosophers like Derrida, in the spirit of Nietzsche, abandon the quest and embrace the fact that language structures experience in such a way that the subject is alienated from itself and from the world. What this position has in common with the philosophical tradition it rejects, however, is precisely the idea that language functions either to represent the world to the subject (and hence not to structure the subject) or to fail to represent the world to the subject (and hence to "structure" subjectivity). Wittgenstein denies the idea that language, or the thought that language expresses, in any special sense *represents* the world to consciousness, and hence to say it *mis*represents the world to consciousness and structures that relation makes no sense either. The view of language as representation or failed representation misconstrues the nature of language and its relationship to consciousness.

It is difficult to summarize Wittgenstein's approach to consciousness without doing it an injustice, but Charles Altieri has done so as well as anyone. For Wittgenstein, he writes,

[C]onsciousness is essentially not a way of relating to objects but of relating to actions we learn to perform. The basic condition of human experience is not minds facing a world of objects but a wide variety of activities constituting a complex interrelated web of cultural and natural forms toward which we can behave in a creative way if we need or care to.[44]

In this context, language is a tool that facilitates our interaction with the world and with other people. Since there are myriad ways in which language can function – such as to make commands, questions, and exclamations – description is only one of language's uses and certainly not a privileged one. Equally, since there are myriad ways of interacting with the world and thereby defining ourselves, there is not one essential self at stake in any of our interactions but a self that is defined by change and adaptation. These are perhaps obvious points to make, but they are points entirely lost in contemporary theories of the literary and the cinematic that view the operation of the text within the Procrustean mold of the construction and deconstruction of "the subject." The freezing of this opposition within film theory between the classical Hollywood text and the avant-garde text only serves to dramatize its absurdity.

It may be pointed out that although I have spent extensive time criticizing a philosophical conception of the subject, the conception of the subject that underpins contemporary film theory is a psychoanalytic one. While I have shown that this psychoanalytical conception of the subject is often cast in terms of a philosophical conception of the subject, the former is not reducible to the latter. Indeed, as I have indicated, psychoanalysis may offer a diagnosis of why this essentially theological quest for certainty has had such a grip upon the life of the human mind. It suggests that such a search manifests an aspiration toward plenitude or wholeness that is felt to be unrealized in the life of the human being because of the division between consciousness and the unconscious. Psychoanalysis suggests that, in the life of the mind, a subjective drama plays out that *does* undercut our conscious action and interaction in the world, and thus seems to offer a challenge to a Wittgensteinian conception of the subject. Where I would argue with contemporary uses of psychoanalytic theory is over how that challenge is conceived. Psychoanalytic theory certainly offers a challenge to any humanist conception of the subject that identifies subjectivity or the ego with consciousness. However, to recognize that the subject has an unconscious as well as a conscious relationship to language is not to concede to the idea that the subject is merely an "effect of language": To say that mental life is informed by unconscious processes does not mean to say that we are imprisoned by them.

Nonetheless, Lacan does conceive psychoanalysis in a way that offers a fundamental challenge to a humanist conception of the subject. Lacanian psychoanalysis suggests a foundation for a Derridean critique of the subject, such that it no longer rests upon a principle of deconstruction that remains wedded to the very premises it seeks to undermine. Consider, once again, the subject before the mirror, the no-thing. Perceiving himself in the mirror of the other, the subject appears to himself as an entity; but if this entity in the mirror were actually a reflection of something outside the mirror, then a reference to that which is before the mirror would be retained. The reflection in the mirror would be a straightforward representation of what is before the mirror; yet what is before the mirror is the no-thing, which is unrepresentable. Thus what is represented in the mirror, although it appears to represent something, actually functions as a signifier relating to the no-thing before the mirror as a stand-in for something that cannot be reflected. The subject constituted in misrecognition is thus constituted through the figure of *différance*. The mirror image is both a spatial figure in which representation and signifier are condensed (to form the imaginary) and a temporal figure in which the two forms of representation are displaced or deferred (to form the symbolic). The two aspects of the figure never coincide but remain in a relationship of permanent displacement or deferral. The signifier of the subject always already stands in for the representation of the subject that refers to it; thus the subject figures in representation only as an absence or lack. The subject's ability to represent himself and to represent "reality" – his concept of identity and difference – is attained, paradoxically, at the cost of the necessary loss of the subject represented. It is thus impossible to refer to the primordial condition of the subject, qua no-thing, that subsists in the real.

Lacan's theory of the subject arguably gives Derrida's theory of *différance* a grounding that it lacks in Derrida's own philosophy. Lacan provides a reason why an epistemology grounded upon the empiricist conception of knowledge must fail: From a Lacanian perspective this conception fails, as Derrida claims it fails, because it is founded on *différance;* but what supports this claim in Lacan's philosophy of the subject is the fact that the real relation of subject and object, signifier and substance, lies entirely elsewhere. It lies in the condition of the no-thing, a state marked by a much more profound identity of symbol and substance (the *objets petites autres*) than that implied by the empiricist conception of knowledge, where the symbol is already distinguished from substance and the subject is already distinguished from the object. *Différance* describes how this philosophical conception of the subject comes into being from the no-thing. It describes the possibility of experience itself, the condition under which there could exist an object known and a subject who knows. The laying bare of *différance* becomes an act of revelation. Psychoanalytic "deconstruction" thus exposes the vanity of the subject who inflates the material signifiers of language with "sense" and thereby circumscribes itself as a subject in a world of objects, only to deflate back into the no-thing-ness whence it came.

Lacan reconstructs Freudian psychoanalysis as a solution to metaphysics. However, I would suggest that psychoanalysis, in this way, offers an alternative to a humanist conception of the subject only by itself becoming a theology. The bedrock of existence thereby lies in an imaginary identity between subject and object, language and the world, that preexists the formation of the subject and the distinction between language and the world. Theology suggests that this bedrock is given by God, and God's Word provides the original ontological bond between word and thing. Subjectivity represents the fall of humanity into the world and severance of word and thing. Like the prelapsarian world of theology, the "identity" of subject and object that preexists humanity's fall into identity and difference cannot be described as such, and its effects are only inferable retrospectively. Of course, the difference between Lacan and the theologians is that the God of theology represents unity, synthesis, harmony, and life, whereas Lacanian psychoanalysis offers a negative theology premised upon radical fragmentation, dispersion, negativity, and ultimately death. At a certain point one cannot argue with Lacan's view of the subject other than to say that, like the theologian, he provides no reason for us to assent to it: One either believes or one does not. Despite Lacan's alleged return to Freud, his is a view of psychoanalysis that profoundly diverges from that of Freud, and ultimately trivializes the insights of psychoanalysis; for the importance of psychoanalysis as a theory of the human mind that can contribute to the understanding of culture is precisely that it provides a way of understanding the place of irrational mental life in relationship to rational mental life. Lacan's theory reduces rational mental life to the irrational.

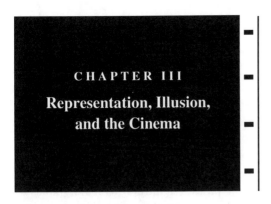

CHAPTER III

Representation, Illusion, and the Cinema

Contemporary film theory's characterization of the cinema as a form of illusion bears a certain resemblance to Plato's criticisms of art in *The Republic*. Plato considers that art is essentially illusory because, rather than being master of what we see, we are placed at the mercy of a point of view upon the world that is dictated to us by the artwork. Furthermore, he believes art tends to indulge sensation at the expense of reason by undermining the self-control of the viewer. The history of Western aesthetics since the Enlightenment could be viewed as an attempt to rescue art from the debased position assigned to it by Plato. This goal has been achieved by drawing an evaluative distinction between art and mass culture. Mass culture is designated illusory, regressive, and sensational; high art is considered authentic, ennobling, and moving.[1] As I suggested in Chapter 1, contemporary film theory reproduces this opposition and the hierarchy it implies, though it is recast as an opposition between an ideological mass culture and an emancipatory modernism. It could be argued that since the idea of illusion has played a central role in sustaining the negative characterization of mass culture against high art, the idea of illusion should be abandoned entirely as a way of understanding the effect that forms of cultural practice such as the cinema have upon the spectator. In this chapter and the next I shall pursue a different line of argument: Illusion, I suggest, is central to our experience of diverse forms of cultural practice and especially important to our experience of cinema. While the experience of cinema as a form of illusion is closely identified with popular cinema and, in particular, classical Hollywood cinema, it nonetheless also plays a central role in our experience of forms of cinema that define themselves as artistic practices.

In this context, then, one value of contemporary film theory is that it analyzes in some detail our experience of the cinema as a form of illusion, although it does so on the basis of an erroneous conception of what that experience entails. The argument of contemporary film theory about cinematic illusion is also important in another respect: It draws attention to the way in which the cinema, as a form of projected moving image produced by an apparatus, bears a relationship to illusion that is different from traditional art forms and occupies a preeminent place in mass culture by virtue of its form. In this chapter and the next I shall attempt to describe the way in which the cinema is experienced as a form of illusion that I will call "projective illusion." I do not claim that this form of illusion is unique to the cinema, but I do claim that it is uniquely promoted by the cinema and forms of image-making apparatuses that are akin to it. Before I discuss its character in the cinema, I shall begin by contrasting projective illusion with other kinds of illusions that are associated with pictorial representation, and then consider its place within a wider conception of illusion. I should emphasize that my concern is less to demonstrate that the experience of projective illusion *is* a form of illusion, than to illuminate the character of this experience by comparing it with other forms of visual experience that are readily considered illusions.

Representation and Illusion

In order to isolate the character of projective illusion, we must understand the relationship it bears to other forms of pictorial and dramatic illusion. In a trompe l'oeil painting I see the painting as if it were an object and not a pictorial representation at all; the trompe l'oeil thus entails a loss of medium awareness. The trompe l'oeil is readily produced through representational painting, although a photographic or cinematic version could be produced under the right conditions. Live-action performance affords a distinctive kind of illusion that is akin to the trompe l'oeil, where an actor masquerades as a real person: a member of the audience. In a reproductive illusion – so named because it is created by forms of mechanical or electronic reproduction (photography, film, video) – I mistake the fictional referent of a pictorial representation for an actual one. Reproductive illusion may be considered a form of trompe l'oeil in the sense that it entails a fictional object taken for a real object; but I wish to emphasize its difference from the trompe l'oeil illusion as I have defined it. This difference lies in the fact that the spectator of a reproductive illusion remains medium aware. In projective illusion I experience a pictorial or dramatic representation as if it were a fully realized world of experience and not a representation. Projective illusion is not a form of trompe l'oeil: The reality experienced is a "virtual" one. Yet, like the trompe l'oeil, it entails a loss of medium awareness. It is an experience that can be engendered by all forms of pictorial or dramatic representation, but I shall argue that the experience is facilitated by the cinema.

The particular qualities of representational painting readily afford the possibility of trompe l'oeil illusion. In a representational painting the object that is perceived is constituted out of the surface of the paint. Paintings can thus mimic a condition in which the object does not seem to be constituted out of the surface of the paint but actually seems to be in front of the viewer. On the other hand, the medium-aware viewer of a representational painting – the viewer who looks at a painting as a *painting* of something – looks at the way in which the surface of the painting has been marked in order to produce an image of the object. Richard Wollheim has characterized this experience as "seeing-in": "[W]hen seeing-in occurs, two things happen: I am visually aware of the surface I look at, and I discern something standing out in front of, or (in certain cases) receding behind something else."[2] In a traditional trompe l'oeil such as the cabinets of stuffed birds painted by Leroy de Barde (Fig. 1), the two aspects of this experience are pried apart. Initially, and in the photographic reproduction printed here, we perceive the painting as a cabinet. Upon closer inspection we see that the apparent cabinet is in fact a configuration of marks on a surface – a painting. However, we are unable to reconcile our perception of the apparent object with our perception of the surface of the painting and see the apparent object itself in the surface of the painting. A similar effect is achieved by a photorealist painting such as *White Chevy, Red Trailer* by John Salt (Fig. 2), although in the case of photorealist painting there is one particular object – a photograph – with which the painting is always confused. When we experience the trompe l'oeil, our customary perception of the painting as a painting (our medium awareness) is inhibited. We experience a difficulty or an uncanniness in our perception. What we take for granted in our normal experience of representational painting – that our perception of how the object is depicted enters into our perception of the object – is thrown out of kilter. We experience shock or surprise; our interest in the painting is consumed by exploring this effect.

For a photographic trompe l'oeil to occur when I perceive a photograph, I would have to believe either (1) that what I see is really an object and not a photograph, or (2) that what I see is a nonphotographic representation of an object. It is hard to imagine a photograph being confused for its referent, since the construction of an effective trompe l'oeil requires very precise control over the configuration of the elements within an image that photography, for reasons that I shall explain below, does not readily afford. However, a photograph might under the right circumstances be confused with a nonphotographic representation, say a sketch. In the early years of photography, photographers sought to mimic the conventions of academic painting. Certain of these photographs succeed in conveying a sense that they are

Figure 1. N. Leroy de Barde, *Réunion d'Oiseaux étrangers placés dans différentes caisses* (ca. 1810). Musée du Louvre, Paris. Photo Réunion des Musées Nationaux.

Figure 2. John Salt, *White Chevy, Red Trailer* (1975). Published by permission of the Birmingham Museum and Art Gallery.

sketches when, in addition to the fact that the photograph mimes a genre painting, two other factors obtain: highly textured paper reminiscent of a painter's canvas and an out-of-focus image that muffles the contours of the referent. Whether or not these images deserve to be called trompe l'oeil illusions is another question; I have not seen an example that possesses the uncanny force that is the hallmark of the best trompes l'oeils.[3] However, it should be noted that if a photograph that looks like a representational painting is possible, then so is a photograph that looks like a traditional trompe l'oeil painting. A photograph that successfully mimicked a traditional trompe l'oeil painting would be a trompe l'oeil photograph.

It is just as difficult to conceive of a trompe l'oeil in the photographically based medium of cinema. In order for the cinematic image to be experienced as a trompe l'oeil, we would have to mistake the film for real life in the manner of the proverbial spectators of the Lumières' *Arrival of a Train at the Station* (1895).[4] The size of the image (its largeness) and its character (its lack of three-dimensionality), in relationship to its varied content and the context where it is seen (the auditorium), make the possibility of trompe l'oeil illusion extremely unlikely. The exception that proves the rule is a demonstration of Showscan conducted by special effects master Douglas Trumbull. With the house lights still up, the audience saw a screen that appeared to be illuminated from behind while the shadow of a workman moved toward it until he appeared life-size as someone working behind the screen. The audience heard voices, apparently from behind the screen, talking about problems they were having in setting up the screening. After a short period it was revealed to the audience that what they saw and heard was a film, not actual events taking place in the theater prior to the screening.[5]

Reproductive illusion trades upon qualities of the photograph that it does not share with painting. A photograph is produced by the mechanical imprint of the image of an object through the causal process by which light reflected from the object registers on photochemical emulsions. This causal process underlying the production of the photographic image parallels the causal process underlying human vision: The photograph depends upon a direct connection between object and photographic plate, just as what we see depends upon a direct causal connection between object and retina. In this way, as Kendall Walton has suggested, looking at an object in a standard photograph is like seeing an object with a mechanical aid such as a mirror, telescope, or eyeglasses, except that unlike them the camera also has the capacity to document the way in which the object appears to us in sight.[6] When we look at an object in a standard photograph it appears to us in roughly the way it would were we to have actually encountered the object at the particular moment of its being photographed. To capture the transparency of standard photographic depiction, Walton suggests that the medium-aware spectator who sees the photograph as a photograph looks through the frame of the image at a profilmic event, an event that is in front of the camera and hence in the world.[7]

Roland Barthes has drawn attention to the fact that as a result of the causal process underlying the production of the photograph, a photograph necessarily documents how an object looked at a particular moment in the past.[8] However, I think it is mistaken to conclude that a medium-aware perception of a standard photograph entails that we view the profilmic event as something in the past, since there are only certain photographs, at certain times, whose age we can infer from looking at them. Whether or not we infer that a photograph depicts something from the past depends on the kind of photograph it is – that is, whether or not it is an old photograph – and it depends on how the photograph is used – that is, if we value it for its age. Photographic portraits of deceased ancestors, for example, meet both requirements. However, many photographs do not reveal their age, in particular those in which we are interested not for the singularity of the object depicted but for its being an illustration of a type. An awareness of pastness does not accompany our perception of a nature photograph, such as a dew drop on a rose petal; neither does it accompany our perception of an illustrative photograph such as a cereal bowl on a box of cornflakes. Of course, these photographs do not carry with them a temporal index of presentness. They lack a temporal index altogether.

Reproductive illusion depends upon the transparency of the photograph or the relationship that the photograph bears to reality, and hence it is not a form of illusion to be found in representational painting. A painting can only mislead us about its own status, not about the status of reality. A photograph rarely misleads us about its own status, but it can indeed mislead us about the status of reality. A photograph may simply reproduce an illusion; for example, we may see a photo of a bowl of fake oranges that looks like a photo of real fruit. In this case the photograph reproduces the confusion in perception set up in the crafting of the object. However, the contribution of the photograph may be greater than this. Face to face we may see that the trompe l'oeil painting of the cabinet in Figure 1 is, in fact, a painting; but in the photographic reproduction it looks like an object, and we cannot confirm that it is a painting. A stage set of a city street is a fabrication, but carefully photographed it may look like a real street. The minimal contribution of the photograph, then, is to record an illusion, but it may also contribute to the production of an illusion by presenting the phenomenon in a way that disguises its fictive status. Reproductive illusion does not preclude looking through the photographic image at the object and hence the form of medium awareness that characterizes our perception of the standard photograph. On the contrary, it trades on the ability of the photograph to provide a transparent access to the referent.

There is a second kind of reproductive illusion manifested by the trick photograph, such as that of Woody Allen as Zelig posing with Hitler in the film *Zelig* (1983). In the form of reproductive illusion I have described, the illusion is produced through the reproduction of something staged that appears to be real. The deception in the trick photograph is achieved by a reconfiguration of the image so the photograph is *constituted* as an illusion. The trick photograph is deceiving regardless of whether what it depicts is staged or real. The deception is more fundamental than the simple case of reproductive illusion: We are deceived into believing that the photograph is pointing to an object array in the world that is not in fact in the world. However, like the photograph of a staged event that looks real, the trick photograph trades on our understanding that it is a recording of reality in order to deceive us about the nature of that reality. In this sense, despite the fact that this deception is produced by melding together two or more images, trick photography is akin to other kinds of reproductive illusion that involve deception. Trick photography becomes central to cinematic representation through the techniques of special effects.

I have suggested that when we look at a representational painting as a painting we see the figure or landscape therein. We may of course simply attend to the surface features of the painting, in which case we will continue to look at the painting as a painting but not as a representation of anything. However, there is a third possibility: Our awareness of the painting as a painting may be eclipsed entirely, and we may imagine or visualize that the object of the painting is before us, unmediated by representation. When we entertain the painting in this fashion we do not think that the represented object is actually before us in the space of the real world, yet we visualize that the object in the painting is fully realized before us. We imagine that we inhabit the world of the painting in the manner of an internal observer. Likewise, a photograph can be experienced as a projective illusion: Instead of looking through a photo at the object depicted within it, we may perceive the object as one that is fully realized before us and be unaware of the fact that what we perceive is a photograph of something. Equally, we may look at a play as a medium-aware spectator and appreciate the artifice of the set and the craft of the actor's performance and delivery while emotionally responding to the performance, but we may also experience the performance as if it were a fully realized world and no longer see the characters as characters or the performance as a performance.

In order to be realized, projective illusion requires the contribution of the spectator in a manner that I shall examine more thoroughly in Chapter 4. Furthermore, the representational cues that engender the experience are not specific to any particular medium. The minimum condition for a picture or drama to be experienced as a projective illusion is simply that the form be representational, that is, it must contain pictorial elements that a spectator can recognize as standing for individuals or types of things. Moreover, different media provide different kinds of cues that facilitate the viewer's capacity to experience them as a projective illusion. Each of the cues provided by different media, sometimes separately, sometimes in conjunction, can augment the experience of projective illusion: linear perspective, photographic lifelikeness, projection, movement, sound, color. Either individually or severally, these cues are associated with different representational practices. Rudolf Arnheim's idea of partial illusion illuminates the character of these visual cues, though it is not, as Arnheim seems to imply, the experience of illusion itself that is partial.[9] Partial illusion serves to describe the way in which the method of engendering the experience of projective illusion offered by a given representational practice contributes only one of several possible cues for evoking lifelikeness.

In comparison with the representational painting, the lifelikeness produced by a photographic recording of an object minimizes the contribution required by the spectator's imagination in order to experience the depiction as if it were a fully realized world; yet the standard photograph is impaired by a size that encourages medium awareness, for we are typically aware of its frame. The projected image long predates the history of photography, and though it lacks the indexical aspect of the photograph it has distinct advantages. Other things being equal, its larger size encourages the spectator to be unaware of the frame of the image, an experience that is augmented by the panoramic sweep of the wide-screen image. Furthermore, the projected image lacks a surface. Provided it is projected onto a neutral background, its absence of surface will also promote the loss of medium awareness that is prerequisite to the experience of projective illusion. The movement and sound of theatrical drama afford the spectator a surrogate reality more readily than the static and silent painting or photograph; and yet in comparison with both painting and photograph, the capacity of live theater to engender projective illusion is constrained by the fact that the drama is embodied before us in the auditorium. As Christian Metz has emphasized in comparing theater and cinema, the actors and props in a play are physically present in a way that they are not in a pictorial representation.[10] In order to experience a drama as a projective illusion, as a fully realized world, we must imagine that the actors and props are neither physically present nor a part of this world.

However, these various cues do not simply have equal status with respect to projective illusion or to the media that embody them; projective illusion has a historical character in which some representational cues supplant others in their capacity to evoke lifelikeness. This is the point made by André Bazin in his essay "The Ontology of the Photographic Image," though he casts the question erroneously as one that pertains to realism rather than illusionism.[11] Bazin argues that photography is a more realistic medium than painting because of the causal bond that exists between image and object, and that cinema adds to the realism of photography the extra dimension of movement. However, since realism is a matter of artistic convention, the claim that photography is more realistic by virtue of its basis in mechanical reproduction cannot be defended. Nevertheless, the argument is illuminating if it is taken to describe the historical character of our experience of projective illusion. There is a historical development to projective illusion in which representational cues act as thresholds for the experience that supersede previous thresholds. This supersession is certainly not absolute: The invention of photography does not preclude the experience of representational painting as a projective illusion. However, with respect to its capacity to evoke the experience of projective illusion, a painting, in comparison to a photograph, appears dated because a new technique has superseded it. For a spectator no longer used to looking at painting, painting evokes a medium awareness. Furthermore, this supersession is not a linear one. For example, I have already noted that, in certain respects, painting is superior to photography for the evocation of projective illusion. In addition, before photography was invented, the magic lantern afforded a projected moving image that was superior to both painting and photography in its aura of illusionism.

It may seem arbitrary to suggest a point in the history of pictorial and dramatic representation where the experience of projective illusion is sufficiently guaranteed to warrant attaching the label "projective illusion" to the picture itself. However, I would suggest that the advent of the cinema represents precisely such a decisive threshold in the history of projective illusion. The capacity to generate the experience of projective illusion is perfected by the cinema because it combines the properties of a number of representational practices that had hitherto remained distinct: photographic lifelikeness, projection, and movement, with the later crucial additions of sound and color. Projective illusion was not "invented" with the cinema; rather, the cinema is located within the long history of representational practices. Furthermore, as Charles Musser has pointed out, the cinema takes its place within a wider history of screen practice that has consistently aspired to maximize the spectator's experience of illusionism.[12] Specifically, the cinema has as a precursor the projected moving image of the magic lantern, to which the lifelikeness of photography was also added; but the advent of the cinema brought with it the perfection of the lifelike depiction of movement (and later sound) that allowed a fully realized dramatic enactment to be wedded to the illusionism of the projected moving image. It could become the intention of those engaged in crafting films to engender and sustain the experience of projective illusion.

Reproductive Illusion in the Cinema

Reproductive illusion is a form of illusion that is context dependent. If we are informed that the content of a photographic image is staged, we will not be deceived by it. Conversely, if we are informed that the content of an image is actual when in fact it is staged, we may be deceived by it. However, the most informative case lies in between, where we are presented with a staged photograph without any extraphotographic cues to its status. The fact that a photograph is a recording of real-world objects leads us to assume that what we see in a photograph is actual in the absence of obvious cues to the contrary. This assumption received a fine illustration in a recent royalty case surrounding Robert Doisneau's photograph *Le Baiser de l'Hôtel de Ville* (*The Kiss at City Hall*, 1950). The photograph appears to document a passionate fleeting kiss in an anonymous crowd, thereby encapsulating the romantic, existential aura of postwar Paris. It turns out that the photograph was staged, and the actress involved was finally claiming her share of the profits. The *New York Times* saw fit to editorialize on the disillusionment that such a discovery of the staged character of the photograph brings to our perception of the image.[13] In a subsequent letter to the editor, a photographer tried to argue that the *Times* misunderstood the character of photography, that all photographs are fictions;[14] but the photographer misses the point that, in the absence of cues to the contrary, photographs still carry a presumption of truth for the viewer that rests upon the causal relationship between object and image.

This presumption is crucial when considering the role of reproductive illusion in the nonfiction film, where actuality footage is commonly used by a filmmaker to present her case. In a nonfiction film our ability to evaluate the status of actuality footage as evidence will always be limited by the difficulty of discerning the extent to which the presence of the film unit has affected the filming of events, as Buster Keaton wittily demonstrates in *The Cameraman* (1928). However, we will be deceived outright when the nonfiction filmmaker simply fabricates the events she purports to present as actuality, either by presenting a dramatization as if it were real, or by editing the footage in such a way as to falsify the historical record in the manner of the trick photograph.[15] Of course, the fact that we are watching a nonfiction film does not by itself warrant the assumption that what we see is real. Nonfiction film often combines actuality with staged footage, as in Errol Morris's film *The Thin Blue Line* (1989), which is composed largely of staged scenes. Usually the spectator has no problem discerning which parts of a nonfiction film are staged and which are actuality. However, I would argue that the spectator of a nonfiction film believes that what she sees is real unless there is reasonable evidence to the contrary. Of course, the propaganda film that uses deceptive footage is pernicious in a way that Doisneau's photograph is not, for the deception extends beyond the mere content of the image to the larger argument that the image serves to support. However, both uses of photography exploit the belief in the reality of the image that is played upon by Doisneau.

Noël Carroll has argued that the documentary film should be defined by its rhetorical form as a discursive genre, a genre of filmed essay, rather than as a putative recording of reality. He concludes that nonfiction films in which shots and their sequencing have the status of a record of the events they depict are "neither the whole of the genre nor a privileged or central instance thereof."[16] In general, I find Carroll's emphasis to be important, but he overstates his case in a manner that obscures the role that the spectator's belief in the reality of the image, and the possibility of deception that it entails, actually plays in our experience of the documentary film. At times Carroll implies that the viewer of a documentary should be a singularly skeptical viewer and suspend all assumptions about the character of the image until proven otherwise. He writes that since it is often impossible to tell whether or not an image "physically portrays" its subject matter or, in other words, has an evidentiary status, "we are best advised to treat such images as nominal portrayals," that is, as bearing the same relationship to the recorded material as a character in a fiction bears to the actor playing the role.[17] This state of heightened alertness is no doubt the ideal state for the spectator to be in to avoid being duped by the image, but it is not the characteristic attitude of the documentary viewer. To be sure, the spectator of a documentary film does not naïvely believe in the reality of what she sees. Nevertheless, we are in practice deceived, and in order for this to be possible, there are *some* assumptions about the image's evidentiary status that we bring to bear upon the image. As I have already stated, we believe that what we see is actuality unless there is reasonable evidence to the contrary. Reproductive illusion trades upon this reasonable belief.

Reproductive illusion is particularly prevalent in the genre of pornography because it mixes together actuality and fictional elements and blurs the boundaries between them. The rationale of so-called hard-core pornography is that the acts of sex and violence depicted have actually taken place. Hardcore pornography elicits the spectator's voyeurism by purporting to show us real sexual activity, not the pretense or illusion of a sexual act; but pornography relies on the seamless coexistence of actual sexual activity with simulations of aspects of that activity. Although the so-called meat-shot insert that depicts the act of copulation in close-up is "actuality," it may not depict the activity of the protagonists who are established as the agents of a given sexual act. The porn film often encourages the spectator to believe that the protagonists are not simply performing the sexual act but also are enjoying it, but is the enjoyment of the actors acted or real? As Linda Williams has pointed out, this difficulty of separating reality and illusion is particularly acute in certain forms of sadomasochistic pornography:

[S]adomasochistic sexual acts are . . . problematic as acts: they move us by their sensationalism even more than "hard-core" genital sex acts, and there is every reason to believe that they can really affect the bodies of their participants; yet they can also be acts in the theatrical sense of shows performed for oneself or others.[18]

Is the violence real or pretend? If it is real, is it actually enjoyed (masochistically) or simply painfully endured? Rather than simply deceive the spectator, this kind of pornographic representation seems to challenge the limits of his credulity. The spectator is placed at a kind of loss in relationship to knowledge that is not unlike the masochist's relationship to power. The masochistic spectator's pleasure in being unable to tell replicates the masochistic performer's pleasure in being unable to control.

In an entirely fictional context, reproductive illusion can be used to disguise the fictional character of the work. At its extreme this may completely deceive the spectator. The most famous example of reproductive illusion comes not from film but from radio: In 1938, Orson Welles broadcast H.G. Wells's *War of the Worlds* in the form of a news report that the Martians had landed in New Jersey, and many listeners truly believed that this event was occurring, having either missed or ignored the notice that it was a dramatization.[19] In her book on pornography, Linda Williams discusses the case of a horror film called *Snuff* (1976) that caused a major public scandal upon its release. Trading on rumors that porn films existed that actually killed off their female protagonists, the filmmakers of *Snuff* added a coda consisting of the director stepping out from behind the camera, having sex with a "script girl," and then killing her in an orgy of violence. According to Williams,

the sequence culminates in the director cutting open the woman's abdomen, pulling out her inner organs, and holding them over his head in triumph while the sound track mixes heavy panting with the beat of a throbbing heart. The organs seem to convulse. The image goes black as a voice says, "Shit, we ran out of film." Another says, "Did you get it all?" "Yeah we got it, Let's get out of here." No credits roll.[20]

The public outcry promoted an investigation by New York's district attorney that revealed the scene was fabricated.

Reproductive illusion may be exploited for more subtle dramatic or aesthetic purpose than is evident in these examples. In a series of photographs by Cindy Sherman called *Untitled Film Stills* (1977–80), Sherman poses like a heroine from American and Italian movies, mostly from the fifties and sixties. In one, Sherman has made herself up to look like Marilyn Monroe, and the lighting, framing, and pose of the figure, together with the caption of the photograph, "Untitled Film Still #54," suggest an actual still from a movie (Fig. 3). In this sense the image functions as a reproductive illusion in which one staged event, the imaginary film still, is perceived as another staged event, the shot of a scene from a movie. Once one sees the photograph in the context of the series and realizes that this image is posed and in fact a "self-portrait" of the photographer, those aspects of the image that are real versus imaginary become legible. Sherman exploits the relationship between the staging of the illusion and the fact that the illusion is staged in order to suggest both that the reality of female identity is as an image that exists for the (male) gaze, and that this identity as an image is an illusion, a masquerade controlled by the female as agent.

Jim McBride's *David Holtzman's Diary* (1968) is a fictional film of the life of one David Holtzman of New York City, but it is filmed as if it were the autobiographical diary of an actual filmmaker named David Holtzman. The spectator is lured into believing that the film is a documentary through its verisimilar mise-en-scène that is complemented by a range of filmic techniques connoting actuality. The film is shot on location; its reference is contemporary; and its acting style, costumes, and setting are of a contemporary "vernacular." The scenes are shot with a hand-held camera in grainy black and white images. The editing appears improvised, and film leader appears at the end of each apparent scrap of film. At the same time, however, the level of self-consciousness about the cinema exhibited by the protagonist of the film begins to suggest to us that the events are staged. We realize that this is a fiction film whose subject matter – the confusion between film and reality – is performed for the spectator in the presentation of its own fictional staging as documentary actuality. The film's uncanny effect then becomes a source of pleasure, though we are not certain until the final credits roll that the film is scripted and staged.

McBride's film exploits the fact that, since the advent of cinéma vérité, the filmmaker now has a set of techniques and conventions available that actively connote a sense of "being there," particularly via the hand-held camera and live sound recording. Of course, vérité techniques are utilized in a purely fictional context (as in the films of John Cassavetes and Martin Scorsese) to promote a sense of realism without engendering reproductive illusion. However, when these techniques are used in conjunction with other cues that suggest the evidentiary status of the image, and when sufficient cues to the contrary are lacking, they can be used to foster the illusion that

Figure 3. Cindy Sherman, *Untitled Film Still #54* (1980). Metro Pictures.

staged events are actual events captured by the filmmaker. These techniques of illusionism are utilized in sensationalist television current affair programs that dramatize, in the manner of "docudramas," real-life unsolved crime stories, such as NBC's *Unsolved Mysteries.* Although the event is staged, the action is shot with vérité techniques at the actual scene of the crime to give the spectator the illusion of witnessing the event.

A fiction film does not typically mislead us as to its status as a fiction film; but within the context of a fiction film we are consistently deceived about the actual character of the object array that we appear to see. Routinely, we remain uncertain as to what is unadorned location and what is staged in a film. In any film shot on location, that location may be altered in a manner of which the spectator remains unaware. Furthermore, special effects allow for the creation of composite images that deceive us into believing that we perceive before the camera an object array that is not actually there. Composite images can be created in camera through multiple takes, but they are more commonly created in postproduction through the techniques of matte painting and optical printing. Most recently the digital creation of photographic images affords the possibility of manufacturing photographs or parts of photographs that bear no relationship to actual profilmic events.

Figure 4. *Citizen Kane* (1941). In-camera matte shot of the discovery of Susan Alexander's attempted suicide.

Orson Welles's *Citizen Kane* (1941) provides a compendium of traditional special effects techniques, as Robert Carringer has documented.[21] The shot that reveals Susan Alexander's attempted suicide in apparent deep focus (Fig. 4) is an in-camera matte shot in which the foreground was shot in focus with the background dark, the film rewound, and then the background shot in focus with the foreground dark. In the shot of the picnic caravan (Fig. 5), which was actually taken on the beach at Malibu that is surrounded by hills, the hills have been matted out and replaced by a sketch of terrain (and skyline) that evokes the Florida Everglades. Here the matted part of the shot functions as trompe l'oeil in which a painting looks like a photograph. The trompe l'oeil is particularly effective in this image because it is melded with a shot that is obviously a real location. In Susan Alexander's opera debut, what appears to be a continuous camera movement takes us from the stage, up the backstage rigging, to two workmen on a platform high above. In fact, the sequence consists of two separate shots of Susan and the workmen intercut with a miniature of the rigging. The effect is achieved through optical printing, in which developed film running in a projector is exposed on raw stock running through a camera. This setup allows for different images to be melded together through invisible editing, and hence for a composite image to be created in temporal sequence.

Figure 5. *Citizen Kane* (1941). The picnic caravan with and without artist's matte painting.

Sensory Illusion and Seeing Aspects

In order to define the experience of projective illusion more precisely, we need a more fine-grained account of illusion. Noël Carroll defines an illusion as something that "deceives or is liable to deceive" the viewer.[22] By "deception" he means that the illusion provokes the viewer to entertain false beliefs about the object perceived. The experiences of trompe l'oeil and reproductive illusion conform to this definition of illusion, but that of projective illusion does not. When we experience a pictorial representation as a projective illusion we do not believe that what we see is real. Carroll's definition is qualified with the proviso that there might be an "epistemically benign" sense of illusion in which "*x* is an illusion of *y*" simply means "*x* looks like *y*" but deception plays no role.[23] In specifying precisely the character of what I have called projective illusion, I shall begin by taking up Carroll's implication that different kinds of illusion can be distinguished on the basis of the quality of effect they have on the perceiver.

As it stands, Carroll's epistemically benign sense of illusion is uninformative, for calling a picture or drama an illusion in this sense adds nothing to our understanding of a picture or drama as a representation. The key to developing a more fine-grained account of illusion is to differentiate the kinds of deception involved in visual representations that are putatively illusions, rather than to differentiate a form of illusion in which deception plays no role. Most illusions are deceptive in two respects: They deceive the senses, and they lead us to make false inferences. We *see* something that does not really exist, and *believe* that it does exist. These two kinds of deception are distinguishable, however: We may experience a sensory illusion without being deceived into believing that what we see is real. The definition of illusion as deception must be modified. An illusion is something that deceives or is liable to deceive the spectator, but the deception need not be of the epistemic kind. Sensory deception does not entail epistemic deception.

Consider a powerful illusion such as the Müller–Lyer illusion in which parallel lines of equal length are perceived as lines of unequal length (Fig. 6). The Müller–Lyer illusion is one of a species of illusions that trades on our inclination to respond to depth cues. In this case, we see the lines as external and internal corners that appear as different lengths because of the different perspectival cues. We do not see the lines as marks of equal length on a page. What is involved in our experience of this illusion? Initially we may be deceived into *believing* that the lines are of unequal length because what we *see* are lines of unequal length; but even once we are persuaded that the lines are of the same length, by measuring them or by drawing horizontal lines at each end of the verticals, we still *see* the lines as being of unequal length. The Müller–Lyer illusion and similar illusions are always compelling because the sensory deception continues to exert its force even when we know that what we see is contrary to fact. We experience a conflict between our senses and our judgment; the illusion drives a wedge between our perception and belief.[24]

I use the term "sensory illusion" to describe the fact that we still see the lines of the Müller–Lyer illusion as lines of unequal length even though we know they are lines of the same length. By using the term "sensory" I do

Figure 5. *Citizen Kane* (1941). The picnic caravan with and without artist's matte painting.

Sensory Illusion and Seeing Aspects

In order to define the experience of projective illusion more precisely, we need a more fine-grained account of illusion. Noël Carroll defines an illusion as something that "deceives or is liable to deceive" the viewer.[22] By "deception" he means that the illusion provokes the viewer to entertain false beliefs about the object perceived. The experiences of trompe l'oeil and reproductive illusion conform to this definition of illusion, but that of projective illusion does not. When we experience a pictorial representation as a projective illusion we do not believe that what we see is real. Carroll's definition is qualified with the proviso that there might be an "epistemically benign" sense of illusion in which "x is an illusion of y" simply means "x looks like y" but deception plays no role.[23] In specifying precisely the character of what I have called projective illusion, I shall begin by taking up Carroll's implication that different kinds of illusion can be distinguished on the basis of the quality of effect they have on the perceiver.

As it stands, Carroll's epistemically benign sense of illusion is uninformative, for calling a picture or drama an illusion in this sense adds nothing to our understanding of a picture or drama as a representation. The key to developing a more fine-grained account of illusion is to differentiate the kinds of deception involved in visual representations that are putatively illusions, rather than to differentiate a form of illusion in which deception plays no role. Most illusions are deceptive in two respects: They deceive the senses, and they lead us to make false inferences. We *see* something that does not really exist, and *believe* that it does exist. These two kinds of deception are distinguishable, however: We may experience a sensory illusion without being deceived into believing that what we see is real. The definition of illusion as deception must be modified. An illusion is something that deceives or is liable to deceive the spectator, but the deception need not be of the epistemic kind. Sensory deception does not entail epistemic deception.

Consider a powerful illusion such as the Müller–Lyer illusion in which parallel lines of equal length are perceived as lines of unequal length (Fig. 6). The Müller–Lyer illusion is one of a species of illusions that trades on our inclination to respond to depth cues. In this case, we see the lines as external and internal corners that appear as different lengths because of the different perspectival cues. We do not see the lines as marks of equal length on a page. What is involved in our experience of this illusion? Initially we may be deceived into *believing* that the lines are of unequal length because what we *see* are lines of unequal length; but even once we are persuaded that the lines are of the same length, by measuring them or by drawing horizontal lines at each end of the verticals, we still *see* the lines as being of unequal length. The Müller–Lyer illusion and similar illusions are always compelling because the sensory deception continues to exert its force even when we know that what we see is contrary to fact. We experience a conflict between our senses and our judgment; the illusion drives a wedge between our perception and belief.[24]

I use the term "sensory illusion" to describe the fact that we still see the lines of the Müller–Lyer illusion as lines of unequal length even though we know they are lines of the same length. By using the term "sensory" I do

Figure 6. The Müller–Lyer illusion. The height of the corner adjacent to the distant figure is equal in length to the central section of the corner adjacent to the foreground figure.

not mean to imply that the experience of sensory illusion is merely sensory. Our perception of the lines as being of different length cannot be divorced from the *thought* that the lines are of unequal length. The distinction between sensory illusion and epistemic illusion thus overlaps with a distinction drawn by Noël Carroll between entertaining a thought about something and believing something:

[T]o have a belief is to entertain a proposition assertively; to have a thought is to entertain it nonassertively. Both beliefs and thoughts have propositional content. But with thoughts the content is merely entertained without commitment to its being the case; to have a belief is to be committed to the truth of the proposition.[25]

Of course, entertaining a thought about an object does not entail our imagining that we actually perceive that object, but in sensory illusion it does. Sensory illusion thus involves entertaining the thought that the object perceived is before us, but, unlike seeing in general, it does not entail that we believe the object is before us.

Projective illusion, in which we imagine we are witness to the events depicted in a visual or dramatic representation, may be characterized as a form of sensory illusion. We imagine, or entertain in thought, that we are seeing the object or event portrayed in a representation. This thought is promoted by the qualities of the object that we do see in a way that is analogous, in certain respects, to the way that the thought that the Müller–Lyer lines are of unequal length is promoted by their spatial configuration. However, unlike our experience of the Müller–Lyer illusion, the experience of projective illusion is context dependent. The Müller–Lyer illusion is artfully constructed in such a way that it is compelling even when we no longer believe it. However, context-dependent illusions like mirror illusions are not compelling in this way: Even if we are momentarily deceived by a mirror image, once we know that it is a mirror image and no longer believe the illusion, our senses are not deceived either. Projective illusion is like mirror illusion in that our knowledge about what we are seeing can break the hold of the illusion; but as we have seen, projective illusion, unlike mirror illusion, does not involve epistemic illusion. So in the case of projective illusion it is not simply that knowledge about what we are seeing breaks the hold of the illusion, but that the illusion might not be experienced at all.

Consider the example of the fiction film. We may always watch fiction films in the manner in which we remain medium aware in the relevant sense; that is, what we see conforms to what we know to be the case. When we watch a fiction film the film does not compel us to see the events of the fiction as if we were witness to them. As Gregory Currie has argued, our relationship to visual fictions may be no different from our relationship to literary fictions.[26] Watching a film, like reading a book, may simply involve imagining that the fictional events portrayed occur, rather than imagining that we actually see the events occurring. What we see in the film may be actors performing and the sets on which they perform. A film does not require us to perceive it in the form of a projective illusion in order to appreciate it as a fiction. Currie offers his account of visual fictions as alternative to the kind of explanation I am offering here. However, the possibility that we do imagine that we are seeing fictional events is not incompatible with Currie's explanation, as Jerrold Levinson points out in a reply to Currie.[27] Yet how then are we to explain the fact that we can shift from seeing actors in the film

Figure 7. The duck–rabbit figure.

to imagining we see the characters they portray? What is required is an explanation of how we can experience the representation in both ways.

In order to understand how it is possible both to see a representation and to imagine that we see what the representation depicts, it is necessary to isolate how the context of illusion may be defined by a phenomenon of seeing that may be called "seeing aspects" or "seeing-as."[28] This phenomenon involves a change in the way we see an object during the course of our perception of it, although the object itself remains the same. In his later philosophy, Wittgenstein discusses seeing aspects extensively and provides numerous examples, including the following: seeing two separate faces, then seeing a family resemblance between them (seeing one face in another face); seeing a row of four dots (· · · ·) as two pairs of dots side by side; seeing the duck–rabbit figure first as a duck, then as a rabbit (Fig. 7); seeing a plane figure consisting of a square and two rhombuses as the outside or inside corner of a box (Fig. 8).[29] The phenomenon of seeing aspects is defined by the fact that one cannot perceive the new aspect of the object simultaneously with the aspect first perceived; one can only flip-flop, sequentially, between them.

For Wittgenstein, the phenomenon of the dawning of an aspect illustrates the fact that our thoughts about an object cannot be divorced from our perception of that object in the activity of seeing. When the aspect changes, the spatial properties of the figure remain exactly the same, and the change of aspect is subject to the will of the perceiver; thus we can say with justification that we have changed our way of thinking about the object. At the same time, we don't merely interpret what we already see, for there is no more or less room for making a mistake here than there is in any other case of see-

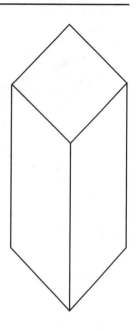

Figure 8. Either a square and two rhombuses or the corner of a box.

ing. When I experience the change of aspect I simply *see* either a duck or a rabbit. The fact that our thought about an object is bound to our perception of it explains why we cannot simultaneously perceive the two aspects of the figure. If our seeing *x* as *y* involves a distinct combination of thought and perception, so does our not seeing *x* as *y*. I cannot discern what it is that marks the change of an aspect when I notice a change of aspect. When we refuse to see *x* as *y,* it is impossible to be aware of the properties of *x* that would be transformed were we to see *x* as *y*. For, as the example demonstrates, what is different in the experience of the two cases (seeing or not seeing *x* as *y*) cannot be factored out from what is common to the two cases. The properties of *x* such that I see *x* as *y* are precisely what I cannot see when I choose to see *x*.

The examples of seeing aspects that Wittgenstein discusses are what might be called "pure" cases of seeing-as: those defined by the fact that there is nothing in our visual field we can identify as marking the change in aspect. However, there is another group of cases involving seeing aspects that are relevant to our discussion in which we *can* identify the aspect of our visual field that marks the change of aspect. Consider the figure of the Necker cube (Fig. 9), in which we may perceive the flat arrangement of lines first as one cube and then as another cube. At first sight this example may seem similar to the box corner in Figure 8. However, a difference resides in the

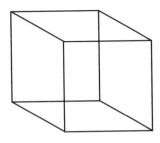

Figure 9. The Necker cube. The foreground outside corner of one cube becomes the background inside corner of the other cube.

addition of the further lines representing the back side of one cube or the front side of the other. When we shift from one cube to the other cube, we can identify a shift in our visual field. One side (or corner) stands in front of or behind the other. In the case of the Necker cube we can identify within our visual field precisely what it is that marks our change of perception. In "pure" cases of seeing-as, we cannot discriminate those aspects of our visual field that sustain one view of the object or the other. In "impure" cases such as the Necker cube, previously unseen features of our visual field – the change in the relative positions of the sides of the cube – are newly perceived;[30] yet cases such as the Necker cube are still examples of seeing-as for, like the case of the duck–rabbit, we remain unable to reconcile the two aspects of our visual field. Both the "pure" and "impure" cases of seeing-as are important for considering the relationship between seeing aspects and illusion.

In the duck–rabbit illustration or the Necker cube there is no "correct" interpretation of the figure. We can say of neither interpretation that it is misguided; we can say only that the figure is either a duck or a rabbit, or either one cube or the other, according to that aspect upon which we focus. These figures are apt for illustrating the phenomenon of seeing-as precisely because they do not involve illusion. What happens, then, when illusion *is* involved in seeing-as, as in the example of the eggbox illusion (Fig. 10)? The eggbox illusion is an example of an impure case of seeing-as, for while our perceptions of the eggbox as concave and convex are irreconcilable, we can identify the change in our visual field that marks the shift from one perception to another. Illusion enters into this example of seeing-as because only one perception is the correct one. The eggbox illusion is one of a species of illusions in which contrasts between light and shade give an ambiguity to depth perspective. Once we learn the correct designation – say, that the eggbox is concave – our perception oscillates between seeing the concave eggbox and the illusion of seeing the concave eggbox as convex. In general cases where seeing-as involves illusion, our perception oscillates between seeing x and seeing x as y, where y is the illusion. We leave the safe haven of a congruence between thought and perception to experience an incongruity between the two, rather than the different form of congruity that is experienced in the cases of the duck–rabbit figure or the Necker cube.

The eggbox illusion has the compelling character of the Müller–Lyer illusion in the sense that it is impossible to tell just from looking at the illustration which view is correct. Furthermore, even if we are told the correct view, our knowledge is not of a kind that prevents us from experiencing the illusion when we flip-flop back again. In this sense, the eggbox illusion, like the Müller–Lyer illusion, is one that is necessarily experienced. It is unlike the mirror illusion, in which contextual information breaks the hold of the illusion on our senses altogether. Nevertheless, the fact that this illusion involves seeing-as modifies our relationship to it in a key respect, for we are afforded the possibility of a correct perception of the phenomenon we are viewing. Unlike the case of the Müller–Lyer illusion, we can bring our perception and our belief into line with each other. Furthermore, our experience of the illusion does not end here, for we can also flip-flop back again from the correct perception to the illusion. In a case like this one, which also involves seeing-as, the experience of a discrepancy between what we perceive and what we now know to be the case becomes an option we can voluntarily entertain.

The eggbox illusion provides a model for understanding some forms of pictorial illusion that we have already considered. Both forms of the trompe l'oeil illusion also involve seeing-as. Viewing the traditional trompe l'oeil, we are unable to reconcile our perception of the painting as a painting with our perception of the painting as an object. Viewing the photorealist trompe l'oeil, we are unable to reconcile our perception of the painting as a painting with our perception of the painting as a photograph. The trompe l'oeil is an "impure" case of seeing an aspect, for the shift in our perception of the character of the object we are seeing is caused by the fact that previously unseen features in our visual field, in particular the surface of the painting, are newly perceived. We are alerted to the actual status of what we see by these distinct visual cues. However, the trompe l'oeil still qualifies as an example of seeing-as, as well as an example of an illusion, because we remain unable to reconcile the two aspects of our visual field and see the apparent object or photograph in the painting.

While the eggbox illusion and the trompe l'oeil illusion involve seeing-as and hence allow the form of illusion to be entertained voluntarily, they remain compelling in character. Projective illusion, however, does not have this compelling character; that is, our knowledge of the status of visual and

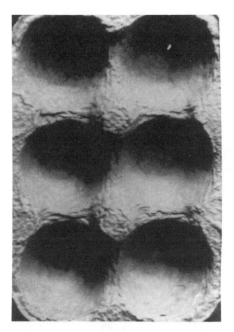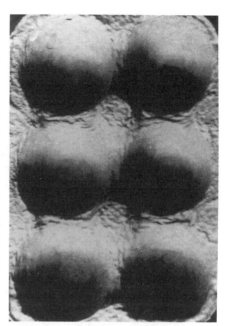

Figure 10. The eggbox illusion. The convex eggbox on the right is simply an inversion of the concave eggbox on the left. If the page is tilted to the side, viewers should be able to find a point where they can oscillate between seeing the eggbox as concave and convex in both images. Photo: John Hyman.

dramatic representations may undermine our capacity to experience projective illusion. The fact that projective illusion is embedded in the context of seeing-as affords the possibility of voluntarily entertaining an image in the form of a sensory deception: We may choose to step through the seeing-as corridor and enter the world of illusion. At the same time, the experience of illusion into which we flip-flop lacks in its own right the epistemic force of, say, the eggbox illusion: We are never confused as to which aspect of the phenomenon is real and which is the illusion, for projective illusion lacks the compelling character of the Müller–Lyer or eggbox illusion.

Projective illusion is also unlike the eggbox illusion in the sense that we cannot differentiate those features of the image that sustain our perception of the image as an image from those that sustain our perception of the image as a projective illusion. When we experience a picture as a projective illusion we cannot isolate what it is in our visual field that has changed, although the way in which we experience our visual field has changed. Unlike the cases of seeing-as involving illusion that I have considered so far, it is a "pure" case of seeing-as. It is this feature of projective illusion, together with the fact that it does not compel us to experience it, that explains its particular relationship to volition. Though our experience of the illusory aspect of the eggbox illusion is sometimes involuntary, it is nonetheless an experience that we can readily control. However, projective illusion has a much "looser" connection with the will. We cannot choose to step through the seeing-as corridor into the world of illusion as we would choose to flip-flop between the two sides of the duck–rabbit figure or between the two views of the eggbox. Although we can allow ourselves to lose medium awareness, we may only be aware of the fact that we are experiencing a projective illusion after the event. Nevertheless, the experience of projective illusion remains a voluntary activity in a crucial sense, for it still involves looking, and looking – in contrast to merely seeing – is something that we actively do rather than something that just occurs.

It is perhaps helpful to summarize the argument of this section. I discriminate between varieties of illusion on the basis of two criteria. Certain kinds of visual illusions, particularly those forms specifically constructed as visual illusions, will always deceive the senses; however, other kinds that are more context dependent will not. Thus the first criterion is whether or not the illusion is necessarily experienced as an illusion when it is perceived. The second criterion is whether or not the illusion is one that also involves seeing-as. Seeing-as opens up the possibility of a limited escape from the hold of an illusion that would otherwise be necessarily experienced. These two criteria allow me to discriminate four different kinds of illusion, represented in Figure 11:

1. illusions that are necessarily experienced but do not involve seeing-as;
2. illusions that are not necessarily experienced as illusions and do not involve seeing-as;
3. illusions that are necessarily experienced and do involve seeing-as;
4. illusions that are not necessarily experienced as illusions but do involve seeing-as.

Projective Illusion and the Cinematic Image

When you see a zombie in George Romero's *Night of the Living Dead* (1968), you may see the image as a medium-aware spectator. That is, you may look through the image at the fictional portrayal of a zombie not only with the knowledge that what you see is only a film, but also by perceiving the way in which the fictional scene is staged for the camera. It is highly un-

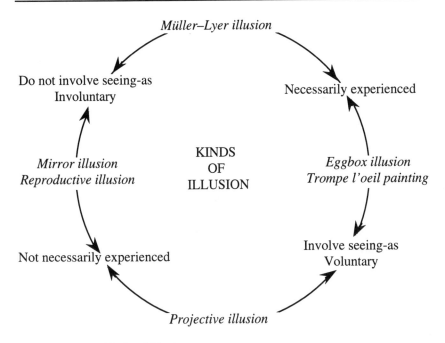

Figure 11. Four kinds of illusion.

likely, but you might perceive the zombie as a reproductive illusion and pre-sume that these creatures were out there in this world, for example, if some-how you thought that the film was a documentary. However, there is a third option: You may imagine that you perceive a world inhabited by zombies. In this third case, you do not mistake a staged event for actuality in the manner of a reproductive illusion; rather, you lose awareness of the fact that you are seeing a film, that is, watching a recorded event that is staged before the camera. Instead of looking "from the outside" upon something staged in this world, you perceive the events of the film directly or "from within." You perceive a fully realized though fictional world that has all the percep-tual immediacy of our own; you experience the film as a projective illusion. When you imagine that you look upon the events of the film "from within," the frame of the image circumscribes the limits of your visual field rather than signaling to you that what you see is the projection of a recorded im-age. We may borrow Metz's formulation here and speak of the spectator's "identification" with the camera. In projective illusion, the spectator occu-pies the perceptual point of view of the camera upon the events of the film.[31]

The cinematic image reproduces the monocular linear perspective inscribed in the camera lens as well as the accurate rendition of reality afforded by the photograph and combines these with the projected image. As I have already suggested, the size and absence of surface of the projected image promote the loss of medium awareness that is prerequisite to the experience of projective illusion. However, it is the addition of movement to the projected image, perfected by motion picture technology, that is decisive to the experience of projective illusion. As Christian Metz noted in an early essay, the image of movement and movement itself are one; there is no image of recorded movement in the cinema, there is only a moving image.[32] This sense of presence that movement brings to the projected image is complemented by the character of diegetic sound. Although transformations do occur from an original sound to its recording, there is no image of recorded sound in the cinema; sound, too, is directly experienced.

A further way in which the projected moving image enhances the experience of projective illusion lies in the relationship it establishes between on-screen and off-screen space. Because the projected image is a moving one, objects and people enter and leave the frame of the image. Furthermore, through sound we are not only made aware of off-screen events, but those events have the same sense of presence as do on-screen events. Thus, our awareness of off-screen space in the cinema is much greater than that which we have, say, when viewing a projected slide. Off-screen space may simply be understood as an extension of the dramatic space of the image (which is solidly a part of the real world) upon which we may look through the image when it is revealed to us. However, when our awareness of off-screen space is combined with the perception of movement that appears present to us and is supported by a sound track that emphasizes both the presence of the image and the continuum between on- and off-screen space, the optimum preconditions for the experience of projective illusion are established. In projective illusion this on–off-screen continuum is, as it were, peeled away or severed from its moorings in the real world. In the live-action film this continuum is coextensive with the real world, but detached from it by the fact that it is perceived no longer as a reproduction of that world but as an original world of its own, or our, making.[33]

The photographic nature of the cinematic image enters into our experience of projective illusion in the cinema in a particular way. Certainly, the animated film affords the experience of projective illusion, especially when it models itself on the narrative and stylistic conventions of the classical Hollywood fiction film. Yet the fact that a live-action projective illusion is coextensive with the real world lends live-action projective illusion a quality of realization that the animated film lacks. This quality of realization is fostered by the way in which projective illusion in the cinema supervenes upon reproductive illusion. I have emphasized the fact that we are not customarily deceived by a reproductive illusion as it occurs in the fiction film into believing that what we see is real. However, we are commonly deceived by special effects in the cinema into perceiving what appears to be an object array that is not actually there, and, as I have already noted, digital processing now allows for the manufacture of photographs whose contents bear no relationship to actual profilmic events. In this way the capacity of the cinema for reproductive illusion in the form of special effects greatly increases the scope of projective illusion, allowing for the experience of fully realized fictional worlds that extend far beyond the boundaries of our own. This capacity of the cinema to foster the experience of projective illusion through special effects is exploited through the genres of science fiction, horror, and fantasy.

My arguments about projective illusion in the cinema coincide at certain points with Stanley Cavell's conception of film. Cavell emphasizes what I have called the transparency of the photographic image, which is enhanced by the absence of surface that characterizes the projected image. However, he follows Bazin in claiming that the significance of the role of the transparency of the cinematic image lies not in its contribution to our experience of illusion, but in affording a more direct experience of reality. The basis of his claim seems to lie in a rejection of the idea that the photographic image is a recording of what it depicts. He points out correctly that there is a difference between a recording of sound and the manufacture of a photographic image. In a sound recording, one discrete event (the recorded sound) replicates another (the actual sound); but what does a photograph record? One is inclined to say "a sight," but one cannot record the sight of an object in the same sense. There is no original with which to compare the recording. The photograph cannot be said to *record* a sight of the world; rather, it automatically *manufactures* a sight of the world. Cavell concludes that what we see in the cinema as medium-aware spectators (although he does not use this term) is not a profilmic event shot and framed in a particular way, but "a succession of automatic world projections."[34] Cinema is, as the title of Cavell's book implies, "the world viewed."

I concur with Cavell's emphasis on the transparency of the photographic image and the absence of a surface that is internal to the projected moving image. However, I have argued that the importance of these features is not that they somehow bring us to an encounter with reality, but that they uniquely afford the experience of projective illusion. My understanding of projective illusion in the cinema rests on the distinction I have drawn between viewing the cinema as a fully realized world and viewing it as medium-aware spectator, where medium awareness entails that we see the film as successive shots of various profilmic events. Cavell seems to reject this conception of medium awareness on the grounds that a film is not a recording, but he gives metaphysical weight to the distinction between recording and image making that overlooks the central attribute they share: The standard photograph, like the recording, affords us transparent access to an object in *this* world. When we see a film as "a succession of automatic world projections," however, we do not see a series of profilmic events enframed by a camera and edited together; we perceive a fully realized world of experience that we seem to witness directly. This is not the experience of a medium-aware spectator but of a spectator who has suspended medium awareness and experiences the film as a projective illusion in the manner I have characterized.

I referred earlier to Roland Barthes's observation about the necessary pastness of the photographic image, an argument that has provided the basis for a contention that cinematic illusionism consists in the presence of something that is past. For example, John Ellis writes that

the cinematic illusion is a very particular one: it is the illusion of something that has passed, which probably no longer exists. The cinema image is marked by a particular half-magic feat in that it makes present something that is absent. The moment shown on the screen is passed and gone when it is called back into being as an illusion.[35]

However, this contention seems to me mistaken on the grounds that the medium-aware spectator of a film is no different from the medium-aware spectator of a photograph. Just as with a photograph, we only infer that a film is old when it looks dated or aged. Usually when we look at contemporary films, and often when we look at old films too, the age of what we see does not enter into our experience. Since medium awareness does not entail that we see the image as something that is past, the experience of projective illusion is not based on a denial of the pastness of the image; rather, it is based upon a denial of the fact that the image is an *image* of something at all. In projective illusion the spatial absence of the scene depicted in the image is denied in favor of the illusion of its spatial presence. However, since spatial absence is a necessary attribute of temporal pastness (though *not* vice versa), awareness of the datedness of a film is one way that our attention may be drawn to the photographic basis of the medium and may be sufficient to break the hold of projective illusion. This is one reason why some spectators have a low tolerance for black and white or silent films.

The minimal threshold of projective illusion in any pictorial medium is whether or not the picture provides a legible representation. In the history of film, this threshold was relentlessly interrogated by the "ontological" avant-garde of the sixties and seventies, whose concern was to explore the material and spatiotemporal properties of the medium. Peter Kubelka's flicker film *Arnulf Rainer* (1958–60) consists entirely of light and dark frames in succession. Paul Sharits explores the same idea using colored filters in his film *N:O:T:H:I:N:G* (1968), though he adds a narrative interest to the film by periodically including a number of graphic images and sound effects that can be loosely related to one another. An image with a potential representational content can be rendered illegible through a number of means: cinematographic (extreme camera movement); photographic (multiple exposure or overexposure of the image, use of the negative image, manipulation of the camera lens, lensless or cameraless photography); nonphotographic (manual manipulation of the lens and manual or chemical manipulation of the film strip); or a combination of the above. Michael Snow's film *Back and Forth* (1968–9) demonstrates the moment at which projective illusion is made impossible by extreme camera movement and the noise of the camera boom. The film consists of a camera panning back and forth across a children's classroom at progressively increasing speed and noise. The camera finally reaches a velocity in which the image is blurred and ambient sound is blotted out by the noise of its own movement. Peter Kubelka's film *Schwechater* (1957–8) demonstrates the threat posed to legibility, and hence to projective illusion, by photographic means. The images depicted in the film are the head and shoulders of a woman, a hand, and groups of (bourgeois) people sitting at a table drinking. The images are reversed from positive to negative, overexposed, superimposed (e.g., the hand periodically obliterates the woman's figure), combined in very rapid succession, and periodically shot through red filters. At times the image fragments into illegibility and at times it consists of an empty frame. Stan Brakhage's film *Dog Star Man* (1961–4) provides a rich source of manual manipulations of the film strip, such as scratching, dyeing, and growing mold on the film, that together with rapid camera movement, montage, and superimposition impede our capacity to discern of what the images in the film are comprised.

Certain films challenge our capacity to experience projective illusion because they offer images that require us to see them differently from the way we customarily look at films as medium-aware spectators. I suggested earlier that the characteristic way we perceive photographs is by looking through the photograph at the object, whereas the characteristic way in which we perceive paintings is to see the object in the painting. We expect photographs, unlike paintings, to be transparent in the manner that is captured by the term "looking through," and this expectation carries over into our experience of cinema. However, in certain projected images – for example, many of the images in *Schwechater* and *Dog Star Man* – when we do recognize what is depicted in them, we see them in the manner in which we look at paintings. The images produced in these films often appear as a configuration of lines and light on a surface, in the same way that we see the object in the surface of the photograph when looking through is precluded. Because these films defy our customary expectations about looking at photographs (and the cinema), they encourage medium awareness and discourage the experience of projective illusion. Brakhage's *Mothlight* (1963) takes the challenge to our expectations one stage further by abandoning photography entirely in the production of the cinematic image. The original of the film was literally made of moth wings, leaves, and flowers taped onto a strip of clear film with transparent editing tape.

As I have already suggested, following Metz, the distinctive cue or threshold for the experience of projective illusion in the cinema is movement. More accurately, as Noël Burch has suggested, the source in the cinema of projective illusion, or what Burch calls the "diegetic effect," lies in the expectation that movement *could* occur rather than in its actual presence.[36] The question of expectation is central here, for if, as I have argued, projective illusion is an experience afforded by any medium of representation, then it is the way in which a cue specific to a given medium or several media alters the spectator's expectation of what she is to see, that makes that cue into a distinctive threshold of projective illusion. In creating a form of experience that affords the possibility of movement, the cinema engenders the expectation of movement. If that expectation is disappointed, then the spectator will be less disposed to experience the film as a projective illusion. When her expectations of what the medium should afford are let down, the spectator becomes medium aware in the sense that undermines the experience of projective illusion. Of course, with the advent of sound a further threshold was introduced: the presence – or rather, the expectation – of profilmically motivated sound. A similar argument applies to color. Indeed, in this respect the cinema dramatizes the historical character of projective illusion in a way that no other medium does. A film may appear dated in a manner that is not dependent on its content but upon its technology. The spectator interested in film primarily for the experience of projective illusion is interested largely in current cinema, which provides, so to speak, the latest model. A silent or black and white film seems old-fashioned in the manner that an old car appears out of date.

Burch has drawn attention to the way in which the threshold of movement is systematically explored in the work of Michael Snow. Either camera movement or profilmic movement, together with a legible image content, are sufficient to produce the diegetic effect characteristic of the cinema. In his film *La Region Centrale* (1970–1), Snow's camera was on a special mechanical tripod that allowed it to rotate 360 degrees in one continuous movement on top of a peak in the Canadian tundra. The camera traces a series of figures across the landscape and sky – arcs, zigzags, 360-degree rotations, and figures of eight – at varying distances and speeds. The movement of the camera in the film is accompanied by electronic bleeps that mark alterations and adjustments in its trajectory. Burch writes:

[B]esides establishing what may be one minimal threshold of diegetic production, the film indicated, by the very strength of its diegetic effect in the absence of any animate beings or of any natural sound, that the production of that effect depends neither on direct sound (an apparently "natural" sound produced "by the image") nor even on profilmic movement – the landscape is completely static – but can be generated by the camera alone and a "nonfigurative sound," a simple digital translation of the camera's movements.[37]

One particular repeated figure illustrates the relationship between camera movement, legible content, and the diegetic effect. The camera makes a 360-degree vertical rotation over an empty gray sky and the ground beneath. The camera movement across the empty gray sky is not legible; it thus appears as a blank, depthless image without diegetic effect. The moment the camera movement hits the horizon line and the image becomes legible, the camera's trajectory becomes visible and the diegetic effect is restored. However, as the movement gets closer to the camera tripod, the image goes out of focus. While the camera movement remains discernible, the content of the image is no longer legible, and the diegetic effect is once again lost.

Snow's film *Wavelength* (1966–7) is best known for its apparently continuous forty-five-minute zoom across the space of a Manhattan loft; but in this context what is interesting is the way the film secures the spectator's imaginary involvement in the interior space it depicts by creating an expectation that something will happen there. This expectation, raised simply by the camera being trained on the loft space, is augmented by the fact that through the loft windows we see and hear, in what appears to be sync sound, cars and trucks passing on the street outside. After some time, events are staged in the loft space: movement of furniture, the death of a man, a telephone call. Of course, the medium-aware spectator may view what takes place in the film as a meditation upon the relationship between actuality and staged event. However, it is equally possible that, "identifying" with the point of view of the camera, the spectator may view the film as a fully realized fictional universe where something is waiting to happen.

Projective Illusion and Cinematic Narration

I have described those characteristics of the image that encourage loss of awareness of the cinematic image as a photographic reproduction of a profilmic event in favor of a perception of the image as a fully realized world through "identification" with the perceptual point of view of the camera. Narrative encourages the spectator to sustain the experience of projective illusion over a longer period of time. In a fiction film the significance of any given image lies in relationship to events that have already been portrayed and those that are about to occur in the film. Any given image embodies or is embedded within a narrative – a series of events taking place in a causal chain – that motivates both the contents of the image and its duration. The way in which narrative motivates the content and duration of the image offers an incentive for the spectator to sustain the experience of projective illusion. It also sets up for the viewer further expectations that, if unmet, will break the hold of illusion.

Narrative brings a dimension of temporal illusion to our experience of projective illusion because it encourages us to experience projective illusion over time. Since, in projective illusion, what we perceive appears spatially present to us, it also appears temporally present. If the experience of projective illusion is sustained, the film appears to unfold before our eyes as we watch, as if it were live, created in the moment of projection. The temporal illusion that this sense of temporal presence creates is not, as I have argued, the temporal presence of something that is past; it is the illusion that time is not passing or the illusion of a perpetual present. One of the customary pleasures of narrative film is, in the words of Ben Singer, "to construct illusory time, to annihilate time, to make hours go by like minutes (a capacity confirmed and lauded by the bygone Mutual Film Co.'s motto 'Mutuals make time fly')."[38] When the experience of projective illusion is sustained we lose our awareness of time. The everyday experience of shock or surprise at emerging from a matinee performance into darkness outside attests to this experience.

Spectators of the commercial fiction film have become accustomed to narrative motivating the content and duration of the image in a certain way: the manner of storytelling exemplified by classical Hollywood cinema. Historically, classical Hollywood narration has provided the benchmark of filmmaking practice against which other traditions of filmmaking have defined themselves. Classical Hollywood narration can be defined as a form of narration that rigidly subordinates the spatial and temporal parameters of a shot to the causal logic of a story, ensuring a clear and continuous line of narrative action.[39] The space of the shot and its duration is "used up" by narratively significant elements, and the transition between shots is disguised in such a way that tends to preserve medium *un*awareness and encourage an experience of the image–sound sequence as if it were a continuous present. In this way the rationale of classical Hollywood narration is precisely to maximize the possibilities of filmed drama as projective illusion, although classical narration does not ensure that a spectator will experience a film as projective illusion or that the experience of projective illusion will be sustained over time. Furthermore, Hollywood cinema allows for moments of medium awareness in which the spectator's knowledge that it is only a film comes to inform the activity of seeing; but as Stephen Heath suggested and David Bordwell has elaborated, classical Hollywood cinema seeks to conventionalize those moments of medium awareness, to contain them within predictable boundaries.[40]

The rationale of maximizing the spectator's experience of projective illusion underlies Hollywood's attachment to genre. Genres mitigate the difficulty of understanding a given text by providing a framework of expectations within which that text can be understood. Genres specify in advance the content of the narrative. Any given genre film, such as the western or horror film, draws on themes and images from other texts (the generic intertext) that blur the boundaries of the individual text. Because the generic intertext already forms a part of the spectator's stock of knowledge, the individual genre film simply taps into a reservoir of themes and images already possessed by the spectator. Genre conventions also specify the form of the narrative, providing conventions for permissible deviations from classical norms – for example, "decorative" camera movements in the musical film, direct address to the audience in film comedy. Genre conventions thus minimize the effort required by the spectator to understand a film in its singularity and maximize his capacity to enter into the film's narrative world.

The primary means through which the spectator's attention is focused or centered in narrative cinema is through character. As David Bordwell writes,

"In classical filmmaking, the overriding principle is to make every instantiation of technique obedient to the character's transmission of fabula [story] information, with the result that bodies and faces become the focal points of attention."[41] The conventions of classical narration are designed to maximize the extent to which the events of the story are conveyed to the spectator through the actions of characters. Cutting on a character's actions limits a shot to a narratively salient duration, and matching on that action ensures the seamlessness of a cut. Reverse-field cutting through an eyeline match motivates shot transitions through character action, while the 180-degree rule ensures a constant spatial relationship between character and environment and a consistent direction of movement on the screen. Reframing and centering of the frame ensures that the spectator remains focused upon the characters and their actions. Finally, sound is matched to the content of the image and placed at the service of character dialogue. The conventions of narrative cinema allow us to comprehend readily the events of the narrative through a conception of human agency that we bring to the film from everyday life. Thus character plays a central role in facilitating and sustaining our experience of projective illusion in the cinema.

In a manner that complements the effect of genre conventions upon the spectator's perception of narrative film, star persona constitutes "a rough character prototype" for the character within a film.[42] The spectator need not become acquainted with the character from scratch, but views him in terms of a set of familiar traits. Already acquainted with the star's role in the film, the spectator need not see it as a role: Star persona encourages the audience to fuse the role of the character with the real-life body of the actor, conflating the distinction between "nominal" and "physical" portrayal. In our identification with, say, the star persona of Robert de Niro, we may fuse the particular role of Jake La Motta in the film *Raging Bull* (1980) with the range of intertextual associations that accrete around the body of Robert de Niro, the actor, to form Robert de Niro, the star. We may switch from the realistic perception of Robert de Niro the actor, who is playing Jake La Motta, to the projective illusion of Robert de Niro as "Jake La Motta."

Classical cinema readily affords the experience of projective illusion because its conventions are so familiar. To some extent the experience of projective illusion is simply a function of audience familiarity with the conventions of classical narration. For example, the conventions of art cinema, once learned, afford the experience of projective illusion to the same degree as classical cinema; yet, the conventions of art cinema are more difficult to learn than those of classical narration. In this sense, there is a privileged relationship between classical narration and illusionism, for its conventions, although learned, are easily comprehended. All systems of narration afford the experience of illusion if the audience is familiar with the conventions upon which they are based, but classical narration promotes that experience more readily than others. Those narrative films that promote the experience of projective illusion least readily, those that lie on the threshold, are films that purposely subvert our expectations of narrative and character. Even so, subversion of illusion itself has its own conventions that, if learned, neutralize the subversion.

The work of a second wing of the avant-garde of the sixties and seventies was defined by its challenge to the conventions of narrative filmmaking. This second avant-garde was contrasted with the "ontological" avant-garde of that period by Peter Wollen in his influential essay "The Two Avant Gardes." Wollen identifies this second avant-garde with the films of Straub-Huillet and Godard, but the works of Chantal Akerman, although they show the influence of the "ontological" wing of the avant-garde, also lie within this tradition. No narrative film more consistently challenges our customary expectations of narrative cinema than her film *Jeanne Dielman, 23 Quai du Commerce, 1080 Bruxelles* (1975). *Jeanne Dielman* explores, with minimal dialogue, three days in the life of a single mother and part-time prostitute. Generically, the film invokes the domestic melodrama in its depiction of a female heroine who, unable to transform social constraints that are iniquitous to her well-being, experiences those constraints in the form of internal suffering. However, the "expressionistic" conventions of the genre that allow the spectator to identify with the character as performed by a star such as Barbara Stanwyck or Joan Crawford are completely undercut in this film. The film's "star," Delphine Seyrig, is resolutely denied the possibility to perform her suffering; indeed, she shows no emotion at all. The genre of melodrama requires the performance of an inner life to dramatize the depredations of the external world, but the inner life of Jeanne Dielman is thoroughly impoverished. The central character is so completely alienated that she can no longer be said to experience her world at all.

As Ben Singer has pointed out, *Jeanne Dielman* draws attention to the stylistic conventions of storytelling in narrative cinema by "amplifying" them or placing them in quotation marks. Akerman follows Warhol in making the duration of a shot far exceed the amount of time required to convey the narrative information it contains. We are thus made to feel time passing as Jeanne performs her everyday household chores, including sex with paying clients. Akerman's fixed, frontal, low-angle camera eschews the variable framing that helps to articulate character motivation through reverse-field cutting and eyeline matches, and that, more generally, focuses the spectator's attention upon what is narratively salient. Shot transitions are made overt by what Singer calls the trope of standardization: "the film establishes a consistent and conspicuous cue to signal an impending cut."[43] Rather than cutting on action, Akerman waits until the protagonist has completely finished her task, and the camera often lingers on the objects that remain after the protagonist has left the scene. Finally, Akerman draws attention to the elision of narrative time that classical narrative customarily affords. In a film that is based on shots of long duration, the montage of three shots in quick succession depicting a walk that Jeanne takes with her son around the block stands in relief. In another sequence, Akerman draws attention to narrative time by showing an event that requires an ellipsis in one continuous shot: Jeanne and a client enter her bedroom with the camera remaining outside; then the corridor darkens and a few seconds later they leave as if they have just had sex. The challenge that a film like *Jeanne Dielman* poses to our narrative expectations may undermine our capacity to experience projective illusion, but like all films, *Jeanne Dielman,* too, affords such an experience once we are familiar with its conventions.

In this chapter I have attempted to characterize the experience of projective illusion in the cinema, and have explored some of the factors of the cinematic image and cinematic narration that govern the capacity of the spectator to entertain this form of experience. Why, however, do we experience projective illusion when that experience is not dictated to us by the object we perceive? One answer is that the perception of a represented object as a real one is required for us to have an emotional response to that object. That is, the theory of projective illusion can be offered as a solution to what Noël Carroll dubs the "paradox of fiction."

How is it, Carroll asks, that we can be afraid of the Green Slime in a horror movie? "Emotional response is thought to require belief in the existence of its object; but with fictions we know that the Green Slime does not exist. So our fear in this case seems inconsistent with our knowledge."[44] The theory of projective illusion solves the paradox of fiction by elaborating a sense in which our knowledge that the object does not exist is suspended. Yet Carroll himself argues persuasively that the experience of representation as an illusion is not required for a spectator to respond emotionally to a fiction; an emotional response to an object can be generated simply by entertaining in thought the object that evokes this response. In order to be afraid of the Green Slime we simply have to reflect upon its properties; we are not required to see the Green Slime in the form of a projective illusion. Our capacity to be frightened by the thought of the Green Slime explains how we can respond emotionally to written fiction, where the Green Slime is not visually represented. However, to argue that such a perception of the Green Slime is not required in order to have an emotional response to it does not refute the fact that we may, in addition to entertaining the Green Slime in thought, experience it as a projective illusion. Indeed, I have argued that the idea of entertaining the thought of an object is built into our experience of illusion. When we perceive a projective illusion, the manner in which we perceive it involves entertaining the thought that what we perceive is real.

Still, the question remains, Why have recourse to this further theory of illusion if our emotional response to pictorial and dramatic representations can be adequately explained without it? The answer lies in the explanation of what it is to respond emotionally to something that we entertain in thought. When Carroll describes entertaining the Green Slime in thought, I take it that, for Carroll, the representation of the Green Slime is a nominal one. That is, we experience the Green Slime in our imagination as a portrayal of the Green Slime, rather than as if the Green Slime were real. However, psychoanalytic theory suggests that when our thoughts are governed by our emotions they tend to take on a more primitive form in which the object entertained in thought disguises the fact that it is merely a representation and takes on a form that is fully realized: Thought becomes fantasy. This more primitive form of emotional response is facilitated in general by such activities as play and consuming fictions where a functional, problem-solving use of the mind is in abeyance. Furthermore, pictorial and dramatic representations afford precisely the disguise of representation that is encouraged by our emotions in their primitive form. They afford a fully realized object that conforms exactly to the qualities of the object of our fantasy. Thus, though our emotions do not require that we experience pictorial and dramatic representations in the form of projective illusion, they do encourage us to experience them in that way. It is to this predisposition of the mind to entertain film in the form of projective illusion that I now turn.

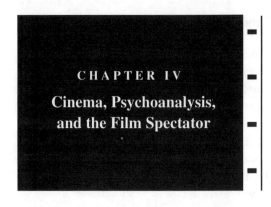

CHAPTER IV

Cinema, Psychoanalysis,
and the Film Spectator

Contemporary psychoanalytic film theory is grounded in two related theses: the thesis of primary cinematic identification and the thesis of mirror misrecognition. As we saw in Chapter 1, both these theses received their initial articulation in Baudry's essay "Ideological Effects of the Basic Cinematographic Apparatus." They were later adopted, more circumspectly, by Metz, in his essay "The Imaginary Signifier."[1] The thesis of primary cinematic identification states that the spectator's "identification" with character and, more generally, with what is seen in a film, presupposes the spectator's "identification" with the camera and hence with the gaze of a transcendental subject. In Metz's elaboration of the thesis of primary cinematic identification the gaze of this transcendental subject is characterized as voyeuristic. The thesis of mirror misrecognition states that the apparent mastery the spectator exercises over the image in the cinema is an illusion. Like Lacan's young child before the mirror, the cinema spectator invests in the illusory reality of the image through primary cinematic identification in order to prevent his own disintegration as a subject.

I have suggested that the theses of primary cinematic identification and mirror misrecognition should be abandoned on the grounds that the spectator's response to the image is not passively determined in the manner required by the theory. In Chapter 3 I offered a description of the spectator's experience of illusion in the cinema that takes account of the spectator's role in entertaining this experience. In this chapter I shall develop this argument by offering a conception of film spectatorship that is based upon a refinement of the analogies between film and dream and film and daydream. These analogies were also pursued by Metz in "The Fiction Film and Its Spectator: A Metapsychological Study," and Baudry pursued the film–dream analogy in his second essay on the apparatus, "The Apparatus: Metapsychological Approaches to the Impression of Reality in the Cinema."[2] However, neither of these essays had the influence of their authors' earlier works. Following the lead of these latter essays, I argue that the cinema does promote a regressive experience on the part of the spectator analogous to the experience of dream or fantasy. The cinema, like dream and fantasy, recalls the child's experience of "primary identification" – the young child's first encounter with the other when the boundaries between the me and not-me are not yet firmly established. However, unlike the thesis of primary cinematic identification, the psychoanalytic conception of spectatorship I propose here places identification with character on an equal footing with "identification" with the point of view of the camera, and gives equal importance to a sense of merger with the image and loss of self, as well as to a sense of control and mastery over the image. Furthermore, unlike the thesis of mirror misrecognition, the understanding of spectatorship that I propose here also takes proper account of the place of consciousness in the spectator's experience of a film. I do not propose psychoanalytic theory as an explanation of every aspect of spectatorship in the cinema; rather, I seek to isolate exactly which aspects of watching films psychoanalysis can appropriately explain.

Either separately or together, the theses of primary cinematic identification and mirror misrecognition lay the foundation for feminist arguments that the psychical mechanisms invoked by the cinema are gender bound. While acknowledging that apparatus theory is patriarchal in its formulation of spectatorship, feminist film theorists have also argued that apparatus theory illuminates the sense in which the "subject position" of the spectator in the cinema is a male one. The cinema is thus said to reinforce a gender hierarchy in which female pleasure is defined in relationship to male pleasure. Within feminist film theory, these arguments have been challenged on the grounds that they establish the gender-bound nature of the psychical mechanisms invoked by the cinema at the cost of rendering immutable the gender hierarchy they appear to inscribe. A number of feminist film theorists have suggested that an understanding of spectatorship in terms of fantasy could provide a way out of the apparent gender hierarchy inscribed in theories of the cinematic apparatus.[3] In this chapter I conceive of the spectator's experience of projective illusion in the cinema as a form of fantasy predicated upon a gender-neutral suspension of disbelief or disavowal whose psychoanalytic origins lie in separation from the mother. I argue that gender bias is produced not by the structure of the look in the cinema, but in the way that Hollywood cinema produces normative versions of subjectivity and gender identity through the stories that it tells (usually heterosexual, white, and middle class). The forms of identification that depend upon looking – voyeurism and fetishism – may be mobilized in the cinema to reinforce these normative versions of subjectivity, but they may be equally engaged in by a spectator predisposed to experience the portrayal of subjectivity in cinema in a manner that runs counter to its normative, manifest content. Psychoanalysis can thus illuminate both the normative fantasies that are produced in the cinema and an aspect of how and why it is that different spectators can see the same film differently.

Dream, Fantasy, and Projective Illusion

In Chapter 3 I offered an explanation of the capacity of the cinema to be experienced as a form of illusion in terms of properties of the cinematic apparatus itself. However, this characterization of the cinema as an object that engenders the experience of illusion only establishes one part of my argument; for if the sensory deception of projective illusion in the cinema is something that is not necessarily experienced by the spectator, an enumeration of the features of the object, however subtle, is not sufficient to explain that deception. What is also required is an explanation of our predisposition to entertain the image as a projective illusion or to entertain in thought that the object is real. There must be a propensity in the mind itself to seek out or even create the form of experience afforded in the cinema, since that experience is not dictated to us by the medium. I shall argue that a psychoanalytic view of the mind can illuminate our predisposition to entertain projective illusion and hence the quality and character of our involvement in the cinema that fosters this experience. Of course, this argument is not a new one; as we have seen, it is put forward in the writings of Baudry and Metz. However, the argument requires reassessment and restatement in order to redeem a psychoanalytic approach to the cinema from some of the ambiguity and equivocation that beset the arguments of contemporary film theory, and to answer the criticism that psychoanalytic theory ignores the fact that cinemagoing is a conscious and rational activity.[4]

The conception of spectatorship I propose in this chapter is based upon a clarification of the analogies between film and dream, and film and daydream. Dreams and daydreams or fantasy, together with visual imagination, form a group of iconic mental states that I shall term "iconic imagination." Psychoanalysis offers an explanation of the psychic function that iconic imagination plays, by virtue of its iconicity, in our mental life.[5] This psychic function is wish fulfillment. Iconic imagination is possessed of psychic force; it has the capacity to evoke, to varying degrees, the effect of an event through which we have actually lived, even though the event is merely depicted or represented to us in our imagination. However, iconic imagination need not have this psychic force: It may be nominal in character; that is, we may experience the events we imagine as portrayals rather than as if they were real. Thus, psychoanalysis is concerned with understanding the conditions under which iconic imagination realizes its psychic force and thereby expresses the fulfillment of a wish. How is this relationship between the psychic force of iconic imagination and its psychic function as wish fulfillment forged in mental life?[6]

Clearly, we may fulfill our wishes without recruiting iconic imagination in order to do so. In rational action, when we wish something to be the case, we form a disposition to act and realize our wish. Autonomous beliefs we hold about the world will determine whether we can satisfy the wish and what specific actions will lead to its satisfaction. Beliefs about the world may also contribute to the formulation of further or related wishes. Freud called this kind of adjustment and readjustment of desires to autonomous beliefs about the world "reality testing." In this context, iconic imagination may be recruited in order to help us realize our wish. For example, we may use iconic imagination in order to test out a real-world situation, such as different ways of getting to a conference of film scholars, and use the results of our mental experiment in deciding which mode of transport to use. When iconic imagination enters into rational deliberation in this way, the imagined satisfaction of the wish takes place against the background of other competing desires and our beliefs about how they can be fulfilled. Iconic imagination, in this context, will not characteristically exhibit the psychic force that it may possess in other circumstances.

Contrast this case with the case of a wish-fulfilling fantasy, such as an erotic daydream. Here, I entertain the satisfaction of a wish for its own sake. The wish expresses itself in the form of iconic imagination precisely because iconic imagination possesses the requisite property of lifelikeness. Beliefs enter into such a wish-fulfilling fantasy, but they are no longer independent of the wish that is to be satisfied. Beliefs inform the fantasy only insofar as they conform to the wish; those that are contrary to the wish are excluded. Wish-fulfilling fantasy contrasts with a problem-solving use of the imagination in the effect it has upon us, since it will characteristically leave the person who entertains the fantasy in a state of heightened pleasure. What is striking about the role of fantasy in mental life, even in this simple case, is that it serves at once to feed upon and nurture the desires that it appears to satisfy. The particular desires that fantasy tends to nurture are desires that would otherwise fail to find expression or realization in reality. Insofar as these desires are unrealizable, they are unsatisfiable. Fantasy affords the possibility for unsatisfiable desires to appear to be realized and hence to evoke the pleasure that would attach to their satisfaction. However, the pleasure evoked by the appearance of desires' satisfaction in fantasy carries with it a sense of incompletion or lack of fulfillment since fantasy cannot actually satisfy those desires. By sustaining the possibility of desires' fulfillment, yet always falling short, fantasy actually promotes the desires it appears to satisfy, and thus promoted, these desires cause fantasy to repeat itself and reinforce the hold of fantasy on psychic life. In this sense, as Elizabeth Cowie puts it, following Laplanche and Pontalis, fantasy is "the *mise-en-scène* of desire, the putting into a scene, a staging, of desire."[7]

In this description of wish-fulfilling fantasy, desire and iconic imagination are inextricably interwoven: Through imagining her desires satisfied, a person can achieve a state of pleasure that simulates to some degree her state of satisfaction were her desires actually to be satisfied. According to Freud, dreams also secure the apparent satisfaction of unrealizable desires; the way in which they do so further illuminates the function of wish-fulfilling fantasy. Consider a transparent wish-fulfillment dream, such as an erotic dream. Because I am asleep my imagination is free to conjure up scenes with an intensity and a completeness that waking life precludes, and the dream may arouse in me the kind of pleasure that would accompany my actual experience of the events that it depicts. The dream of satisfaction thus simulates the satisfaction of desire to a degree that the daydream cannot. When we dream, what we desire becomes what we believe: We believe that what we want to happen actually happens. We imaginatively experience as an actual occurrence the events of which the dream is merely a representation. Desire recruits the full psychic force of iconic imagination and simulates its own satisfaction.

Freud suggested that in this way dreams manifest, or at least provide the occasion for, a primitive form of mental functioning that he labeled the "primary process," and which his patient, the Rat Man, felicitously called the "omnipotence of thought." When thoughts are omnipotent, desires operate under the aegis of what Freud called the wish. Richard Wollheim describes the wish in this way: "I wish for something rather than merely desire it, when I desire it: and because I desire it I tend to imagine (in the appropriate mode) my desire satisfied: and when I imagine my desire satisfied, it is for me as if that desire were satisfied."[8] When desire regresses to the form of the wish, desire misrepresents itself as being satisfied by the mimicking of its satisfaction. Furthermore, the inevitable shortfall in the satisfaction of our desire seems counterbalanced by the fact that the satisfaction, when mimicked, can be reproduced endlessly. When the mind operates under the aegis of the wish, the difference between conscious desires that could achieve realization and unconscious desires that are idle or impossible to fulfill no longer obtains.

How, then, can the relationship between desire and iconic imagination, as it is illuminated by psychoanalytic theory, explain the spectator's experience of projective illusion? When we experience a film as a projective illusion, the fictional or imaginary character of the events represented to us in the film are obscured in a manner that has the psychic force of dream. In the cinema we are able to experience events depicted in a film with some of the psychological closeness and somatic intensity of our own dreams; it is this that affords us pleasure over and above the content of an individual film that we happen to see. "Cinema," as Baudry writes, "mime[s] a form of archaic satisfaction experienced by the subject by reproducing the scene of it."[9] The idea that we experience motion pictures with the psychic force of dream explains the particular quality of moviegoing: the power that movies can exercise over the imagination, to be sure, but also the evanescent quality of the experience of projective illusion and hence the desire to repeat it. The experience of projective illusion in the cinema is undoubtedly facilitated, as Baudry suggests, by certain contingent features of the theater-viewing situation that recall those of sleep – darkness, relative immobility, and so on – but these features do not cause the experience of projective illusion, and they are not necessary to the experience.

The analogy of film and dream may immediately be challenged on the grounds that in the cinema we are awake, whereas the psychic force of dreams, as I have described it, depends on the fact that we are asleep. Since we dream the experience of satisfying our wishes, the simulation of satisfaction can be completely realized. However, if we are awake, as when we experience a daydream, the psychic force of iconic imagination is attenuated, and while the satisfaction is consciously experienced, it is not fully simulated. Why then claim that the cinema has the psychic force of dream, rather than the attenuated psychic force of conscious fantasy or daydream? To my mind, the analogy is appropriate because the lifelikeness of projective illusion is as complete as the lifelikeness of dream. This lifelikeness is not that of real life. It is, as Baudry suggests, a more than real world. It is a fully realized yet fictional universe that we experience with the quality of affect that characterizes our experience of dream. The fact that we are awake must be taken into account when considering the analogy between dream and projective illusion, but it does not undermine the analogy. We experience projective illusion with the psychic force of dream, but being awake, we do not misrepresent our desires as actually satisfied and believe that what we see is real.

We experience projective illusion in a manner that is akin to the psychic force of dream. However, because we are awake, projective illusion fulfills the psychic function of wish fulfillment in a manner akin to that of the day-dream or fantasy. As we have seen, in fantasy, unlike in dream, the satisfaction of our desire, although consciously experienced, is less intensely felt and requires a greater cooperation of the ego in order to be sustained. Fantasy thus makes manifest the way in which the psychic force of iconic imagination is dependent on the character of what it represents to us. The repertoire of events that we visualize in our fantasies must be such that we are actually afforded some measure of satisfaction if that repertoire is to act as wish fulfillment. Since cinemagoing is a part of waking life, whether or not the occasion for the satisfaction of desire with the psychic force of dream is actually realized depends on the extent to which what is depicted and narrated in the film conforms to those desires. Like fantasy, the cinema may provide a forum for the substitute gratification of desires in such a way that it tends to leave us in a state of pleasure that intimates a condition in which our desires are actually satisfied. However, in order to fulfill this psychic function, the cinema must provide the spectator with depictions and stories whose content corresponds to the spectator's own fantasies. In this respect, the cinema is not unlike other media, such as popular fiction, that seek to address the spectator's fantasies through the kinds of stories they tell. However, in the cinema, the psychic function of fantasy may be conveyed with something like the psychic force of dream. The spectator may experience the substitute gratification of her desires in the form of projective illusion.

The spectator's requirement that the fantasy conform to her wishes in order to be experienced with the psychic force of projective illusion is not simply a question of content, but it is also a question of form. Noël Carroll has discussed the capacity of variable framing to focalize or direct the spectator's attention to the salient features of a narrative in a way that enhances the viewer's sense of absorption in the narrative world.[10] Carroll argues that his analysis of variable framing offers an alternative to a psychoanalytic understanding of the power of movies. However, I would argue that it complements a psychoanalytic understanding of that power, for it clarifies one of the ways that movies sustain the experience of projective illusion by virtue of their form: What characterizes the experience of fantasy and dreams is that the scenes they depict seem absolutely pertinent to the person who is experiencing them, even if their meaning is opaque. The size of the movie image further contributes to this sense of psychological relevance. Movies conform to the spectator's fantasy not simply by offering the spectator narratives that conform in content to her fantasy, but by offering these narratives in a way that gives the spectator an impression that what is being presented to her is of maximum psychological significance.

Identification, Voyeurism, and Projective Illusion

The relationship between the psychic force of mental states and their psychic function is secured through their characteristic psychic form or phenomenology. There are two types of visualization. Often my dreams or daydreams have a protagonist whose thoughts, feelings, and perceptual point of view of events I share. Usually, though not always, the protagonist of the dream will be myself, the dreamer. Wollheim describes this form as "centered iconic imagination."[11] When I centrally imagine a dream or fantasy, I experience it from the standpoint of someone internal to the scene; that is, the mental states I experience are embodied in a person. This contrasts with "acentered iconic imagination." When I acentrally imagine a dream or fantasy, I may emotionally react or respond to events that I visualize, but I do not adopt the emotional response and point of view of a person within the scene. One is inclined to say that I still have a point of view upon the events that I visualize but that my point of view is disembodied.[12] However, as we saw in Chapter 2, the idea of a disembodied point of view can mislead one into conceiving a point of view that is disembodied yet maintains a consistent location in space. However, the disembodied point of view that characterizes acentrally imagining a dream does not have a consistent location in space; it is not, in the sense of a physical vantage point, a *point* of view at all.

In the distinction between centered and acentered imagination, there is a correlation between whether or not the mental state I inhabit is the embodied mental state of a protagonist or a mental state that is internal to the scene, and whether or not the point of view that I occupy is the perceptual point of view of the protagonist. The reason for this correlation may be expressed in the following way. When we centrally imagine our dreams and fantasies from our own point of view, as we customarily do, we inhabit a point of view through inhabiting a given mental state to which a point of view is also attached. After all, it is the attachment of a point of view to a mental state that defines the difference between centrally and acentrally imagining an event. Centrally imagining an event from someone else's point of view is modeled in the same way as centrally imagining an event from my own; for what identifies or marks the fact that I am occupying someone else's mental state is the fact that I am occupying the point of view I imagine that person to have.

The distinction between central and acentral imagining breaks down when we attempt to apply it to our experience of projective illusion in the cinema, because of the differences between the experience of the dreamer who visualizes the dream and the cinema spectator who perceives a film. In the cinema, the correlation between the mental state I inhabit and the perceptual point of view I occupy no longer obtains. Unlike the case of iconic imagination, point of view is not required in order to mark a mental state as someone else's; this is established by the simple fact that I am watching a character in a film. I may identify with a character by adopting his psychological point of view upon events as my own without thereby adopting his perceptual point of view. Conversely, I may adopt the perceptual point of view of a character as my own, through the point-of-view shot, without identifying at all with the beliefs and feelings of the character to whom the point of view of the shot belongs. Furthermore, the fact that I experience projective illusion in the cinema in a form that is clearly demarcated from my body and beyond my physical control precludes the possibility of experiencing film in the manner of centrally imagining a dream or fantasy with myself as protagonist. The illusion of inhabiting an imaginary world as a protagonist within it defines the experience not of cinema but of virtual reality, afforded by interactive computer programs in a context where the physical distance between spectator and screen is eliminated.

If we are to distinguish forms of projective illusion in the cinema, the distinction must be based upon an independent consideration of the question of the emotional response of the spectator to a film in relation to the mental state of a character, and the question of whether or not the spectator occupies a point of view upon the scene. I shall address first the emotional response of the spectator. Wollheim himself clarifies the difference between centered and acentered imagination by analogy with the emotional response of a theater audience to the protagonist of a play. He suggests that centered imagination is analogous to "empathic identification" with a character in a play, in which an audience's response to that character is unconstrained by judgment: "The empathic audience is that audience whose reaction to the hero is that it feels what he feels. Thus: if he feels terror, it feels terror: if he feels brave, it feels brave." In contrast, acentral imagination is analogous to "sympathetic identification." The audience who sympathizes with a character does not simply adopt the feelings of a character as its own, for its emotional response is mediated by its judgment – favorable or unfavorable – as to a character's worth: "If the judgement is favorable, then if the hero feels terror, it will feel pity: if the hero feels brave, it will feel admiration. But, if the judgement is unfavorable, then, if the hero feels terror, it will feel delight: if the hero feels brave, it will feel terror."[13] In his later version of this argument, Wollheim suggests that acentered imagination may be construed upon the model of a sympathetic or detached spectator. Detachment entails no emotional involvement whatsoever, though it is not incompatible with favoring one character over another.[14]

Wollheim's use of the distinction between the empathic and sympathetic audience remains wedded to his primary distinction between centered and acentered imagination, which is drawn according to whether or not we inhabit a point of view within the scene. However, in the experience of projective illusion, where we can identify empathically with a character's feelings without occupying her perceptual point of view, the distinction between empathic and sympathetic identification no longer assumes the place it has in Wollheim's account. With respect to our emotional response to a character during the experience of projective illusion, the crucial distinction rests between identification with the character (whether empathic or sympathetic) and detachment. The detached spectator responds emotionally to what he experiences, but his emotional response is an autonomous one; it is not predicated upon identification with the feelings of the character. The form of projective illusion experienced through identification with character I shall call "character-centered projective illusion"; the form detached from an identification with character I shall call "spectator-centered projective illusion."

Our emotional response to film is fostered by the experience of projective illusion, but a theory of projective illusion is not usually required to explain that response. In particular, the structure of character identification can be explained outside the framework of projective illusion.[15] The distinction between sympathy and empathy rests on the degree to which we suspend judgment *about* a character, but the experience of projective illusion is defined by our suspension of judgment *that* the character is a character. In the case of empathic identification, at least, it is hard to imagine that a spectator who failed to discriminate between a character's feelings and her own would nevertheless continue to see the character as a character. It is likely, instead, that she would fuse the traits of the character with those of the star and perceive the character as a person fully embodied by the actor in the world of projective illusion. Character identification runs on a continuum from detachment to sympathy to empathy that is defined by the role that reason plays relative to the emotions. We may reasonably speculate that the more a spectator's judgment is eclipsed in her response to character, the more likely she is to slip through the "seeing-as" corridor into the world of illusion.

Since character-centered projective illusion is defined by emotional identification with character, it does not depend on whether or not we occupy the perceptual point of view of a character. Indeed, we may experience projective illusion from a character's psychological point of view even if the character is absent from or physically marginal within a shot or sequence. Character-centered perception is simply one form that character-centered projective illusion may take. It is a privileged form in the films of Alfred Hitchcock. In *Rear Window* (1954), for example, the spectator often occupies the point of view of James Stewart as L. B. Jeffries; but Hitchcock's cinema is uncharacteristic in precisely this rigorous emphasis on perceptual point of view. As film historians have taught us, classical Hollywood cinema does not consistently narrate character actions through perceptual point of view.[16] On the other hand, spectator-centered projective illusion may occur in shots or sequences where I experience projective illusion and characters are not involved, as well as those in which I do not identify with any of the characters and yet experience the film as a projective illusion. Since I may occupy the perceptual point of view of a character without identifying with his feelings – as in, say, those "slasher" films in which I occupy the perceptual point of view of an anonymous stalker – projective illusion may remain spectator-centered even though the spectator occupies the perceptual point of view of a character.[17]

In general in a fiction film there are at least two contexts in which a spectator's emotional response may be autonomous from an identification with character; both of these will therefore privilege a spectator-centered experience of projective illusion over a character-centered experience. The first context is where film emphasizes the physical attributes of the human body at the expense of personality in such a way that the spectator fails to be offered a "character" that elicits emotional response. Due to the capacity of the cinema to present the human body to the spectator in a manner that is fully realized, from its inception the cinema has offered the spectator the spectacle of the human body and, in particular, isolated body parts, rather than the portrayal of a person (a body with a mind); it has offered us the spectacle of human behavior rather than the portrayal of motivated action. This emphasis is characteristic of certain genres, such as silent comedy and the musical, as well as certain films of the avant-garde, such as those of Andy Warhol and the films of Chantal Akerman.

Where spectator-centered projective illusion is privileged in this way over character-centered projective illusion it may give rise to voyeurism. Scenes that involve the depiction of sexuality and violence in the cinema not only short-circuit identification with character and encourage a spectator-centered emotional response, but also foster an emotional response predicated upon an emotional intensification of the act of seeing itself. In a voyeuristic response to an image, the spectator's emotional response to the scene arises out of the experience of projective illusion. Ordinarily, as I have suggested, the spectator's emotional response to a scene is explicable without assuming that projective illusion is experienced, although projective illusion may accompany the emotional response. Voyeurism, however, is a special case of projective illusion in which the spectator's emotional response to the scene is predicated upon her act of imaginarily seeing the events portrayed in the film; it thus necessarily takes the form of spectator-centered projective illusion. The converse does not hold: Spectator-centered projective illusion does not entail a voyeuristic response on the part of the spectator, for voyeurism requires a particular staging of the human body that acts as a lure for the eye.

The second context in which spectator-centered projective illusion may be privileged is where the filmic elements of the shot – camera movement, framing, and distance – are not anthropocentrically organized. Typically in classical Hollywood cinema, camera movement, framing, and shot distance afford us a point of view upon the scene that corresponds to the eyeline of an adult human witness to that scene. On the other hand, auteur cinema, for example, characteristically departs from this norm, as in the extended camera movements of Max Ophuls or Stanley Kubrick, or the unusual camera angles of Alfred Hitchcock and Joseph Losey. In commercial cinema, especially the "exploitation film," overt camera angles or movement often accompany the display of scenes of sex and violence in a way that encourages voyeurism by fostering the spectator's detachment from an identification with character.

A film that explores the threshold between spectator- and character-centered projective illusion, and the role of voyeurism in sustaining that division, is Chantal Akerman's *Jeanne Dielman,* which I discussed in the previous chapter. *Jeanne Dielman* is a film that contains characters and tells a story about them, but that, by virtue of the relationship between its form and content, systematically privileges spectator-centered projective illusion over the character-centered variety. *Jeanne Dielman* maximizes the effectivity of spectator-centered projective illusion by insistently combining a representation of character in which interiority is absent, with the distant detached stare of an unmoving camera. For those audience members who remain with the film after it has defied their initial expectations about character, the fixed stare of the camera affords an emotional response that is singularly intense, yet not dependent upon identification with a character whose inner life is so absent. It is true that as the narrative of *Jeanne Dielman* progresses, the protagonist's psychology begins to inform more completely the actions that we see, and the rigid structure of the narrative begins to break down while its pace quickens, "using up" more dead space and time. However, this psychology is a thoroughly "abnormal" one. The character's actions do not appear internally motivated, but external to her, compelled by a cause over which she has no control. In this sense her actions remain behavior from which we are detached, although our fascination is increased by the fact that this behavior is no longer routinely predictable.

As I have emphasized, the privileging of spectator-centered emotional response does not entail that the emotional response be a voyeuristic one. This film, however, does strongly evoke the voyeuristic gaze by staging the classical representation of a woman alone in a domestic interior whose life we catch seemingly unawares, through a frame whose angle, distance, and stasis evokes the keyhole.[18] The signal scene in the film in this respect is where Jeanne bathes naked. She is partially concealed from our gaze by the insistent low angle and long-shot of the camera that fills the lower part of the frame with the floor and side of the bath. Of course, what is singular about *Jeanne Dielman*'s staging of the voyeuristic gaze is that it refuses any measure of satisfaction to it. At the simplest level Jeanne's body is never fully revealed (we are given only a partial view of her as she bathes, and the sex takes place behind closed doors), but more important, her body is reduced by the work it performs and its association with the household objects that surround it to the status of a thing, rather than a living being. *Jeanne Dielman* thus exposes the impossibility of gratification that underlies voyeuristic fantasy but that is denied by the voyeur. In this way the film replicates for the viewer the emotional alienation experienced by the protagonist that results from her social position within a patriarchal culture.

With respect to the relationship between spectator-centered projective illusion, character identification, and voyeurism, Stanley Kubrick's film *A Clockwork Orange* (1971) provides an illuminating contrast to *Jeanne Dielman*. Kubrick's work is also a fiction film that foregrounds the relationship between spectator-centered projective illusion and voyeurism, but it does so from the opposite extreme. First, *A Clockwork Orange* makes every effort to align the spectator with the pathologically violent central protagonist, Alex, through his ingratiating and witty voice-over narration and his footloose and fancy-free persona. Second, Kubrick mimics the techniques of the exploitation film so as to maximize the spectator's voyeuristic gratification. For example, the rape scene in which Alex assaults the wife of the writer to the tune of "Singin' in the Rain" is filmed through a wide-angle lens with a hand-held camera, which maximizes the spectator's sense of being involved in the scene. A scene such as this may prompt the spectator to see the image as a staged event; however, I would speculate that such a response would have the character of a defensive "its really only a movie" reaction to the intensity of the projective illusion engendered by it.

For the first twenty minutes of the film at least, Kubrick invites the spectator to experience the events of the film through the lavish way they are choreographed with all the relish that the central character, with whom we are encouraged to identify, experiences them. However, as I shall argue in the final section of this chapter, it makes no sense to speak of identifying with a character's voyeurism: Voyeurism is always spectator centered rather than character centered. Still, Kubrick provides an experience for the spectator that attempts to approximate that of the character. In *Jeanne Dielman,* voyeuristic pleasure is consistently invoked and denied in a manner that recalls and mimics the obsessional neurosis of its protagonist. By contrast, in *A Clockwork Orange* we voyeuristically experience the apparent satisfaction of the desires that we impute to the character with whom we are encouraged to identify. Of course, later in *A Clockwork Orange,* as Alex enters prison, the pace of events radically slows down, the color becomes a uniform institutional gray-blue, the music stops, and we become aware of the fact that what we are watching is only a film. It is as if the spectator is punished for succumbing to the sensory lure of those opening scenes in a manner that parallels the way that Alex is punished for the activities those scenes depict. However, the effect of boredom here is not to expose the illusion of satisfaction that voyeuristic pleasure depends upon. On the contrary, it attests to the permanent allure of the voyeuristic pleasure that corresponds to the impulses of the protagonist, which neither conventional punishment nor new fads in "treatment" can eradicate or diminish.

One of the major fallacies of contemporary film theory has been to imply that spectatorship in the cinema is inherently voyeuristic. This emphasis on the cinema's voyeuristic character results from an overvaluation of the role that vision plays in determining the emotional responses of the spectator. To my mind, this overvaluation stems, in large part, from the adoption of Metz's distinction between primary and secondary cinematic identification (introduced in Chapter 1), which implies that all forms of emotional identification in the cinema are dependent upon identification with the camera's point of view. In primary cinematic identification, according to Metz, the spectator takes up the position of the camera and identifies "with himself as a pure act of perception."[19] In relationship to this primary identification with the camera, the spectator's emotional identification with character, and more generally, his "identification" with the content of what is viewed, is a secondary one. Metz suggests that there is a hierarchy between the two ways of experiencing the cinema: Secondary identification presupposes primary identification; that is, the activity of seeing is privileged over what is seen.

If Metz were correct, what I have called projective illusion would be equivalent to primary cinematic identification, and spectator- and character-centered projective illusion would comprise two forms of secondary cinematic identification; but as I have argued, the emotional response of the spectator to what she sees is not predicated ordinarily upon the fact that she has adopted the visual field of the camera as her own. In particular, character identification occurs independently of the experience of projective illusion, although our experience of projective illusion can be encouraged through that identification. Hence the character-centeredness of character-centered projective illusion does not presuppose camera-centered perception. Nor does the spectator-centeredness of spectator-centered projective illusion presuppose camera-centered perception: I may have an emotional response to an image that is autonomous from my identification with character, regardless of whether or not I experience the image in the form of projective illusion. The failure within psychoanalytic film theory to draw a distinction between our capacity to respond emotionally to a film and our capacity to imagine that we are witness to the events of the film, has misled a whole generation of film theorists. Our capacity to respond emotionally to a film may engender the experience of projective illusion, but it does not presuppose that experience, save for the special case of voyeurism.

While Metz conceives of primary identification in the cinema as the spectator's occupancy of the camera's point of view in the act of seeing, he also gives a further specification of the mental state of the spectator that has its origins in Baudry's essay "Ideological Effects of the Basic Cinematographic Apparatus." Baudry and Metz argue that when we experience the impression of reality, it is as if we constitute the world that we perceive through the act of perceiving it in the manner of the subject of a transcendental or idealist philosophy. This characterization of the cinema spectator provides a basis for defining the nature of the look that is fostered by projective illusion in the cinema as a controlling or sadistic look. Clearly, this is not the manner in which we experience character-centered projective illusion. At best, Baudry and Metz could be taken here to be describing one way in which spectator-centered projective illusion is experienced; but even this type of projective illusion is not necessarily experienced in this way. As I have already suggested, I may experience projective illusion in such a manner that my point of view is dispersed over the field of the image. I may feel overwhelmed or engulfed by a world that exists independently of my intention, in the same manner that I may feel overwhelmed or engulfed by iconic imagination when I experience it in an acentered form. Rather than experiencing ourselves in control of the image, we experience the image as if it controls us – as a prolonged swoon, so to speak. I understand Gaylyn Studlar's "masochistic aesthetic" to be a celebration of this sublime form of spectatorship.[20]

The experience of seeming to control what we see or of being controlled by it are alternative ways of experiencing spectator-centered projective illusion, just as they are two ways of experiencing acentered imagination. Metz associates the experience of control with a recognition of the apparent omniscience of our gaze in a moving camera shot. When we see what a moving camera sees in the form of a projective illusion, we see it without moving our bodies or turning our heads. Studlar associates a loss of control with our experience, for example, of Josef von Sternberg's mise-en-scène, which is often cluttered beyond our capacity to assimilate its contents. When we experience such a mise-en-scène in the form of a projective illusion, the space may seem to overwhelm us in its detail and density. Where spectator-centered projective illusion is privileged over character identification and a voyeuristic gaze is elicited, this voyeuristic gaze may either be controlling or submissive, depending on the precise context of narrative and mise-en-scène in which the look is registered. However, it can never be specified definitively whether spectator-centered projective illusion is experienced as a control or loss of control over the image. The quality of a spectator's look at a film is never dictated or determined by the film; it is only, at most, fostered or encouraged by it.

Varieties of Disavowal

I have tried to explain the quality and character of our experience of projective illusion in terms of the psychic force of our iconic imagination and its function as wish fulfillment; but how can a psychoanalytic theory of the mind illuminate the fact that even while we experience projective illusion, we know that what we are watching is only a film? Contemporary film theory turned to the psychoanalytic theory of disavowal in order to understand this phenomenon. Unfortunately, the account of disavowal put forward in the writings of Metz and invoked by subsequent film theorists is plagued with ambiguity due to a failure to discriminate between normal and pathological forms of disavowal. This failure reflects the dependence of psychoanalytic film theory on Lacanian psychoanalysis. Furthermore, following Freud's own usage in certain essays, contemporary film theorists discuss disavowal in the context of fetishism, and thus the two terms have become conflated; but the mechanism of disavowal, as Freud recognized, is as characteristic of the neuroses as it is of the perversions.[21] I shall elucidate the mechanism of disavowal in the context of neurosis rather than fetishism to make clear the distinction between disavowal and fetishism. By clarifying a distinction between normal and pathological disavowal, I also seek to redeem the concept from the context of Lacanian film theory.

In a conscious wish-fulfilling fantasy of the kind I have already discussed, I imagine a state of affairs that is contrary to fact. I imagine, say, that I am having an erotic encounter with Shelley Winters. In order for me to entertain the fantasy with the psychic force required for the fantasy to register the fulfillment of my wish, I must suppress awareness of the fact that I am only imagining the event in order to circumvent both my knowledge that I am not the lover of Shelley Winters and my belief that such a state of affairs is highly unlikely to occur. Following Anna Freud, we may speak in this case of a denial or disavowal of reality through fantasy.[22] In fantasy, I affirm what I know not to be the case; but do I believe, when I entertain the fantasy, that I am Shelley Winters's paramour? Of course not, for I am conscious. When I imagine myself the lover of Shelley Winters, I am entertaining what I know not to be the case. Fantasy here is akin to play, and the disavowal it entails is a benign one. One might put it this way: When disavowal is benign, I entertain the fantasy all the while knowing that it is not really the case.

When our conscious desires are realized in fantasy, they merely circumvent belief in order to find expression while leaving our true beliefs essentially intact. As we have seen, in conscious fantasy the psychic force of the daydream is attenuated due to the fact that the wish animating it is a conscious one. When we are conscious of our desires, desire is not assimilated to belief with the psychic force of dream. However, desires that would otherwise fail to find expression are not simply conscious desires, but also wishes that we would not readily admit to, such as incestuous desires and their kindred, rage (the wish to destroy the object that is wished for). Fantasy actively promotes and sustains these desires because it not only affords their simulated realization, but it does so in a manner that actively shields them from consciousness, as well as from the frustration of desire and the conflict among desires with which reality testing is associated. Fantasy performs this function by exploiting the properties of narrative to link irreconcilable desires and disguise the relationship in which they stand to one another in the manner that Freud first described in relationship to dreams. It is because fantasy can disguise the unrealizable, unconscious desires animating it that it enables those desires to receive expression in the form of the wish. As we have seen, when desire receives this expression as a wish, I believe that what I wish for really occurs.

However, it may still be objected: How can wish-fulfilling fantasy function with the psychic force of dream, since when we entertain such a fantasy we are awake and hence know all along that it is only a fantasy? It can function in this way because the mind disguises not only the unconscious desires that animate fantasy, but also the fact that it is through fantasy that these desires are realized; that is, fantasy itself is also disguised. This disguise enables the mind to protect wish-generated belief from the fact that it is only a product of wish fulfillment. How, then, is fantasy disguised? It is disguised through the process of acting out, which consists in the projection of fantasy onto the world in such a way that one's actions are dictated by the fantasy. When fantasy is acted out it no longer appears to the subject as a fantasy. Once it is normalized in this way, as Richard Wollheim writes, "the person will be required to find good reason for these actions, but, more than this, he will be required to make it seem to himself as though he is acting on such reasons."[23] Where fantasy is normalized, desire is actually assimilated to belief, and the world does seem, for the time being, to be cut to the measure of desire.

Freud's patient known as the Rat Man was tormented by powerful and ambivalent feelings toward his dead father, feelings to which he could not readily admit. According to Freud's interpretation of his symptoms, in his fantasy that was sustained by acting out, his father was alive and hence available for the expression of the Rat Man's feelings. During the time that the Rat Man was studying for an examination, he worked long hours late into the night. After midnight he would interrupt his work to open the front door of the house as if his father were waiting outside to come in. Then he would return to the hall and inspect his genitals. Believing, in this way, that his father was alive, he was able to express his feelings to his father: his love, by being a good boy and studying late into the night, and his rage, by being a naughty boy and exposing his genitals. He could thereby take revenge upon his father, who had chastised him for masturbating when he was a child, while at the same time disguising the expression of his anger.

When desire assimilates itself to belief, as it does in the case of the Rat Man, the mind's grasp upon reality is undermined. Of course, the Rat Man knew that his father was dead, and in this sense his case is no different from the case of wish-fulfilling fantasy where we entertain in fantasy something that we know not to be true. However, where a wish is consciously fulfilled in fantasy, the fantasy is merely entertained and does not encroach upon belief. In the case of a wish-fulfilling fantasy, disavowal is the means by which the mind can continue to indulge in the pleasures of fantasy; but for the Rat Man, in the grip of powerful, unacknowledged desires, reality is threatened with foreclosure, and disavowal is a mechanism of last resort that prevents reality's being foreclosed. When disavowal functions in this way, the part of the mind that maintains contact with reality splits itself off from the part where belief has been swallowed up by desire. Freud called this form of disavowal a "splitting of the ego."[24] The mind divides in two and holds, simultaneously, mutually contradictory beliefs about the world. In the sense that such a split prevents reality from being foreclosed, it acts as a defense against the encroachment of desire in the form of the wish upon mental functioning. However, by separating the part of the mind that maintains a relationship with reality from the part that has succumbed to the wish, this splitting of the ego, like other so-called defense mechanisms, lies at the service of desire and acts as yet another layer of protection against reality testing. Disavowal in the form of a splitting of the ego could be taken to describe disavowal in its pathological form. Freud does not make a distinction, as I have done, between entertaining something in thought and believing that something exists; he does not draw a distinction between disavowal per se and disavowal in the form of an ego split. However, such a distinction seems consistent with his own thoughts on the subject.

Contemporary film theory has failed to distinguish between these two forms of disavowal. This is no doubt in part because the distinction between normal and pathological forms of disavowal is not explicitly provided by Freud, and in part because the boundary between the normal and abnormal is a relative one. However, although these forms of disavowal lie at either end of a continuum of cases, and the boundary between the two is thus a relative and fluid one, it is nevertheless necessary to draw this distinction in a context where the activity being described – watching films – clearly lies within the range of rational behavior. Of course, it is quite possible that going to the cinema could become a pathological form of behavior and cause the kind of splitting Freud associates with severe forms of neurosis. A spectator of a given disposition might respond to a film as if it were real and behave as if the world on the screen and the world of experience formed an undifferentiated continuum. Fraught with the anxiety correlative to such an acting out of fantasy, this pathological spectator would at once ward off the anxiety and keep his experience intact through a splitting of the ego: I know this is a film, but all the same I believe it to be real. A case like this may illuminate the character of cinemagoing in general, but it would be absurd to claim that this is really the way in which the cinema spectator characteristically behaves. The situation of the spectator in the cinema is not that of Freud's Rat Man in relationship to his fantasy, for cinemagoing is a conscious activity. The movies do not cause the ego to lose its grip on reality and unconsciously defend against this loss by splitting.

However, to argue that cinemagoing is a conscious and rational activity does not entail abandoning a psychoanalytic understanding of spectatorship, as some critics of psychoanalytic theory maintain. It simply requires taking account of the conscious and rational dimension of the experience when characterizing the irrational or noncognitive experience it promotes. Disavowal in the cinema takes the same form as our cognitive relationship to conscious fantasy or daydream, although, as I have argued, it is a conscious fantasy experienced with the psychic force of dream. When we experience projective illusion in the cinema, we make believe that the experience is real, or suspend our disbelief, but we do not believe that the illusion is real. The experience of projective illusion is like a trompe l'oeil: We see the illusion while we know it to be an illusion. However, trompe l'oeil illusion has a level of objectivity that projective illusion in the cinema does not. Projective illusion requires a contribution of the spectator, a predisposition to see the image as a fully realized world. Psychoanalysis illuminates this contribution of the spectator to the experience of the cinema.

The pleasure afforded by projective illusion is a form of pleasure akin to children's games of make-believe; it is not a form of experience that stops just short of psychosis. The cinema meets halfway the spectator's predisposition to stage fantasy and gratify her desire in the form of the wish. In this way, as Ira Konigsberg has pointed out, the spectator's experience of film conforms to the child's experience of the world of transitional objects and phenomena described by D. W. Winnicott.[25] The transitional object, such as a blanket or toy, lies, for the child, on the boundary between the subjective and objective, the me and the not-me, comforting him in the absence of the caregiver and allowing him to master that absence. The transitional object remains part of the child's subjective, imaginary world, and is recruited by him to fulfill desire in the form of the wish. At the same time it is a part of the objective world, and its recruitment by the child to serve his fantasy marks a recognition of the boundary between the me and not-me, and between fantasy and reality. The child is able to reject or disidentify with the object as well as to identify with it. He can experience separation and autonomy, yet all the while retain the capacity to merge with the object. In this way, wish fulfillment is given free reign but does not impinge on the child's sense of reality; rather, it is placed benignly at the service of creativity and play. The pleasure of entering in and out of the imaginary world afforded by

the transitional object describes precisely the pleasure of the cinema spectator as she enters in and out of the world of projective illusion. Like the child
playing a game of make-believe, the spectator who entertains the film as a
projective illusion does not simply give herself over to the screen; she toys
with the experience of presence and absence as in a game of *fort–da* or
peekaboo.

The most important reason the function of disavowal in the cinema has
remained so obscure is the role that Lacanian theory has played in conceptu-
alizing "identification" in the cinema. I have distinguished normal disavowal
from a pathological disavowal or a splitting of the ego on the grounds of
whether or not the false reality or illusion is merely entertained in thought
(visualized in iconic imagination, perceived in the cinema), or is actually
believed. The distinction rests on the degree to which the fantasy is unconscious and structures the life of the individual in such a way that beliefs are
colonized by belief-indifferent desires. However, a third sense of disavowal
can also be distinguished – disavowal as misrecognition – as articulated by
Jacques Lacan through the concept of the mirror stage.[26] As we have discussed in previous chapters, for Lacan, the child's sense of self-identity
emerges in his early life only through his representation in a mirror and, less
metaphorically, through the gaze of the mother.[27] Initially the subject is
fragmented. Upon perceiving himself as a self through his representation in
the mirror or in the gaze of the mother, the subject is constituted as a coherent entity. However, since the subject really is a fragmentary and undifferentiated libidinal puddle and not the unified body image he appears to be in
the mirror, he is constituted in a state of disavowal or misrecognition of his
true nature. Self-knowledge is founded upon a radical self-alienation of
which the ego qua ego is necessarily unaware.

For Lacan, then, a splitting between reality and the fantasmatic is not just
one possible consequence of experience that is equal and alternative to a
more benign relationship of the self to fantasy: It founds experience itself.
Whereas in the cases of disavowal that we have been considering the normal
and pathological are at once related but distinguishable, Lacanian misrecognition allows no meaningful distinction to be made between the normal and
the pathological. The Lacanian ego is the normalized pathology of a subject
who projects an object world and thereby constitutes her own being in order
to cover up the division and dispersal from which she emerges. However, if
experience itself is founded upon a division in which the self is forged in the
form of an alien other, then misrecognition is not, strictly, an *experience*
that the subject can have at all. Before the mirror, spatially and temporally,
there is the subject as no-thing. After the mirror, there is a subject as an entity. The no-thing is not in a position to *mis*recognize itself in the mirror be-

cause it is not yet an entity with recognition capacities. After the mirror there *is* an entity who recognizes herself as a subject, but this recognition is always and necessarily a misrecognition, for the subject really is a no-thing. Thus, as Joan Copjec has pointed out, from the point of view of Lacanian theory, Lacanian film theory mistakenly literalizes the mirror metaphor in the spectator–screen relationship.[28] The thesis of mirror misrecognition in film theory implies that there is something – the spectator – before the screen-mirror, when from the point of view of Lacanian theory what is really there is the no-thing. In film theory the subject is given a spatial position, a point of view upon events, that in Lacanian theory it lacks. The Lacanian conception of misrecognition might be characterized as an epistemically pernicious form of disavowal in the sense that the subject cannot have knowledge of the essential lack that founds her. Lacanian misrecognition does not involve the splitting of belief that characterizes Freud's splitting of the ego, in which two contradictory facts about the world are simultaneously held to be true. It entails that (self-)knowledge is a fiction; experiential reality is structured, through representation, as an illusion.

As we saw in Chapter 1, Baudry applies the thesis of mirror misrecognition to the cinema in the context of the thesis of perspectival subject positioning informed by Althusser's theory of ideology. Metz does not explicitly endorse the thesis of perspectival subject positioning and the theory of ideology upon which it is based, but, like Baudry, he does invoke Lacan's concept of mirror misrecognition in the context of discussing the thesis of primary cinematic identification. The spectator in the cinema, perceiving the cinematic image in the form of an illusion of reality, is given what appears to be a transparent, unmediated perception of that world. Although this spectator does not perceive her reflection in the screen-mirror (she has already passed through the mirror stage), her gaze is endowed with an omnipotence that is like the gaze of the child before the mirror. However, the analogy between screen and mirror also demonstrates that the spectator's sense of authority and mastery is really only a function of an apparatus. It is the cinematic apparatus that simultaneously engenders the illusion of reality for the spectator to experience and the spectating subject to experience that reality in a manner that endlessly reproduces the founding moment of the ego. Subsequently, the spectator in front of the screen emotionally invests in this illusion of reality to prevent her own dissolution, just as the subject in front of the mirror invests in the image in the mirror in order to preserve his identity.

The spectator conceptualized in terms of Lacanian theory is certainly different from our imagined pathological spectator who takes the image for reality and defends against the anxiety caused by this perception by splitting.

The pathology of the Lacanian spectator is thoroughly normalized; she seems to take for granted the idea that the image is real. Nevertheless, the Lacanian spectator is defined by the pathology she shares with my pathological one: her essential anxiety about the status of the image. The Lacanian spectator is faced with the constant threat of being "torn to pieces" if the status of the image qua image is revealed to her.[29] If my pathological spectator were confronted with the real status of the image, the results would be catastrophic, given the fact that his ability to function depends on maintaining this disavowal; but such a catastrophe equally befalls the Lacanian spectator every time she is faced with an awareness of the image. The idea of the Lacanian spectator rests upon the unlikely hypothesis that the dissolution of the ego is at stake not simply every time we go to or leave the cinema, but every time there is a cut![30]

That this catastrophe is always averted, even by the Lacanian spectator, is due to the fact that the Lacanian spectator retains aspects of the non-Lacanian spectator, who has supposedly been redefined. Thus Metz writes that while the spectator's position in front of the image reproduces the position of the subject before the mirror, at the same time the spectator knows that what she is watching is only a film. The spectator's awareness that the film is only a film therefore does not have the catastrophic effect entailed by the scenario of mirror misrecognition. Quite the contrary: This effect has often been construed within contemporary film theory as liberating, releasing the spectator from the tyranny of an apparatus that dupes the spectator into believing that the illusion it produces is real. The Lacanian spectator of film theory turns out to be less Lacanian than an amalgam of the Lacanian and the non-Lacanian spectator. This spectator, like the child before the mirror, has an illusion of omniscience and omnipotence that is fortified by the belief that what she sees is real. Yet, at the same time, this spectator synthesizes both extremes of the non-Lacanian spectator. She is a spectator with an ego that is divided: She believes in the reality of what she sees even while she knows that it is only a film. She also voluntarily enters and leaves the cinema and does not, in general, confuse projective illusion with the external world.

The thesis of mirror misrecognition in the cinema should be abandoned on the grounds that it is a fundamentally contradictory idea that fails to recognize the discrimination between normal and pathological disavowal. It should also be abandoned on the grounds that it depends upon the thesis of primary cinematic identification, which I have already argued is indefensible. Our emotional response to the cinema is not necessarily embedded in the act of looking, other than in the trivial sense that it presupposes our capacity to recognize visually the events and characters to which we respond. When we go to the cinema, we do not necessarily experience the film as a projective illusion. When the thesis of primary cinematic identification takes the form of the transcendental ego, it is open to further objections. When we do experience projective illusion, we do not necessarily experience it in the form of a transcendental ego. Character-centered projective illusion does not involve the experience of a transcendental ego; neither does the form of spectator-centered projective illusion, described by Studlar, in which the ego swoons before the image.

Voyeurism, Fetishism, and Sexual Difference

I have defended the importance of psychoanalytic theory for understanding spectatorship in the cinema, but I have argued that the central theses of contemporary psychoanalytic film theory – primary cinematic identification and mirror misrecognition – should be abandoned. Arguments about the representation of sexuality in the cinema have often relied, implicitly or explicitly, on these two theses. In this final section of the chapter I would like to explore the implication of abandoning them in the context of the arguments of feminist film theory.

The general argument of contemporary feminist film theory is that the psychical mechanisms invoked by the cinema, and, in particular, the classical cinema, are gender bound. The way in which this general argument is made varies from author to author, but I shall identify a cluster of theses that have been used to support this argument, either individually or collectively, in the work of a number of authors.

1. The gaze in the cinema is a voyeuristic gaze, either:
   a. because the spectator's gaze is aligned with the look of the camera in primary cinematic identification; or
   b. because the "position" of spectator in the cinema is constituted through mirror misrecognition.
2. The voyeuristic gaze in the cinema is an active, male gaze, either:
   a. because the equation voyeurism = active = male is made by psychoanalytic theory; or
   b. because the gaze is relayed through the spectator's "secondary identification" with the active male narrative agent.
3. The voyeuristic gaze in the cinema confronts the male spectator with the threat of castration, either:
   a. because the play between awareness of and immersion in illusion evokes castration; or
   b. because the voyeuristic gaze confronts the fetishized, castrated female body.

I shall examine each of these arguments in turn.

Thesis 1a is based on the thesis of primary cinematic identification, the assumption that regardless of the particular content of what is depicted in a film, the spectator's emotional response presupposes that he adopts the gaze of a transcendental subject and perceives the world of the film as if it were constituted by that gaze. As Christian Metz makes clear, the gaze of this transcendental subject is also a voyeuristic one. Metz writes that "the voyeur is very careful to maintain a gulf, an empty space, between the object and the eye, the object and his own body."[31] But this gulf between object and body is precisely what is presupposed by the gaze of the transcendental subject. As an all-perceiving, disembodied eye, the transcendental subject is never threatened with entering into physical proximity with what it perceives.

I have argued that experience of the cinematic image as an illusory presence is not necessary to an emotional response to narrative cinema. Nonetheless, it is certainly an experience that is encouraged and fostered by the narrative forms of classical Hollywood cinema, although not an experience exclusive to it. In this sense Laura Mulvey's more cautious formulation of the voyeuristic potential of the cinema is more helpful than Metz's, which relies on the thesis of primary cinematic identification. Mulvey writes:

[T]he mass of mainstream film, and the conventions within which it has consciously evolved, portray an hermetically sealed world which unwinds magically, indifferent to the presence of the audience, producing for them a sense of separation and playing on their voyeuristic fantasy. . . . Although the film is really being shown, is there to be seen, conditions of screening and narrative conventions give the spectator an illusion of looking in on a private world.[32]

However, when a film is experienced as "unwinding magically" before the spectator in the form of a projective illusion, it does not necessarily entail a voyeuristic response to the image. Two further conditions need to obtain: First, the object looked at must be a human being or a creature or thing that is capable of being endowed with anthropomorphic features or associations; second, the form that projective illusion takes must be spectator centered. This second claim deserves some comment.

I have already suggested that voyeurism occurs when spectator-centered identification is privileged over character identification and the spectator responds to the character's body in a manner that is detached from an identification with the character's beliefs and feelings. Unless the character is specifically exhibitionist, I project upon him (or her) a specific intention that I desire him to have: I imagine that the character is presenting his body for my privileged gaze and allowing me to survey it with impunity. However, it may be countered, surely a voyeuristic response to the image can be produced through identification with a character in a film if that character himself is a voyeur? Indeed, voyeurism in the cinema is most often discussed in relationship to films such as *Peeping Tom* (1960) or *Rear Window,* in which the central characters are voyeurs and we are invited to share their acts of voyeurism through our occupying their optical point of view. However, what could an "identification" with a character's voyeuristic gaze mean? A voyeuristic gaze is not a feeling held by that character, and hence it is not something with which one can identify.

If I identify with the desire of Anthony for Cleopatra, I may feel something of that desire for Cleopatra myself, but my desire is dependent upon the feelings of Anthony. If Anthony gazes voyeuristically at Cleopatra, then his gaze is something I see. If I then also look voyeuristically at the image of Cleopatra, I may do so because Anthony has done so, but I may also do so anyway. My gaze is not dependent on his gaze: It is my gaze and is completely autonomous. Films like *Peeping Tom* and *Rear Window* are interesting because they explicitly thematize the act of voyeurism. To the extent that they encourage us to explore the complexity and ambivalence of the voyeur, they actually discourage a voyeuristic response in the spectator; they are better understood as films about voyeurism than voyeuristic films. Of course, films about voyeurism can be viewed voyeuristically if that is the spectator's concern, and the very capacity for this kind of engagement illustrates the spectator-centered autonomy of the voyeuristic gaze. For any spectator, voyeurism may enter into her experience of any film to a greater or lesser degree and in a way that is acknowledged by her or not. Conversely, the spectator's gaze may not be voyeuristic, even when she identifies with a character who is a voyeur.

Thesis 1b is less an alternative to thesis 1a than a supplement to it. As we saw in Chapter 1, the thesis of primary cinematic identification and the thesis of mirror misrecognition are closely related. Thesis 1b supports thesis 1a. By exposing the position of the transcendental subject as a defense against lack, as an illusory fiction of coherence and control engendered by image and narration in the cinema, the thesis of mirror misrecognition exposes the fiction upon which the voyeuristic gaze is constructed. Thus Kaja Silverman points out the way in which Lacan's mirror scenario emphasizes the fact that subjectivity is "from the very outset dependent upon the recognition of a distance separating self from other – on an object whose loss is simultaneous with its apprehension." She goes on to imply that voyeuristic investment of the spectator in the presence of the object in the cinema is only a precarious defense against the loss or lack that underpins subjectivity.[33]

Because the thesis of mirror misrecognition depends on the thesis of primary cinematic identification, and the thesis of primary cinematic identification is insupportable, the thesis of mirror misrecognition cannot be sustained either. Furthermore, I have argued that the thesis of mirror misrecognition is not coherent on its own terms, as it conflates two contrary notions of disavowal and subjectivity, and erroneously privileges one way of experiencing projective illusion in the cinema – that of an active, controlling, transcendental ego – over the others. Thus thesis 1b should be abandoned.

Thesis 2a contains two arguments: that the voyeuristic gaze in the cinema is active and sadistic, and that this active, sadistic gaze is a male one. I shall deal with each argument in turn. As Gaylyn Studlar has argued, the thesis that the voyeuristic gaze is an active gaze is not supported by psychoanalytic theory in general, nor, incidentally, by Lacan's conception of mirror misrecognition. In a wide-ranging paper called "The Scopophilic Instinct and Identification," the German analyst Otto Fenichel suggests in some detail the way in which the libidinally invested glance, like the other drives identified by psychoanalytic theory, has its origins in the earliest forms of identification, where the self is conceived in relationship to the possibility of merger with the other.[34] Governed by a corporeal conception of mind, the infant experiences her sense of self–other relation in terms of the physical incorporation or expulsion of objects through the orifices of the body. When the locus of this process of identification with the object is the look itself, the look is charged with the ambivalence toward the object that characterizes primary identification in general. To look entails controlling and ultimately seeking to destroy the object, but it also entails that the subject is enthralled and transfixed by the object that she desires to be, and is placed in a passive or masochistic relationship to it. Libidinally invested looking is never simply active or passive but always a mixture of both. The active, sadistic look and the passive, masochistic look circumscribe the continuum of possibilities that are encouraged by particular viewing situations in the cinema.

The general thesis that an active or sadistic voyeuristic gaze is a male gaze is also not supported by psychoanalytic theory, and this has been argued effectively by David Rodowick in his book *The Difficulty of Difference*. Through a detailed discussion of Freud's paper "A Child is Being Beaten," Rodowick demonstrates how, at least for Freud, the psychosexual organization of human beings simply cannot be reduced to an opposition, drawn up along the lines of gender, between an active, sadistic, male psyche and a passive, masochistic, female psyche.[35] I have noted that scopophilia cannot be reduced to either an active or passive, sadistic or masochistic drive; equally, it cannot be reduced to a drive that is primarily male or female. In this respect it is instructive to note that the case study Fenichel uses to illustrate the vicissitudes of scopophilia is that of a female voyeur. He describes a voyeuse who is held transfixed by figures within imagined or real pictorial representations that appear to come to life in three dimensions before her. Sometimes, benignly, these figures diminish into two-dimensional forms, and the experience becomes one that she can pleasurably control; yet, at other times, they come to life with a force that threatens to overwhelm her. The significance of this case study for thinking about spectatorship in the cinema is obvious.

Thesis 2b suggests that the voyeuristic gaze in the cinema is active and sadistic because of the way in which that gaze is relayed through the active male narrative agent. Although this thesis may coincide with the assertion of thesis 2a – as it does, for example, in Mulvey's "Visual Pleasure" essay – it is not dependent on this thesis. It *is* dependent on thesis 1b, which I have defended in the qualified terms of my theory of projective illusion. In my modification of thesis 1b, I claim that the cinema has the capacity to elicit a voyeuristic response from the spectator. Since thesis 2b follows from thesis 1b, it too must be modified. It is undoubtedly true of classical cinema, and of cinema in general, that the voyeuristic gaze of the spectator is characteristically promoted by the look of a male character at a female one, although the male character too can be the subject of a voyeuristic gaze. However, since our gaze is distinct from the gaze of the character, it makes no sense to speak of the gaze being controlled or determined by the agency of that character. The active, male protagonist does not necessarily produce an active, voyeuristic gaze for the spectator. It makes no sense to speak of the voyeuristic gaze of the spectator as either male or female.

I have already defended the claim that the experience of projective illusion is sustained through the mechanism of disavowal. However, thesis 3a claims that the play of presence and absence that defines the experience of projective illusion functions to remind the spectator of the threat of castration or lack. This argument can be derived directly from the thesis of the Lacanian spectator. Since I have argued already that the concept of the Lacanian spectator is incoherent, I shall focus upon the comparison that has been made between the spectator's experience of disavowal in the cinema and Freud's account of fetishism. Freud argues that the male child creates the fetish as a response to the anxiety provoked by the absence of the female genitals, given his belief that all people possess a penis. Upon viewing female genitals in the light of this belief, the little boy assumes that the female penis has been removed and fears the removal of his own. The child's reaction may be to refuse simply to accept what he now knows to be the case – that females lack a penis – and create instead an imaginary, idealized stand-in for the missing female penis in the form of the fetish. The fetish allows him to believe in the phallic woman and deny the threat of castration, even as it attests to his knowledge that women do not have a penis and functions as a permanent reminder of that fact. Freud's account suggests that fetishistic disavowal is defined by the fact that the contradictory beliefs are maintained or held in equilibrium by a prop – the fetish – that is perceived as being at once the same as (a part of) and different from (a substitute for) its referent. Of course, the idea of fetishistic disavowal is derived from the context of societies in which fetish objects are used to sustain magical beliefs. Freud applies this idea to the specific case of sexual fetishism, where he contends that the magical belief sustained is that of the phallic woman.

In "The Imaginary Signifier," Metz suggests that the perception of the cinematic image is equivalent to the spectacle of a phallic lack that confronts the male child. He writes:

[B]efore this unveiling of a lack (we are already close to the cinema signifier), the child, in order to avoid too strong an anxiety, will have to double up its belief (another cinematic characteristic) and from then on forever hold two contradictory opinions (proof that in spite of everything the real perception has not been without effect).[36]

As Ben Singer has argued, however, film does not involve the sudden perception of a lack or absence, along with the attendant trauma, that characterizes the perception of the woman as castrated.[37] We do not enter the cinema and first see the image before us as a projective illusion, only later to confront the fact that it is only an image; we know all along that it is only an image. Furthermore, following Jacqueline Rose, Singer also points out that the scenario of fetishism in the context of Freud's writings only has meaning in relation to sexual difference, whereas in the cinema in general beliefs about sexual difference are not at stake.[38] The absence of trauma and the absence of the perception of sexual difference in the cinema preclude the association proposed in thesis 3a between disavowal in the cinema and the experience of castration.

However, all of this does not preclude the possibility that disavowal in the cinema could be characterized as fetishistic in a more general sense of the fetish that is not reducible to the phallic scenario identified by Freud. Since Freud, the understanding of fetishism within the psychoanalytic tradition itself has undergone considerable revision. As psychoanalysts after Freud turned to the analytic study of children and, more generally, of the relationship between the child and its primary caregiver, they have identified a wide range of fetish objects used to substitute not for the missing penis, but for the absent mother. The fetish, in this more general sense, hearkens back to the moment of primary identification in which the child first separates from the mother and differentiates the me from the not-me. I have already referred to Winnicott's analysis of the transitional object that acts as a comforter for the child in the absence of the mother and is a normal way for the child to master that absence. The transitional object is a prototypical fetish that allows the child to maintain the fantasy that the objective world conforms to her subjective reality, even while it marks an acknowledgment of the boundary between the me and the not-me and the reality of the objective world. Post-Freudian psychoanalysis suggests that the phenomenon of fetishism covers a family of cases in which the fetish object becomes pathologized when the pre-Oedipal fetish becomes overlaid and invested with Oedipal anxieties.[39]

Winnicott's analysis of the transitional object illuminates the psychological foundations of the fetishistic belief that informs magic and religious ritual; it is this more general sense of fetishism that is significant for understanding our experience of the cinema. If cinema affords us the possibility of experiencing the realization of our fantasies with the psychic force of dream, it does so because it is an apparatus, a mechanism, that allows two contradictory beliefs about the world to be maintained. However, Singer offers a further objection to such an identification of apparatus and fetish:

The fetish . . . redeems the threatening sight . . . by deflecting attention away from the traumatic absence and by filling the absence with a physical surrogate for the supposedly castrated penis. It seems rather perverse, therefore, to locate the cinematic fetish in the appreciation of technology, since this guides attention toward the critical absence and would then presumably rekindle trauma and defeat the very purpose of the fetish.[40]

Singer is talking here of the Freudian fetish, but the same point might be stated in a more general way. Any fetish object allows us to maintain contradictory beliefs about the world through its relationship of similarity and difference to the object believed in: We maintain our true beliefs by virtue of the difference of the fetish from the object believed in, and our false beliefs through its similarity. In this sense we never, as it were, lose sight of the fetish. However, perception of the cinematic apparatus precludes, or at least tends to undermine, the false belief that the apparatus can be used to maintain. Conversely, our experience of the film as a projective illusion is premised upon our lack of awareness of the film as a film. The cinematic apparatus allows us to experience an entire narrative universe as a simulacrum of our own, even as we know all along that it is only a simulacrum. Once the spectator is predisposed to entertain the illusion that the apparatus affords, the illusory world is completely realized, and we lose sight of the fetish.

This distinction between the cinematic apparatus and the fetish does not force us to abandon the identification between apparatus and fetish, but it does point to the particular character of the cine-fetish and the cine-fetishist. The cine-fetish is a transparent fetish, and the cine-fetishist is one who is obsessed with this effect of transparency and how it is achieved. As Metz writes, "The cinema fetishist is the person who is enchanted at what the machine is capable of, at the *theater of shadows* as such."[41] Just as not all cinemagoers are voyeurs, or not voyeurs all of the time, so too not all cinemagoers are fetishists, or not fetishists all of the time. The cine-fetishist, like the cine-voyeur, is a spectator who enters into the world of projective illusion in a resolutely spectator-centered way. The interest of the cine-fetishist lies precisely in how projective illusion is achieved through film techniques, art and costume design, the sound track, and special effects. The cine-fetishist is interested in the story only insofar as it acts as a vehicle for the achievement of projective illusion. The early cinema spectator, whose fascination with the apparatus Tom Gunning has described as an "aesthetic of astonishment," was a cine-fetishist;[42] and so too, as Metz recognized, is the theorist who writes obsessively about projective illusion in the cinema!

I have defended the claim that spectator-centered projective illusion is fetishistic, although not in a manner that invokes phallic fetishism and the scenario of castration. Thesis 3b claims that the scenario of phallic castration is specifically invoked through the depiction in the cinema of the fetishized female body that signifies castration. There is undoubtedly a historic link between the apparatus of the cinema and the fetishized female body, alternately veiled and unveiled, or, alternatively, broken up into separate body parts. This link is apparent in the prehistory and early history of the cinema as well as in certain genres of film, such as the musical films of Busby Berkeley.[43] However, because the voyeuristic gaze can be both active and passive, there is no intrinsic link between the fetishized female body and an active sadistic gaze. Furthermore, just as the voyeuristic gaze in the cinema is not a gendered gaze, there is no intrinsic link between fetishism in the cinema and the body of the woman. Indeed, it has become apparent how thoroughly the male body is fetishized in the cinema, from the contemporary beefcake of Sylvester Stallone and Arnold Schwarzenegger, back to the silent matinee idols, such as Rudolph Valentino and Douglas Fairbanks, Sr.

However, if psychoanalytic theory rejects the idea that the voyeuristic and fetishistic gaze is intrinsically active and male, why has it been given such authority by feminist psychoanalytic film theory? While feminist film theorists have sought to criticize the way in which the cinema offers pleasure for the male spectator that operates at the expense of women, they have also been keen to discern the gender bias that underpins the discourse of male theorists both in the field of film theory and psychoanalysis. In the case of film theory this involves demonstrating, to my mind with some truth, the patriarchal character of apparatus theory. However, with few exceptions, this criticism has stopped short of investigating the logical and empirical flaws of these theories. On the contrary, the theory has been accepted mistakenly as a valid description by one patriarchal institution – theory – of another – the cinema. In like manner feminist film theorists have been rightly concerned to point out the gender bias in both Freudian and Lacanian psychoanalysis that consigns woman to lack and renders her unrepresentable; yet, at the same time, they have lent these aspects of psychoanalytic discourse a historical validity, rather than identifying those aspects of the theories that might challenge a gender-bound understanding of identity and pointing out the logical or empirical failings of gender-bound explanations.

I offer as a paradigm case of this kind of reasoning Mary Ann Doane's discussion of Metz's theory of primary cinematic identification in a section of her book *The Desire to Desire* entitled "Freudian Scenarios and 'Ours.'" Doane writes of Metz's analysis:

> The psychical process of identification would . . . . appear to be sexually indifferent. But the use of terms such as "all perceiving," "all powerful," "transcendental subject," and "ego" in the descriptions of primary cinematic identification already indicate a difficulty in this respect. For the female subject quite simply does not have the same access as the male to the identity *described* in this manner. [My emphasis.]

The last sentence might be taken to imply that what is wrong here is film theory itself because it misdescribes the phenomenon of the cinema in patriarchal language. However, in the next sentence, through reference to the arguments of Luce Irigaray, which she appears to endorse, Doane implies that this model correctly describes the actual relegation of women:

> In the theory of Luce Irigaray, for example, the woman is relegated to the side of negativity, making her relation to the process of representation and self-representation more problematic.

Yet, having apparently endorsed Irigaray's theory, Doane hints that it speaks of the patriarchal discourse of psychoanalysis that misdescribes the subordination of women rather than describe the actual subordination of women. She continues:

Because she is situated as lack, nonmale, no-one; because her sexuality has only been *conceptualized* within masculine parameters (the clitoris understood as the "little penis"), she has no separate unity which could ground an identity. [My emphasis.]

Yet Doane concludes in a manner that, once again, seems to confirm the male character of the apparatus:

The male alone has access to the privileged specular process of the mirror's identification. And it is this confirmation of the self offered by the plane-mirror which, according to Irigaray, is "most adequate for the mastery of the image, of representation, and of self-representation." The term "identification" can only provisionally describe the woman's object relations – for the case of the woman "cannot concern either identity or non-identity." Hence, the scenarios which ground the theory of the cinematic apparatus are all aligned in some way with the delineation of a masculine subjectivity.[44]

As David Rodowick points out, by arguing in this way feminist film theorists have produced a logical schema in which a binary definition of sexual identity is "characterized by the assumption that maleness can be associated with a sense of imaginary coherence and fullness of consciousness as opposed to the unrepresentability or negativity of femaleness." But, he continues, "this logical schema is a product of film theory. It has produced a framework through which psychoanalytic theory is made to conform."[45]

Once the theses of primary cinematic identification and mirror misrecognition are abandoned as logically flawed and empirically incorrect theories of spectatorship, psychoanalytic theory can no longer support the thesis that the psychological mechanisms invoked by the cinema are gender bound. I would suggest that the collapse of this central argument of feminist psychoanalytic film theory is something that should be welcomed, because it releases the potential of psychoanalytic theory as a tool for feminist film history and criticism. One task of a psychoanalytically informed feminist film history and criticism is to understand the way in which the stories told by the cinema and the characters portrayed in those stories reproduce or subvert stereotypical gender roles through portraying fantasies of identity formation and sexual difference. Naturally, these fantasies tend to be stereotypical because the film industry endeavors to maximize the experience of projective illusion for the largest number of people, and this plugs into the most conventional expectations. Of course, to a great extent it has always been the task of a psychoanalytically informed feminist film history and criticism to understand the structure of these fantasies even as it was overlaid by the larger claims of an insupportable theory of the cinema. In addition, as film scholars have begun to understand, these fantasies of identity formation are fantasies that can also involve class, race, and sexual orientation.

The mechanism of projective illusion that serves to embody so effectively for the spectator fantasies of subject formation and sexual difference also affords the possibility for the spectator to experience even the most stereotypical of these fantasies differently. The consumer of any literary fiction is able to incorporate a work into her own fantasies, but in the cinema this possibility takes on a very immediate and concrete form. For example, the male spectator, and in particular the gay male spectator, may experience the homosocial environment of a buddy movie such as *Thunderbolt and Lightfoot* (1974) in homoerotic terms. However, it would be an oversimplification to pose a simple opposition between a normative story content and the way that story may be experienced. One can assume that an industry seeking profit maximization would seek to address the repressed as well as the overt desires of its heterosexually oriented audience members, and thus cues for a nonnormative reading of a film, such as a buddy movie, may be planted in the text. Furthermore, an industry that does not view its audience in monolithic terms would seek to cultivate partially, if tentatively and unevenly, a diversity of response to a single text. Thus Miriam Hansen suggests the manner in which, in an industry whose spectator was yet to be conceived in homogenous terms (and perhaps this never has been the case), the figure of Rudolph Valentino addressed female spectators in ways that transgressed cultural norms of male heterosexuality and female comportment.[46] Equally, Carol Clover in her book on horror demonstrates how, despite the regressive characteristics of the genre, the figure of "final girl" (i.e., the last character alive) affords a kind of character identification that defies traditional gender norms.[47] In this kind of study, psychoanalytic theory helps articulate the way in which a text affords more than one kind of response on the part of the spectator.

A psychoanalytic understanding of spectatorship can illuminate the beholder's share in sustaining the experience of film as a projective illusion. Psychoanalysis cannot hope to answer every question we might ask about the cinema, but I have argued that it can help answer a central question: how and why we experience projective illusion or the impression of reality in the cinema. I have also argued that on the basis of this theory of projective illusion – and once the twin cornerstones of contemporary feminist psychoanalytic film theory are removed – psychoanalysis has an important contribution to make to feminist film history and criticism. The implication that psycho-analysis has for understanding the effect of the psychic mechanisms invoked by the cinema upon the spectator is precisely the reverse of the construction of rigid or immutable gender roles according to a binary logic of male and female. Psychoanalysis illuminates the manner in which spectatorship may deviate from normative assumptions of subject formation and gender identity embodied in the text, either through an autonomous response on the part of the spectator, or through a response to cues that are planted in the text itself.

Notes

Introduction

1. See Noël Carroll, *Mystifying Movies: Fads and Fallacies in Contemporary Film Theory* (New York: Columbia University Press, 1988), p. 1.

2. In the light of my adoption of the views of Wittgenstein, the psychoanalytic conception of the spectator's experience of cinema that I also offer is contentious, for Wittgenstein was highly critical of Freudian psychoanalysis. The views of Wittgenstein and Freud appear, at first sight, to be incompatible. However, I do not claim that the conception of the cinema I offer here is a Wittgensteinian one: It does not conform with the later Wittgenstein's overall view of philosophy. Instead, my use of Wittgenstein is limited to the endorsement of certain arguments from his later philosophy and the use of other arguments to support my own. While I do believe that Wittgenstein's later philosophy can complement a psychoanalytic theory of the mind, my limited use of Wittgenstein does not presuppose such a claim. For Wittgenstein's criticisms of Freud, see *Lectures and Conversations on Aesthetics, Psychology, and Religious Belief* (Berkeley: University of California Press, n.d.), compiled from notes taken by Yorick Smithies, Rush Rhees, and James Taylor, ed. Phil Barrett, pp. 41–52.

I. Althusser, Lacan, and Film Theory

1 For a history of the impact of the events of May 1968 and their aftermath upon the formation of a radical film culture in France and Britain, see Sylvia Harvey, *May '68 and Film Culture* (London: BFI, 1978).

2 For a detailed history and analysis of the impact of Marxist literary modernism upon film theory in France and England in the 1970s, see David Rodowick, *The Crisis of Political Modernism: Criticism and Ideology in Contemporary Film Theory* (Urbana: University of Illinois Press, 1988).

3 The comparison between the "ontological" and "Brechtian" avant-garde is developed by Peter Wollen in his essays "The Two Avant Gardes" and "Ontology and Materialism in Film," in *Readings and Writings: Semiotic*

Counter-Strategies (London: Verso, 1982), pp. 92–104, 189–207. For a critical examination of Wollen's arguments, see Rodowick, *Crisis of Political Modernism,* pp. 147–79.

4   The way in which contemporary film theory reproduces the traditional dichotomy between high art and mass culture is noted by Colin MacCabe in "Class of '68: Elements of an Intellectual Autobiography," in *Tracking the Signifier* (Minneapolis: University of Minnesota Press, 1985), p. 11.

5   The classic statement of Marx's theory of ideology is to be found in Part I of Karl Marx and Frederick Engels, *The German Ideology,* ed. C. J. Arthur (New York: International Publishers, 1970).

6   Louis Althusser and Etienne Balibar, *Reading Capital,* trans. Ben Brewster (London: Verso, 1979), p. 35.

7   Ibid., p. 59.

8   Louis Althusser, "Freud and Lacan," in *Lenin and Philosophy and Other Essays,* trans. Ben Brewster (New York: Monthly Review Press, 1971), pp. 218–19. For further reference to the concept of misrecognition see Althusser and Balibar, *Reading Capital,* p. 53. Althusser explores the idea of ideology as an "imaginary relation" of individuals to their conditions of existence at greater length in "Ideology and Ideological State Apparatuses (Notes Toward an Investigation)," in *Lenin and Philosophy and Other Essays,* pp. 162–70. See also an essay that has only recently been published, "Theory, Theoretical Practice and Theoretical Formation: Ideology and Ideological Struggle," trans. James H. Kavanagh, in *Philosophy and the Spontaneous Philosophy of the Scientists and Other Essays* (New York: Verso, 1990), pp. 22–31.

9   See Jacques Lacan, "The Mirror Stage as Formative of the Function of the I," in *Écrits: A Selection,* trans. Alan Sheridan (New York: Tavistock Publications, 1977), pp. 1–7.

10   Althusser, "Ideology and Ideological State Apparatuses," pp. 185–6.

11   Louis Althusser, "Marxism and Humanism," in *For Marx,* trans. Ben Brewster (New York: Verso, 1990), p. 227.

12   The antirevolutionary nature of Althusser's theory of ideology is a standard charge leveled against him by Marxists. See Jacques Rancière, "On the Theory of Ideology: The Politics of Althusser," trans. Martin Jordin, in *Radical Philosophy* 7 (Spring 1974): 4; Alex Callinicos, *Althusser's Marxism* (London: Pluto Press, 1976), p. 101; Paul Q. Hirst, *On Law and Ideology* (Atlantic Highlands, N.J.: Humanities Press, 1979), p. 53; Ted Benton, *The Rise and Fall of Structuralist Marxism: Althusser and His Influence* (New York: Macmillan, 1984), p. 107; Gregory Elliott, *Althusser: The Detour of Theory* (New York: Verso, 1987), pp. 231–2.

13   This has been emphasized most recently by Michael Sprinker, who conducts a spirited defense of Althusser from his Marxist critics in *Imaginary Relations: Aesthetics and Ideology in the Theory of Historical Materialism* (New York: Verso, 1987), pp. 193–9.

14 See, for example, Thomas Kuhn, *The Structure of Scientific Revolutions,* 2d ed. (Chicago: University of Chicago Press, 1970).

15 See Noël Carroll, *Mystifying Movies: Fads and Fallacies in Contemporary Film Theory* (New York: Columbia University Press, 1988), pp. 79–80.

16 See Michel Foucault, "History of Systems of Thought: Summary of a course given at Collège de France – 1970–71," in *Language, Counter Memory, Practice,* ed. Donald F. Bouchard (Ithaca: Cornell University Press, 1977), pp. 199–204.

17 Terry Lovell, *Pictures of Reality* (London: BFI, 1983), p. 51.

18 Carroll, *Mystifying Movies,* p. 85. For his source data and his argument Carroll draws on Nicholas Abercrombie, Stephen Hill, and Bryan S. Turner, *The Dominant Ideology Thesis* (Boston: George Allen & Unwin, 1980). Carroll's views on ideology coincide with those of Lovell, although he does not refer to her work in his book.

19 Althusser, "A Letter on Art," in *Lenin and Philosophy,* p. 223.

20 Jean-Louis Baudry, "Ideological Effects of the Basic Cinematographic Apparatus," in *Narrative, Apparatus, Ideology,* ed. Philip Rosen (New York: Columbia University Press, 1986), p. 289. Marcelin Pleynet's comments on the ideological character of perspective are to be found in "Economical, Ideological, Formal" (an interview with Marcelin Pleynet and Jean Thibaudeau by the editors of *Cinéthique*), trans. Elias Noujaim, in Sylvia Harvey, *May '68 and Film Culture,* p. 159.

21 Pleynet and Baudry's argument is reiterated by Jean-Louis Comolli in "Technique and Ideology: Camera, Perspective, Depth of Field," trans. Diana Matias, in *Cahiers du Cinéma 1969–1972: The Politics of Representation,* ed. Nick Browne (Cambridge, Mass.: Harvard University Press, 1990), pp. 215–16; and in "Machines of the Visible" in *The Cinematic Apparatus,* ed. Teresa de Lauretis and Stephen Heath (New York: St. Martin's Press, 1980), pp. 125–6.

22 Carroll, *Mystifying Movies,* pp. 127–38.

23 Baudry, "Ideological Effects," p. 292.

24 Ibid., p. 295.

25 Ibid.

26 Paul Hirst makes this criticism against Althusser's theory of ideology in *On Law and Ideology,* p. 65.

27 Baudry, "Ideological Effects of the Basic Cinematographic Apparatus," p. 293.

28 Carroll, *Mystifying Movies,* p. 146.

29 For a good representation of the position against which Lacan is arguing, see Heinz Hartmann, "Comments on the Psychoanalytic Theory of the Ego," in *Essays on Ego Psychology* (New York: International Universities Press, 1964), pp. 113–31.

30 Jacques Lacan, "The Subversion of the Subject and the Dialectic of Desire in the Freudian Unconscious," in *Écrits,* 315–16. For my understanding of Lacan's conception of subjectivity prior to the mirror stage, I have drawn on Ellie Ragland-Sullivan, *Jacques Lacan and the Philosophy of Psychoanalysis* (Urbana: University of Illinois Press, 1986), 16–30.

31 See Melanie Klein, "A Contribution to the Psychogenesis of Manic Depressive States," in *The Selected Melanie Klein,* ed. Juliet Mitchell (New York: Free Press, 1987), pp. 116–45. Klein draws on suggestions Freud makes in his essay "On Negation," *Standard Edition* XIX, pp. 233–9. Klein's understanding of the corporeal conception of mind receives careful elaboration in the writings of Richard Wollheim: See "The Mind and the Mind's Conception of Itself," in *On Art and Mind* (Cambridge, Mass.: Harvard University Press, 1974), pp. 31–53; and "The Bodily Ego," in *The Mind and Its Depths* (Cambridge, Mass.: Harvard University Press, 1993), pp. 64–78.

32 Jane Gallop, *Reading Lacan* (Ithaca: Cornell University Press, 1985), p. 86.

33 Lacan, "The Mirror Stage as Formative," p. 4.

34 Jacques Lacan, *The Four Fundamental Concepts of Psychoanalysis* (New York: Norton, 1981), p. 96. See also Joan Copjec, "The Orthopsychic Subject: Film Theory and the Reception of Lacan," *October* 49 (Summer 1989): 69.

35 Sigmund Freud, *Beyond the Pleasure Principle, Standard Edition* XVIII, pp. 14–17.

36 Lacan, *Four Fundamental Concepts,* p. 62.

37 Jacques Lacan, *The Seminar of Jacques Lacan, Book 1: Freud's Paper on Technique 1953–54,* ed. Jacques-Alain Miller, trans. John Forrester (New York: Norton, 1991), pp. 172–4; "The Function and Field of Speech in Language and Psychoanalysis," *Écrits,* pp. 103–4.

38 Freud's text itself suggests this comparison. Freud notes that the same boy played a game of peekaboo in a mirror. He writes: "It soon turned out, however, that during this long period of solitude the child had found a method of making himself disappear. He had discovered his reflection in a full-length mirror which did not quite reach to the ground, so that by crouching down he could make his mirror-image 'gone'" (Freud, *Beyond the Pleasure Principle,* p. 15).

39 Lacan, *Four Fundemental Concepts,* pp. 62–3.

40 As Pamela Grace pointed out to me, the fact that Lacan's intepretations of the game can differ so in emphasis stems from the fact that Freud himself does not discriminate the degree to which it is the child's physical game of throwing the reel or his vocalization that allows him to master the mother's absence.

41 Lacan, *Seminar of Jacques Lacan: Book 1,* p. 173.

42 Lacan, *Four Fundamental Concepts,* p. 218.

43 Ferdinand de Saussure, *Course in General Linguistics,* ed. Charles Bally and Albert Sechehaye, trans. Wade Baskin (New York: McGraw–Hill, 1966).

44 Jacques-Alain Miller, "Suture (elements of the logic of the signifier)," trans. Jacqueline Rose, in *Screen* 18:4 (Winter 1977–8): 25–6.

45 Jean-Pierre Oudart, "Cinema and Suture," trans. Kari Hanet, in *Cahiers du Cinéma 1969–1972,* p. 54.

46 Ibid., p. 47.

47 Serge Daney and Jean Pierre Oudart, "The Name of the Author (on the "place" of *Death in Venice*), trans. Joseph Karmel, in *Cahiers du Cinéma 1969–1972,* p. 320.

48 For Oudart's theory of the ideology of perspectival representation, see "The Reality Effect" and "Notes for a Theory of Representation," trans. Annwyl Williams, in *Cahiers du Cinéma 1969–1972,* pp. 189–212. The thesis of perspectival subject positioning certainly does not encompass all of Oudart's theory, but it covers a central part of it and one that was most influential in an English-speaking context.

49 Daniel Dayan, "The Tutor-Code of Classical Cinema," in *Movies and Methods,* vol. 1, ed. Bill Nichols (Berkeley: University of California Press, 1976), p. 450.

50 For criticism of Dayan on this point, see William Rothman, "Against the System of the Suture," in *Movies and Methods,* pp. 451–9.

51 David Bordwell, *Narration and the Fiction Film* (Madison: University of Wisconsin Press, 1985), p. 30.

52 Julia Kristeva, *Revolution in Poetic Language,* trans. Margaret Waller (New York: Columbia University Press, 1984), p. 26.

53 Ibid., p. 88.

54 Ibid., pp. 46–7.

55 Emile Benveniste, "The Correlations of Tense in the French Verb," in *Problems in General Linguistics,* trans. Mary E. Meek (Coral Gables, Fla.: University of Miami Press), p. 208.

56 For Barthes's characterization of *écriture classique,* see *Writing Degree Zero,* trans. Annette Lavers and Colin Smith (New York: Hill & Wang, 1968), pp. 29–40. He draws a distinction between the "readerly" and the "writerly" text in *S/Z,* trans. Richard Miller (New York: Hill & Wang, 1974), pp. 3–6.

57 Kristeva, *Revolution in Poetic Language,* p. 58.

58 Stephen Heath, "Narrative Space," in *Questions of Cinema* (Bloomington: Indiana University Press, 1981), p. 48.

59 Ibid., p. 38.

60 Stephen Heath, "On Suture," in *Questions of Cinema,* p. 90.

61 Heath, "Narrative Space," p. 31.

62 Ibid., p. 38.

63 Ibid., p. 44. See also Stephen Heath, "Film Performance," in *Questions of Cinema,* pp. 119–20.

64 For an alternative view of Heath's relationship to Althusser, see Robert Lapsley and Michael Westlake, *Film Theory: An Introduction* (Manchester: Manchester University Press, 1988), p. 145.

II. The Lure of Metaphysics

1 Louis Althusser and Etienne Balibar, *Reading Capital,* trans. Ben Brewster (London: Verso, 1979), p. 53.

2 Jean-Louis Baudry, "Ideological Effects of the Basic Cinematographic Apparatus," in *Narrative, Apparatus, Ideology,* ed. Philip Rosen (New York: Columbia University Press, 1986), p. 293.

3 Julia Kristeva, *Revolution in Poetic Language,* trans. Margaret Waller (New York: Columbia University Press, 1984), p. 32.

4 Ibid., pp. 40–1.

5 Heath does make explicit reference to Husserl's idea of the "natural standpoint" in his book on the *nouveau roman,* however, in order to characterize the way in which the realist novel exemplifies the empiricist conception of knowledge. Stephen Heath, *The Nouveau Roman: A Study in the Practice of Writing* (Philadelphia: Temple University Press, 1972), p. 18.

6 Edmund Husserl, *Ideas: General Introduction to Pure Phenomenology,* trans. W. R. Boyce Gibson (New York: Collier Books, 1962), pp. 242–3.

7 Ibid., p. 243.

8 Ibid., p. 150.

9 For an attempt to find this middle ground and read Husserl as a "realist," see Allan Casebier, *Film and Phenomenology: Toward a Realist Theory of Cinematic Representation* (New York: Cambridge University Press, 1991), pp. 25–34.

10 An important exception is Harry Staten's book *Wittgenstein and Derrida* (Lincoln: University of Nebraska Press, 1984).

11 Edmund Husserl, *Logical Investigations,* vol. 1, trans. J. N. Findlay (London: Routledge & Kegan Paul, 1970), pp. 279–80.

12 Jacques Derrida, *Speech and Phenomenon and Other Essays on Husserl's Theory of Signs,* trans. David B. Allison, with a preface by Newton Garver (Evanston, Ill.: Northwestern University Press, 1973), p. 78.

13 Ibid., p. 50.

14 Ibid., p. 85.

15 Jacques Derrida, *Of Grammatology,* trans. Gayatri Chakravorty Spivak (Baltimore: Johns Hopkins University Press, 1976), p. 49.

16 Derrida himself uses the expression the "reduction of the reduction" to describe the idea of "deconstruction," in Jacques Derrida, *Edmund Husserl's*

Origin of Geometry, An Introduction, trans. John P. Leavey, Jr. (Lincoln: University of Nebraska Press, 1978), p. 70 n. 66.

17 Jacques Derrida, "Différance," in *Margins of Philosophy,* trans. Alan Bass (Chicago: University of Chicago Press, 1982), p. 16.

18 Ferdinand de Saussure, *Course in General Linguistics,* ed. Charles Bally and Albert Sechehaye, trans. Wade Baskin (New York: McGraw–Hill, 1966), p. 66.

19 Derrida, *Of Grammatology,* p. 65.

20 A number of comparisons between Derrida and Wittgenstein exist in the literature. To my mind Newton Garver overstates the similarities between them in his introduction to *Speech and Phenomena* by (mis)reading Derrida's critique of Husserl through the grid of Wittgenstein's *Philosophical Investigations.* From the opposite side, Harry Staten in *Wittgenstein and Derrida,* notwithstanding the value of his book for understanding Derrida's reading of Husserl, misrepresents the relationship between Derrida and Wittgenstein by assimilating Wittgenstein's philosophy to deconstruction! My view of the relationship between Wittgenstein and Derrida is represented most closely by Charles Altieri in "Wittgenstein on Consciousness and Language: A Challenge to Derridean Literary Theory," *Modern Language Notes* 91:6 (Dec. 1976): 1397–1423. See also John M. Ellis's comments on the relationship between the two thinkers in *Against Deconstruction* (Princeton, N.J.: Princeton University Press, 1989), pp. 42–4.

21 Ludwig Wittgenstein, *Philosophical Investigations,* 3d ed., ed. G. E. M. Anscombe and Rush Rhees, trans. G. E. M. Anscombe (New York: Macmillan, 1968), §243.

22 Husserl, *Logical Investigations,* p. 278.

23 P. M. S. Hacker, *Insight and Illusion: Themes in the Philosophy of Wittgenstein,* rev. ed. (Oxford: Clarendon Press, 1986), p. 265. My understanding of the private-language argument is indebted to Hacker's commentary.

24 Husserl, *Logical Investigations,* p. 302.

25 Wittgenstein, *Philosophical Investigations,* §258.

26 Ibid., §265.

27 Husserl, *Logical Investigations,* p. 279.

28 Wittgenstein, *Philosophical Investigations,* §271.

29 Ibid., §293.

30 Ibid., §202.

31 The interpretation of "practice" as "social practice" is common among critical theorists. See Jürgen Habermas, *Theory of Communciative Action,* vol. 2, *Life Worlds and Systems: A Critique of Functionalist Reason,* trans. Thomas McCarthy (Boston: Beacon Press, 1987), pp. 15–22; and see also Terry Eagleton's caricature of Wittgenstein's views in *Against the Grain: Selected Essays* (London: Verso, 1986), pp. 99–130. Analytical philosophers also frequently misrepresent Wittgenstein on this point. See Norman Malcolm, *Wittgenstein: Nothing is Hidden* (New York: Blackwell, 1986), pp. 154–81; and Peter Winch, *The Idea of a Social Science and Its Relation to Philosophy,* 2d ed. (Atlantic Highlands, N.J.: Humanities Press, 1989), pp. 24–33. For a sustained, persuasive argument against this interpretation, see G. P. Baker and P. M. S. Hacker, *Skepticism, Rules and Language* (New York: Blackwell, 1984).

32 Derrida, *Of Grammatology*, p. 62.

33 Husserl, *Logical Investigations,* quotations from pp. 316, 315, 318, 321, respectively.

34 Emile Benveniste, "The Nature of Pronouns," in *Problems in General Linguistics,* trans. Mary E. Meek (Coral Gables, Fla.: University of Miami Press), p. 218.

35 Ibid., p. 224.

36 Kaja Silverman, *The Subject of Semiotics* (New York: Oxford University Press, 1983), p. 199.

37 Derrida, *Speech and Phenomena*, p. 93.

38 Wittgenstein, *The Blue and Brown Books: Preliminary Studies for the Philosophical Investigations* (New York: Barnes & Noble, 1969), p. 63.

39 Ibid., p. 64.

40 For a clarification of Wittgenstein's analysis of the ego, see David Pears, *The False Prison: A Study of the Development of Wittgenstein's Philosophy,* vol. 2 (Oxford: Clarendon Press, 1988), pp. 241–50. Thanks to Christopher Davis for input on this issue.

41 Wittgenstein, *Blue and Brown Books,* p. 67.

42 See G. E. M. Anscombe, "The First Person," in *Mind and Language,* ed. Samuel Guttenplan (Oxford: Clarendon Press, 1975), pp. 45–66.

43 Hacker, *Insight and Illusion*, pp. 282–3.

44 Altieri, "Wittgenstein on Consciousness and Language," p. 1403.

III. Representation, Illusion, and the Cinema

1 Patrick Bratlinger traces contemporary critiques of mass culture back to Plato in *Bread and Circuses: Theories of Mass Culture as Social Decay* (Ithaca: Cornell University Press, 1983), p. 59.

2 Richard Wollheim, *Painting as an Art* (Princeton, N.J.: Princeton University Press, 1987), p. 46.

3 The reason may be that while nineteenth-century photographs were made according to the conventions of painting, they were not necessarily made in order to deceive the spectator into believing that they were paintings.

4 This myth and its legacy is challenged effectively by Tom Gunning in "An Aesthetic of Astonishment: Early Film and the (In)credulous Spectator," *Art & Text* 34 (1989): 31–45. Gunning proposes that, contrary to myth, early film spectators entered in and out of the experience of illusion in precisely the way I try to rationalize here.

5 Thanks to Bill Paul for this anecdote. It was reported by Douglas Trumbull at a conference at MIT on developments in wide-screen technology.

6 Kendall L. Walton, "Transparent Pictures: On the Nature of Photographic Realism," *Critical Inquiry* 11:2 (1984): 252.

7 Roger Scruton connects the transparency of the photograph with the capacity of the cinema to engender an experience of illusion in a manner that has influenced the argument of this chapter and the next. See Scruton, "Photography and Representation," and "Fantasy, Imagination and the Screen," in *The Aesthetic Understanding* (New York: Methuen, 1983), pp. 102–36.

8 Roland Barthes, "The Rhetoric of the Image," in *Image, Music, Text,* trans. Stephen Heath (New York: Hill & Wang, 1977), p. 44. I thank Ben Singer for the argument of this paragraph.

9 Rudolf Arnheim, *Film as Art* (Berkeley: University of California Press, 1957), p. 24.

10 Christian Metz, "The Imaginary Signifier," trans. Ben Brewster, in *The Imaginary Signifier: Psychoanalysis and Cinema* (Bloomington: Indiana University Press, 1982), p. 44.

11 André Bazin, "The Ontology of the Photographic Image," in *What Is Cinema?* vol. 1, trans. Hugh Gray (Berkeley: University of California Press, 1967), pp. 9–16.

12 See Charles Musser, "Towards a History of Screen Practice," in *The Emergence of Cinema* (New York: Scribner, 1990), pp. 15–40.

13 "A Kiss Is Still a Kiss," *New York Times*, 1 May 1993, sec. 1, p. 22.

14 "On Truth, Beauty and the Moment When a Photo Becomes Art," *New York Times*, 16 May 1993, sec. 4, p. 16.

15 Historians are particularly sensitive to reproductive illusion in film. See William Hughes, "The Evaluation of Film as Evidence" in Paul Smith, ed., *The Historian and Film* (Cambridge: Cambridge University Press, 1976), pp. 49–79.

16 Noël Carroll, "From Real to Reel: Entangled in Nonfiction Film," *Philosophic Exchange* 14 (1983): 30.

17 Ibid. For further discussion of the distinction between "nominal" and "physical" portrayal, see Noël Carroll, *Philosophical Problems of Classical Film Theory* (Princeton, N.J.: Princeton University Press, 1988), pp. 149–52.

18 Linda Williams, *Hardcore: Power, Pleasure and the "Frenzy of the Visible"* (Berkeley: University of California Press, 1989), p. 201.

19 For an account of the broadcast, see Frank Brady, *Citizen Welles: A Biography of Orson Welles* (New York: Scribner's, 1989), pp. 162–80.

20 Williams, *Hardcore*, p. 192.

21 See Robert L. Carringer, *The Making of Citizen Kane* (Berkeley: University of California Press, 1985), pp. 87–99. My examples are taken from Carringer's book.

22 Noël Carroll, *Mystifying Movies: Fads and Fallacies in Contemporary Film Theory* (New York: Columbia University Press, 1988), p. 95.

23 Ibid., p. 96.

24 The claim that the Müller–Lyer illusion is always compelling must be qualified. It is only compelling to someone who has learned to see a two-dimensional configuration of lines as a three-dimensional representation.

25 Noël Carroll, *The Philosophy of Horror or Paradoxes of the Heart* (New York: Routledge, 1990), p. 80.

26 Gregory Currie, "Visual Fictions," *Philosophical Quarterly* 41 (1991): 129–43.

27 Jerrold Levinson, "Seeing, Imaginarily, at the Movies," *Philosophical Quarterly* 43 (1993): 70–8. See also Currie's response, "Impersonal Imagining: A Reply to Jerrold Levinson," *Philosophical Quarterly* 43 (1993): 79–82.

28 I follow here a lead of E. H. Gombrich, who suggests that seeing-as can explain the experience of illusion associated with pictorial representations. See *Art and Illusion: A Study in the Psychology of Pictorial Representation* (Princeton, N.J.: Princeton University Press, 1984), pp. 5–6.

29 Ludwig Wittgenstein, *Philosophical Investigations*, 3d ed., ed. G. E. M. Anscombe and Rush Rhees, trans. G. E. M. Anscombe (New York: Macmillan, 1968), II, p. xi.

30 The sense in which the Necker cube and examples like it are distinct from the "pure" cases of seeing-as is discussed by Malcolm Budd, *Wittgenstein's Philosophy of Psychology* (New York: Routledge, 1989), pp. 87–90.

31 Metz, "Imaginary Signifier," p. 49.

32 Christian Metz, "On the Impression of Reality in the Cinema," *Film Language: A Semiotics of the Cinema,* trans. Michael Taylor (New York: Oxford University Press, 1974), pp. 3–15.

33 Other things being equal, this analysis of the cinematic image is also applicable to the television image, which can also be considered as a form of projected moving image. Of course, the quality and size of the television image together with the context in which it is viewed greatly diminish its propensity for projective illusion. However, high-definition, projected television can produce an image whose clarity and size is almost equal to that of the cinema.

34 Stanley Cavell, *The World Viewed: Reflections on the Ontology of Film,* enlarged ed. (Cambridge, Mass.: Harvard University Press, 1979), p. 72.

35 John Ellis, *Visible Fictions* (London: Routledge, 1982), p. 58. This contention is also criticized by Noël Carroll in *Mystifying Movies,* pp. 119–27.

36 Noël Burch, "Narrative, Diegesis: Thresholds, Limits," in *Life to Those Shadows* (Berkeley: University of California Press, 1990), p. 257.

37 Ibid., p. 256. It is not strictly true that the landscape is completely static.

Early on in the film we see some blades of grass moved by the wind. This event appears so striking because of its isolated occurrence.

38 Ben Singer, "*Jeanne Dielman:* Cinematic Interrogation and Amplification," *Millenium Film Journal* 22 (Winter/Spring 1989–90): 58.

39 See David Bordwell, Kristin Thompson, and Janet Staiger, *Classical Hollywood Cinema: Film Style and Mode of Production to 1960* (New York: Columbia University Press, 1985), pp. 162–3.

40 Stephen Heath, "Narrative Space," in *Questions of Cinema* (Bloomington: Indiana University Press, 1981), p. 51; Bordwell, Thompson, and Staiger, *Classical Hollywood Cinema*, p. 70.

41 David Bordwell, *Narration in the Fiction Film* (Madison: University of Wisconsin Press, 1985), p. 162.

42 Ibid., p. 157.

43 Singer, "*Jeanne Dielman*," p. 59.

44 Noël Carroll, *Philosophy of Horror*, p. 79. The example of the Green Slime comes from Kendall Walton, "Fearing Fictions," *Journal of Philosophy* 75:1 (January 1978): 5–27. Walton proposes solving the paradox of fiction by arguing that our emotional responses to fictional objects are not real but pretend. Carroll argues persuasively against this view.

IV. Cinema, Psychoanalysis, and the Film Spectator

1 Christian Metz, "The Imaginary Signifier," trans. Ben Brewster, in *The Imaginary Signifier: Psychoanalysis and Cinema* (Bloomington: Indiana University Press, 1982), pp. 3–87.

2 Christian Metz, "The Fiction Film and Its Spectator: A Metapsychological Study," trans. Alfred Guzzetti in *Imaginary Signifier*, pp. 99–147; Jean-Louis Baudry, "The Apparatus: Metapsychological Approaches to the Impression of Reality in the Cinema," trans. Jean Andrews and Bertrand Augst in *Narrative, Apparatus, Ideology*, ed. Philip Rosen (New York: Columbia University Press, 1986), pp. 299–318.

3 See, for example, Janet Bergstrom, "Enunciation and Sexual Difference," in *Feminism and Film Theory*, ed. Constance Penley (New York: Routledge, 1988), p. 181; and Constance Penley, "Feminism, Film Theory, and the Bachelor Machines," in *The Future of An Illusion: Film, Feminism and Psychoanalysis* (Minneapolis: University of Minnesota Press, 1989), p. 79.

4 Psychoanalytic film theory is extensively criticized on these grounds by Noël Carroll in *Mystifying Movies: Fads and Fallacies in Contemporary Film Theory* (New York: Columbia University Press, 1988), pp. 9–52.

5 My approach to a psychoanalytic theory of the mind is indebted to the writings of Richard Wollheim. See in particular *The Thread of Life* (Cambridge, Mass.: Harvard University Press, 1984).

6 This distinction between psychic force and psychic function is adapted from Wollheim, *Thread of Life*, pp. 42–5.

7 Elizabeth Cowie, "Fantasia," *m/f* 9 (1984): 79; J. Laplanche and J.-B. Pontalis, *The Language of Psychoanalysis,* trans. Donald Nicholson Smith (New York: Norton, 1973), p. 318.
8 Wollheim, *Thread of Life,* p. 90.
9 Baudry, "The Apparatus: Metapsychological Approaches," p. 312.
10 See Carroll, *Mystifying Movies,* pp. 200–8.
11 Wollheim, *Thread of Life,* pp. 71–2.
12 This is the formulation I gave in an earlier version of this chapter. See "Psychoanalysis, Cinema, and the Film Spectator," *Persistence of Vision* 10 (1993): 12.
13 Wollheim, "Wish-fulfillment," in *Rational Action,* ed. Ross Harrison (Cambridge: Cambridge University Press, 1979), p. 50.
14 Wollheim, *Thread of Life,* pp. 69–81.
15 This position is elaborated by Murray Smith in his forthcoming book *Engaging Characters* (New York: Oxford University Press, 1995).
16 David Bordwell, Kristin Thompson, and Janet Staiger, *Classical Hollywood Cinema: Film Style and Mode of Production to 1960* (New York: Columbia University Press, 1985), p. 32.
17 See Vera Dika, "The Stalker Film, 1978–1981," in *American Horrors: Essays on the American Horror Film,* ed. Gregory Waller (Urbana: University of Illinois Press, 1987), pp. 86–101.
18 See Ben Singer, "*Jeanne Dielman:* Cinematic Interrogation and Amplification," *Millenium Film Journal* 22 (Winter/Spring 1989–90): 65–6. I thank Ivone Margulies for drawing my attention to the importance of this film, though she bears no responsibility for my interpretation of it.
19 Metz, "Imaginary Signifier," p. 49.
20 See Gaylyn Studlar, *In the Realm of Pleasure: Von Sternberg, Dietrich and the Masochistic Aesthetic* (Urbana: University of Illinois Press, 1988), pp. 9–49.
21 Freud discusses disavowal in the context of fetishism in the essays "Fetishism" (1927), *Standard Edition* XXI, pp. 147–57, and "Splitting of the Ego in the Process of Defence" (1940), *Standard Edition* XXIII, pp. 271–8. However in *An Outline of Psychoanalysis* (1940), drafted about the same time as "Splitting of the Ego," Freud writes: "It must not be thought that fetishism presents an exceptional case as regards a splitting of the ego; it is merely a particularly favorable subject for studying the question. Let us return to our thesis that the childish ego, under the domination of the real world, gets rid of undesirable instinctual demands by what are called repressions. We will now supplement this further by asserting that, during the same period of life, the ego often enough finds itself in the position of fending off some demand from the external world which it feels distressing and that this is effected by means of a disavowal of the perceptions which bring to knowledge this demand from reality. Disavowals of this kind occur very often and not only with

fetishists; and whenever we are in a position to study them they turn out to be half-measures, incomplete attempts at detachment from reality." See *Standard Edition* XXIII, p. 203.

22 Anna Freud, *The Ego and the Mechanisms of Defence* (London: Hogarth Press and Institute of Psychoanalysis, 1948), p. 78.

23 Wollheim, *Thread of Life,* p. 156.

24 See Freud, "Splitting of the Ego," pp. 271–8.

25 D. W. Winnicott, *Playing and Reality* (New York: Basic Books, 1971), pp. 1–17. Ira Konigsberg drew attention to the importance of Winnicott for understanding film spectatorship in a paper entitled "Transitional Phenomenon and Transitional Space: Creativity and Spectatorship in Film," presented at the 1993 Society for Cinema Studies Conference, New Orleans.

26 Jacques Lacan, "The Mirror Stage as Formative of the Function of the I," in *Écrits: A Selection,* trans. Alan Sheridan (New York: Tavistock Publications, 1977), pp. 1–7.

27 Unlike Winnicott, who also discusses the child's relationship with the caregiver in terms of mirroring, Lacan gives the caregiver no role in the process. Winnicott is interested in the quality of the caregiver's response and its impact on the child's development from a subjective to an objective world. Lacan is interested in the fact of a reflection for which the caregiver's face serves merely as a prop. Winnicott's child sees herself in the mother's face; Lacan's child cannot see the mother's face, for she sees only herself. See Winnicott, *Playing and Reality,* pp. 111–18.

28 Joan Copjec, "The Orthopsychic Subject: Film Theory and the Reception of Lacan," *October* 49 (Summer 1989): 53–71.

29 The phrase "torn to pieces" is used by Daniel Dayan in "The Tutor-Code in Classical Cinema" in *Movies and Methods,* vol. 1, ed. Bill Nichols (Berkeley: University of California Press, 1976), p. 450.

30 See Kaja Silverman, *The Acoustic Mirror: The Female Voice in Psychoanalysis and Cinema* (Bloomington: Indiana University Press, 1988), pp. 11–12.

31 Metz, "Imaginary Signifier," p. 60.

32 Laura Mulvey, "Visual Pleasure and Narrative Cinema," in *Visual and Other Pleasures* (Bloomington: Indiana University Press, 1989), p. 17.

33 Silverman, *Acoustic Mirror,* p. 7.

34 Otto Fenichel, "The Scopophilic Instinct and Identification," *International Journal of Psychoanalysis* 18 (1937): 6–34. Ann Friedberg refers to this paper in "A Denial of Difference: Theories of Cinematic Identification," in *Psychoanalysis and Cinema,* ed. E. Ann Kaplan (New York: Routledge, 1990), p. 39.

35 David Rodowick, *The Difficulty of Difference: Psychoanalysis, Sexual Difference and Film Theory* (New York: Routledge, 1991), pp. 66–94.

36 Metz, "Imaginary Signifier," p. 70.

37 Ben Singer, "Film, Photography, and Fetish: The Analyses of Christian Metz," *Cinema Journal* 27:4 (Summer 1988): 5–6.

38 Jacqueline Rose, "The Cinematic Apparatus: Problems in Current Theory," in *The Cinematic Apparatus,* ed. Teresa de Lauretis and Stephen Heath (New York: St. Martin's Press, 1980), p. 174.

39 For example, concluding the analysis of several case studies, Robert Dickes writes: "the development of a fetishist and the selection of a fetish are extremely complex; numerous factors, including preoedipal experiences, play a vital role in the history of this symptom complex. The fetish itself does not develop *de novo* in the phallic phase; in the patients I have presented, antecedent objects and experiences have been remembered. These earlier objects acquire much significance and transfer this significance to the final fetish. A continuum exists between transitional objects, childhood fetishes, and final adult fetishes" ("Fetishistic Behavior: A Contribution to Its Complex Development and Significance," *Journal of the American Pyschoanalytic Association* 11:2 [1963]: 328). Janine Chasseguet-Smirgel provides a theoretical grounding for this view: "The fetish is an anal phallus which attempts to exclude the genital penis from the sexual stage. I suggest that we consider the fetishist as trying to foil his castration complex by likening it to his previous experiences of separation which had not constrained him to renounce the possession of the mother. The fetish is the deposit of all the part objects lost during the subject's development" (*Creativity and Perversion* [New York: Norton, 1984], p. 87).

40 Singer, "Film, Photography, and Fetish," pp. 10–11.

41 Metz, "Imaginary Signifier," p. 74.

42 Tom Gunning, "An Aesthetic of Astonishment: Early Film and the (In)-credulous Spectator," *Art & Text* 34 (Spring 1989): 31–45.

43 For the prehistory of the woman as fetish object see Werner Nekes's film *Film Before Film* (1989); on early cinema see Linda Williams, "Film Body: An Implantation of Perversions," in *Narrative, Apparatus, Ideology*, pp. 507–34; on Busby Berkeley see Lucy Fischer, "The Image of Woman as Image: The Optical Politics of Dames," in *Genre: The Musical,* ed. Rick Altman (London: Routledge & Kegan Paul/BFI, 1981), pp. 71–84.

44 Mary Ann Doane, *The Desire to Desire: The Woman's Film of the 1940s* (Bloomington: Indiana University Press, 1987), pp. 15–16.

45 Rodowick, *Difficulty of Difference*, p. 45.

46 Miriam Hansen, *Babel and Babylon: Spectatorship in American Silent Film* (Cambridge, Mass.: Harvard University Press, 1991), pp. 245–94.

47 Carol Clover, *Men, Women and Chainsaws: Gender in the Modern Horror Film* (Princeton, N.J.: Princton University Press, 1992), pp. 21–64.

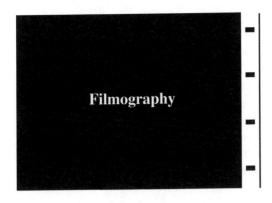

Filmography

Note: This guide to films cited in the text is intended to assist readers wishing to consult any of those films directly. It is not intended to be comprehensive. For avant-garde films, only American distributors have been listed.

Arnulf Rainer, dir. Peter Kubelka (dist. Film-Makers' Co-op / Canyon Cinema Co-op; Austria, 1958–60)

Arrival of a Train at the Station (Arrivée d'un train à La Ciotat), dir. Auguste and Louis Lumière (France, 1895)

Au hazard, Balthazar, dir. Robert Bresson (Parc / Ardos / Athos / Svenska Filminstitutet, France/Sweden, 1966)

Back and Forth (↔), dir. Michael Snow (dist. Film-Maker's Co-op; Canada, 1968–9)

Cameraman, The, dir. Buster Keaton (Keaton–MGM, U.S., 1928)

Citizen Kane, dir. Orson Welles (RKO, U.S., 1941)

Clockwork Orange, A, dir. Stanley Kubrick (Hawk Films, U.K., 1971)

David Holtzman's Diary, dir. Jim McBride (dist. Direct Cinema; U.S., 1968)

Dog Star Man, dir. Stan Brakhage (dist. Film-Makers' Co-op / Canyon Cinema Co-op, U.S., 1961–4)

Film Before Film, dir. Werner Nekes (Kino International / West Glen, West Germany, 1989)

Jeanne Dielman, 23 Quai du Commerce, 1080 Bruxelles, dir. Chantal Akerman (Paradise Films [Brussels] / Unité Trois [Paris]; dist. New Yorker; Belgium, 1975)

Mothlight, dir. Stan Brakhage (dist. Film-Makers' Co-op / Canyon Cinema Co-op; U.S., 1963)

News from Home (Nuit et jour), dir. Chantal Akerman (INA / Unité Trois [Paris] / Paradise Films [Brussels]; dist. World Artists, 1976)

N:O:T:H:I:N:G, dir. Paul Sharits (dist. Film-Makers' Co-op / Canyon Cinema Co-op; U.S., 1968)

Night of the Living Dead, dir. George Romero (Image Ten; dist. Kit Parker; U.S., 1968)

Peeping Tom, dir. Michael Powell (Anglo Amalgamated, U.K., 1960)

Raging Bull, dir. Martin Scorsese (United Artists, U.S., 1980)

Rear Window, dir. Alfred Hitchcock (Paramount, U.S., 1954)

La Region Centrale (The Central Region), dir. Michael Snow (dist. Film-Makers' Co-op; Canada, 1970–1)

Schwechater, dir. Peter Kubelka (dist. Film-Makers' Co-op / Canyon Cinema Co-op; Austria, 1957–8)

Snuff, dir. & prod. Roberta and Michael Findlay (dist. Monarch Releasing Corp.; U.S. / Uruguay, 1976)

Thin Blue Line, The, dir. Errol Morris (BFI / Third Floor / American Playhouse; dist. Films Inc.; U.S., 1989)

Thunderbolt and Lightfoot, dir. Michael Cimino (UA / Malpaso, U.S., 1974)

Trial of Joan of Arc, The (Le Procès de Jeanne d'Arc), dir. Robert Bresson (Agnès Delahaie Prods., France, 1962)

Wavelength, dir. Michael Snow (dist. Film-Makers' Co-op; U.S., 1966–7)

Wind from the East (Vend d'est), dir. Jean-Luc Godard (with Dziga Vertov Group) (Anouchka Films [France] / CCC [Berlin] / Polifilm [Rome], France, 1970)

Zelig, dir. Woody Allen (Rollins–Joffe/Orion, U.S., 1983)

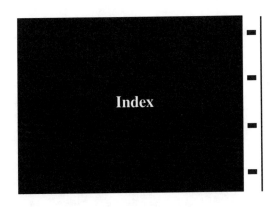

Index

Note: Italic page numbers indicate illustrations.